Ethical Economy

Studies in Economic Ethics and Philosophy

Volume 65

Series Editors
Alexander Brink, Chair of Business Ethics, University of Bayreuth, Bayreuth, Germany
Jacob Dahl Rendtorff, Department of Social Sciences and Business, Roskilde University, Roskilde, Denmark

Editorial Board Members
John Boatright, Loyola University, Chicago, IL, USA
George Brenkert, Business Ethics Institute, Maguire Hall 209B, Georgetown University, Georgetown, Washington, DC, USA
Allan K. K. Chan, Lee Shau Kee School of Business & Administration, The Open University of Hong Kong, Homantin, Hong Kong
Christopher Cowton, University of Huddersfield, Huddersfield, UK
Richard T. de George, University of Kansas, Lawrence, KS, USA
Jon Elster, Columbia University, New York, USA
Amitai Etzioni, George Washington University, Washington, DC, USA
Ingo Pies, Lehrstuhl für Wirtschaftsethik, Martin-Luther-Universität Halle-Wittenberg, Halle (Saale), Sachsen-Anhalt, Germany
Michaela Haase, Marketing, Freie Universität Berlin, Berlin, Germany
Carlos Hoevel, Facultad de Ciencias Economicas, Universidad Catolica Argentina, Buenos Aires, Argentina
Yuichi Shionoya, Hitotsubashi University, Kunitachi, Tokyo, Japan
Philippe Van Parijs, Chaire Hoover d'Ethique Economique, Universite Catholique de Louvain, Louvain-la-Neuve, Belgium
Gedeon J. Rossouw, Hadefields Office Park, Ethics Institute of Africa, Hatfield, Pretoria, South Africa
Josef Wieland, LEIZ, Zeppelin Universität, Friedrichshafen, Baden-Württemberg, Germany

Ethical Economy describes the theory of the ethical preconditions of the economy and of business as well as the theory of the ethical foundations of economic systems. It analyzes the impact of rules, virtues, and goods or values on economic action and management. *Ethical Economy* understands ethics as a means to increase trust and to reduce transaction costs. It forms a foundational theory for business ethics and business culture. The Series *Ethical Economy. Studies in Economic Ethics and Philosophy* is devoted to the investigation of interdisciplinary issues concerning economics, management, ethics, and philosophy. These issues fall in the categories of economic ethics, business ethics, management theory, economic culture, and economic philosophy, the latter including the epistemology and ontology of economics. Economic culture comprises cultural and hermeneutic studies of the economy. One goal of the series is to extend the discussion of the philosophical, ethical, and cultural foundations of economics and economic systems. The series is intended to serve as an international forum for scholarly publications, such as monographs, conference proceedings, and collections of essays. Primary emphasis is placed on originality, clarity, and interdisciplinary synthesis of elements from economics, management theory, ethics, and philosophy.

The book series has been accepted into SCOPUS (March 2019) and will be visible on the Scopus website within a few months.

Ghislain Deslandes

Postcritical Management Studies

Philosophical Investigations

Ghislain Deslandes
Law, Economics and Humanities
ESCP Business School
Paris, France

ISSN 2211-2707 ISSN 2211-2723 (electronic)
Ethical Economy
ISBN 978-3-031-29403-7 ISBN 978-3-031-29404-4 (eBook)
https://doi.org/10.1007/978-3-031-29404-4

Translation from the French language edition: "Critique de la condition managériale" by Ghislain
Deslandes, © Presses Universitaires 2016. Published by Presses Universitaires de France (PUF). All
Rights Reserved.

© The Editor(s) (if applicable) and The Author(s), under exclusive license to Springer Nature
Switzerland AG 2023
This work is subject to copyright. All rights are solely and exclusively licensed by the Publisher, whether
the whole or part of the material is concerned, specifically the rights of reprinting, reuse of illustrations,
recitation, broadcasting, reproduction on microfilms or in any other physical way, and transmission or
information storage and retrieval, electronic adaptation, computer software, or by similar or dissimilar
methodology now known or hereafter developed.
The use of general descriptive names, registered names, trademarks, service marks, etc. in this publication
does not imply, even in the absence of a specific statement, that such names are exempt from the relevant
protective laws and regulations and therefore free for general use.
The publisher, the authors, and the editors are safe to assume that the advice and information in this book
are believed to be true and accurate at the date of publication. Neither the publisher nor the authors or the
editors give a warranty, expressed or implied, with respect to the material contained herein or for any
errors or omissions that may have been made. The publisher remains neutral with regard to jurisdictional
claims in published maps and institutional affiliations.

This Springer imprint is published by the registered company Springer Nature Switzerland AG
The registered company address is: Gewerbestrasse 11, 6330 Cham, Switzerland

To an Unnamed...

"Indeed, everything changes according to whether we conceive of man as a thinking subject dominating the universe of objects (…), or on the contrary as a living being, immersed in life, submerged by it and its needs."

Michel Henry

"Life is what happens to you when you are busy making other plans."

John Lennon

Introduction

If we accept the hypothesis that the word management comes from the Latin *manus*,[1] invoking the role of the hand in driving (especially horses), directing, guiding and controlling, then are we not all engaged, to a greater or lesser extent, in management? Indeed, how can we escape it, in each of the decisions that we take? Are we not "embarked", in the Pascalian sense, to varying degrees and more or less voluntarily, in managerial operations throughout our lives? Everything happens as if it was the "mystery of the economy and management which has literally forged and determined from top to bottom the experience of history, on which we still depend to a large extent", as Agamben argues.[2] As if it were indeed the mystery of management that seems to inspire, stimulate, alter or at least modify the present on which we depend, and the space in which we live, work and think.[3] And if this is the case, then now would appear to be the ideal time to question our ability to manage, offering some new philosophical investigations of this faculty, seeking to understand its rules and laws, to grasp its paradoxes as well as its limits.

Nonetheless, this work cannot be envisaged without recalling two moments in Western history during which the problem of management was posed very clearly: the "proto-management" of Ancient Greece and the phenomenon of modern Taylorian and post-Taylorian management.

For the Greeks, first of all, management primarily concerned the management of private affairs, the domestic universe, the capacity to be a good farmer, head of the family and master of the household.[4] It was also a question of organizing oneself as

---

[1] Giving "main", the French word for "hand".

[2] G. Agamben, 79 and 221: "The economic-governmental vocation of contemporary democracies is not a hitch in the journey; it is an integral part of the theological heritage of which they are the depositaries."

[3] *Id.* p. 46: "Something happened with the term 'economy' that may recall what has happened nowadays with the term 'enterprise', which, with the more or less conscious consent of those concerned, has come to apply to circles that, like the University, have traditionally had no connection with it."

[4] Cf. the French term "ménager", the root of English "management".

x   Introduction

efficiently as possible in order to free oneself from work; management was from the outset an opportunistic and shrewd way of thinking. However, in Aristotle's[5] *Economics*, we find the distinction between management (*oikonomia*) proper – the act of managing one's household, subsequently extended to the public sphere[6] – and "chrematic" affairs, more closely associated with the art of commerce and finance. In Aristotle's view, business management is ultimately a matter of ethical principles; the pursuit of wealth is not as important as the pursuit of those virtues inherent to the genuine exercise of management. Priority is given to what is beneficial over what is profitable. A virtuous individual must therefore constantly "manage" herself and exercise sovereignty over herself; the *phronimos*, or exemplary "ménager", will be prudent as well as discerning and will know how to strike the right balance between self-control and the government of others. She must be capable of stepping back from her own activity in order to offer a clearer account of it, resisting the temptation to forget her own limitations (*hubris*) and recognising her strengths and weaknesses: she will seek to find harmony between her character and the goals she has set for herself.

As far as modern management is concerned, it is worth recalling that it was in a *Bulletin de la Société de l'Industrie Minérale* dated 1916 that an engineer from the coal mines of Commentry, a certain Henri Fayol, set out a few management principles that would become pillars of the discipline. "The task now is to construct an administrative doctrine", remarked Fayol.[7] His wish was soon granted. The idea of management as a scientific and rational process became established within industrial organizations over the course of the twentieth century, notably thanks to the influence of the work of Frederick Winslow Taylor, of which Fayol was aware.

Business Administration According to the "Scientific" Approach

The central elements of this administrative doctrine, set out in a series of principles, would go on to define the structure of the teaching dispensed in management schools (foresee, organise, command, coordinate, control), especially American ones, informing their objectivist and functionalist paradigm. For a long time, this paradigm remained the dominant model among both actors observers of organizational behaviour, even if it was partially contested in social approaches represented by the early experiences of George Elton Mayo (1880–1949) at Western Electric (1924–1932), who noted the importance of the social climate within a working

---

[5] Aristotle 2003.

[6] Dauzat 2003: VI.

[7] Fayol 1916/1999: 51. This presentation includes some of the elements presented by the author at the seminar "Philosophical Variations on the Problem of Management I, II, III, IV", held at the International College of Philosophy from 2013 to 2015.

Introduction

group; or by Abraham Maslow and his theory of needs, which highlighted the existence, beyond formal organization, of an informal organization driven by a desire for personal fulfilment.

It is also worth noting that the Taylorian moment itself is indebted to the developments in managerial thinking that preceded it, particularly during the Renaissance, when management meant first and foremost an *art of caring*, but also of steering and piloting.[8] Already at this early stage, and for a long time subsequently, it was assumed that management involved a plan and a mechanism for achieving certain goals, and a certain prudence in practice as well: Furetière highlighted this aspect in his famous dictionary of 1690, defining *Œconomie* as the "prudent management of one's property, or of that of others".[9]

These early sources also allow us to refute the idea that Taylor is the founder of management.[10] Nevertheless, he can still reasonably be regarded as the (somewhat unconscious) initiator of just-in-time organization, or of what the geographer and economist Diane Perrons insightfully calls *temporalised political economy*.[11] It is Taylor who first ushered humans into the numerically defined domain of constant evaluation[12] and inspired the "dromocratic" revolution in management, in the sense of the neologism proposed by the philosopher Paul Virilio to mean the study of the role of speed in contemporary societies,[13] initiating a new way of understanding time in relation to productive activities.

Taylor's influence can also be felt in the enduring definition of management as a fight against "inefficacy", a conception which wilfully neglects the role of the individual at work. As Taylor himself puts it:

> In all the mechanical arts, the science which explains each act of the workers is so complex that the most gifted worker to carry out the work is incapable of understanding this science, either because he lacks appropriate knowledge or because his intelligence is not sufficiently developed.[14]

In this view, if men and women are inefficient, it is also because they do not like working and are only interested in getting paid for their labour. This vision leads to a division of labour both vertically (*top-down*) and horizontally (the assembly line), since it is a question of putting the right person in the right place, and specialising operators in certain tasks repeated *ad infinitum* under the authority of a supervisor. Behind these new methods, which were "revolutionary" when they were first proposed, there is first and foremost a concern for universality, for the "*one best way*".

This is perhaps better described as "managerialism" rather than management, that is a discourse and a philosophy of action which consider the individual as a

---

[8] Le Texier 2011.

[9] Furetière, 1690.

[10] Deslandes 2014.

[11] Perrons et al. 2005.

[12] Cassin 2014.

[13] Virilio 1977, 1984.

[14] Taylor 1911/1971: 75–76.

"resource", and which have been constantly extending their influence for more than a century.[15] This managerialist "engineering" sees human and social organizations as a timely response to market costs towards greater efficiency, while omitting to ask the political and cultural questions that any form of collaboration implies. It is, moreover, remarkably cyclical in that its conclusions resemble its premises: a shrinkage of the semantic register and a very narrow vision of human beings, incapable of taking an interest in their actions, disarmed in the face of any form of innovation, deprived at last of any deliberative capacity.

Even today, not only can managerialism be glimpsed at work in many industrial, commercial and administrative sectors (from timber to leather, footwear, cardboard, automobile, foundries, the food trade, the fast-food industry, etc.), but it has even inspired the dictionary definition of management as "a set of techniques for directing, organising and managing a company" (*Larousse* dictionary). Management is thus defined by its goal, or more precisely by the techniques that make it possible to achieve that goal, rather than by its nature.[16]

This dominant interpretation of the concept, in its most general sense, is shared by many specialists, for example in the worlds of consulting and executive training. It is also found at the heart of many of the management courses taught in specialised schools and universities, which all too often succumb to the technical temptations of the discipline, to "tools", "mechanisms" and "endogenous disciplines" (marketing, finance, strategy…). All of which tends to reduce the importance afforded to "exogenous disciplines"[17]; that is those that do not belong exclusively to management, such as law, economics, history or philosophy. A more recent definition, such as that proposed by sociologists Luc Boltanski and Ève Chiapello in their essay on *The New Spirit of Capitalism*,[18] presenting management as a "global *mechanism* capable of inspiring all the functions of the company", does not fundamentally contradict this technicist temptation which, combined with the strength of "tools" and "disciplines", remains the dominant interpretation of management in its most general sense.

This mechanical character allows Taylorian/Post-Taylorian management to present itself as axiologically neutral, pretending not to realise that it thus refuses to consider individuals as ends in their own right. The most pressing aim of all is efficiency, a notion which underpins our present calculocracy, the spirit of "all-evaluation", to use the term coined by philologist and philosopher Barbara Cassin,[19] which had come to define our so-called "auditing society". But can this classic form of management – oriented towards optimisation and presented as a method of controlling social relations based on a principle of scientific rationality, removing

---

[15] de Gaulejac 2005, 2012.

[16] Bouilloud 1994.

[17] Bouilloud and Lécuyer 1994: 16.

[18] Boltanski and Chiapello 1999.

[19] Cassin 2014.

Introduction xiii

ethical issues from the field of work – really lay claim to neutrality?[20] How, within such a framework, can the manager ever be protected from the temptation to manipulate social relations to her own benefit, or that of the organization that rewards her?[21]

Towards a Postcritical Approach to Management

The "objective" evaluation of results and "performance" has been adopted and extended by the cybernetic imaginary,[22] promoting a vision of management as a guide and a decision-making tool that even a (more or less) highly developed robot could use. As John Hendry explains, "the dominant conception of the manager is that of a morally neutral technician engaged in a world of rational problem solving".[23] Clearly, the immanent interplay of the powers of subjectivity and their actualisation[24] never enters into this equation. By discounting subjective action out of hand, this dominant conception fails to address the subject of commitment and never questions the deeper motivations of the individual at work.

In its pre-critical period, modern management therefore resembled a set of techniques created to increase objective performance, measured by numbers and requiring neither ethical reflection nor political or cultural treatment. It is at this juncture that we must turn our attention to a current of thought in management research that has developed since the early 1990s, inspired by the work of Mats Alvesson and Hugh Willmott,[25] themselves inspired by the Frankfurt School and a number of post-structuralist authors, and which seeks to highlight the epistemic, political and ethical implications of modern management.

This trend, which is now very influential, has invigorated the various compartments of *management studies* (business ethics, leadership, organizational behaviour, strategy, etc.). It has largely focused on discussing the dominant assumptions in the field of management with regard to values, goals and purposes of organizations, and on identifying alternative (e.g. based on the ethics of *care* for instance) and micro-management methods. This research has also challenged the positivist foundations of knowledge on which the classical models of management are built. Finally, it has helped to expose the "regimes of truth", the unspoken power structures at work within organizations, and to reveal the limitations of the dominant paradigm (masculine, "rational", etc.). Rather than solving so-called management "problems", these authors have sought to problematise the familiar, universal solutions proposed in management handbooks.

---

[20] Grey 1996: 601.

[21] Parker 2002.

[22] Rappin 2014.

[23] Hendry 2006.

[24] Seyler 2010: 61.

[25] Alvesson and Willmott 1992.

xiv Introduction

Nevertheless, considering these two significant moments of the history of management studies identified above, and despite the efforts of critical management researchers, it is quite clear that the question of life as such are never really at the heart of the discussion. In both cases, the individual is represented either as an object,[26] as an image or as a resource. For its part, the "Taylorian science" of management ignores all individual sensitivity or subjectivity. As Thibault Le Texier notes:

> At the beginning of the 20th century, management generally tended to lose interest in individuality as such and concentrate on functions, tasks and operations. Taylor rejects, for example, the idea of personal relationships between managers and managers and the personalisation of functions. For him, management must be objective and depersonalised.[27]

In a collective text published in 1990, Jean-François Chanlat was already criticising the propensity of managerial literature to "treat humans as objects of research devoid of subjectivity and affectivity".[28] In Taylorism and in the studies that bear its hallmark, a disembodied individual emerges, endowed with no affectivity of her own and generally devoid of any capacity for resistance (especially on the political level). We still remain, in different ways, subject to the "tyranny of visibility", to borrow the expression coined by Nicole Aubert and Claudine Haroche.[29] The world of organizations seems beholden to the idea that image is indeed a fair representation of the world, as the jurist Alain Supiot remarks:

> Accounting is a way of accrediting a truth through image. (...) The accounting image thus has a status that could be said to be iconic: just as religious icons weld a community of believers around a religious truth, the accounting image welds a community of merchants around a legal truth.[30]

For their part, critical studies have certainly tried to go beyond the tendency of Taylorian/Post-Taylorian management to define the individual as a "human resource", focusing instead on identity at work and the question of the *self*, particularly from a Foucauldian perspective.[31] But, as Mats Alvesson modestly points out, this field of research is tangled and ever-changing,[32] and one sometimes gets the feeling that identity, as a concept in organization studies, means everything at once and nothing in particular.[33]

From then on, the time may have come to go beyond this opposition between "mainstream" and CMS by trying to give criticism back its positive and creative capacities. This was, for example, the meaning of the question posed by Bruno Latour in 2004 ("Why has critique run out of stream?"), who was already trying to

---

[26] It is worth remembering that those who were "managed" in ancient Greece were also slaves.

[27] Le Texier 2011: 58.

[28] Chanlat 1990/2007: 12.

[29] Aubert and Haroche 2011.

[30] Supiot 2015, p. 122, adding: "Accounting is also the first modern institution to have conferred legal truth on numbers", *ibid.*, p.123.

[31] Rhodes and Wray-Bliss 2013.

[32] Alvesson 2010: 211.

[33] *Ibid.*, 212.

Introduction xv

distance himself from the spirit of deconstruction in a world – traversed by crises of identity as well as of the environment – that is only waiting to be rebuilt on new grounds. And this is also the spirit that animates the ten or so philosophers gathered around Laurent de Sutter (2019) who, in their manifesto entitled *Postcritique*, do not propose to criticise criticism in the form of an endless negative spiral, but try to give it back its active and affirmatory power, in the way suggested by one of the contributors, Dorian Astor, who evokes the Nietzschean *amor fati* on page 76, based on a "gracious and loving kindness" rather than on arrogance and resentment. Thinking not against but for, as proposed by Pacôme Thiellement on page 24, who highlights the fact that criticising has for too long meant loathing, isolating, classifying and, in the end, judging. Critics, he explains, "spend less time loving what they love than not loving what they don't love" (p. 24; Deslandes 2023). This general perspective, which is in many ways plurivocal, as the diversity of approaches described in this collective work shows, nevertheless animates the lines that follow and inspires the tone of this essay.

Besides, the word "love" may be surprising here, but it must be understood in the manner of Platonic eros as a cosmic force that links the elements of the (organizational) world. Eros is not the perfection it seeks, but it is the social feeling par excellence, and in particular the one that best expresses our relationship to work (don't we most often have emotional relationships, of adoration and detestation most often, towards our professional activity?[34]). In short, it is always a sort of "erotic" trade that we have with ourselves and with others, from whom we expect recognition. The question "Do you love me?" is the question that first moves the social relations at work, as the philosopher Jean-Luc Marion remarks in his work *The Erotic Phenomenon*.[35] According to him,[36] love is in first place a desire of elevation which escapes any calculation and which defines us as *Ego Amans* (*I am where I love*).

But how can we go beyond this opposition, and enter fully into postcritical studies in management, other than by returning to the question of the subject and identity? In the classical way adopted by philosophers in the Western tradition, of constantly asking the metaphysical question of the subject. *De facto*, it is usually through living and expressive representations that we can best "grasp how an individual is defined and portrayed in the process of constructing his or her identity".[37] And "business *imperium*", to borrow the expression of the historian and psychoanalyst Pierre Legendre, remains "above all a matter of theatre, the theatricalization of human beings and the world".[38] The individual at work is perceived as a psychological,

---

[34] Not to be confused here with "emotional" capitalism (Illouz 2019), that is the invasion of our sensibilities by industrial neuromarketing.

[35] Marion, 2006.

[36] J-L. Marion whose great philosophical proximity to the one to whom we reserve a central place in this essay Michel Henry must be specified. He was his friend, his editor (Presses Universitaires de France, Coll. Epimethée) and, in a way, his "continuator".

[37] *Ibid.*, 209.

[38] Legendre 2007: 30.

biological and social[39] entity. Management thus appears to be first and foremost a question of "empirically testing and measuring" *a posteriori* the theories in place. Admittedly, the individual belongs to the order of living things, but lived subjectivity is conspicuous by its absence. Even when it comes to dealing with the body this literature, being "mainstream" or critical, is primarily concerned with the mundane body, the visible body or the sensory body, rather than the body as a subjective "matter".[40] Our method here, however, will be to start from that very reality.

Rarely, if at all,[41] have authors in this field ventured to consider the question of what we actually are: a living self which cannot be seen or represented in any fixed manner whatsoever.[42] In management studies, preference is given to "visibility", studies concerned with visualising and comparing "data", etc. The anthropological background of management is generally absent; at times it appears to have been extrapolated from the image of men/women presented by statistics and measurement tools. In this respect, the emerging notion of *quantified self* provides some indication of the extent to which Taylorism has infiltrated our societies: by extending quantitative evaluation to all of our actions and gestures, it gives management almost unlimited power over employee conduct.[43]

As Marie Gueguen recounts in her observations of a supermarket "drive-in" service, where the customer relation procedures in place resemble (according to the author) those introduced by the Post Office in the years 1990–2000 and summarised in the French acronym "BRASMAR" (for "hello-eye contact-attention-smile-thank-you-bye"),[44] the work essentially consists of "running, picking, scanning"[45] under the watchful evaluation of the calculators. As Alain Supiot astutely notes, "new computer tools could be a chance to wrest work from the stupor into which Taylorism had plunged it. But these possibilities are ignored when we insist of thinking of workers in the same terms as computers, considered as a means of humanising work."[46]

---

[39] Chanlat 1990/2007: 15.

[40] According to Michel Henry, "every sensitive body - felt, seen, heard, touched or moved - presupposes another body that feels it, sees it, touches it, moves it, all operations of a second body that constitutes the first and makes it possible - a transcendental body, therefore, and constituting, a subject or 'subjective' body, without which the first, the object-body-of-the-world, would not be possible", Henry 2003, p. 169. See Hassard et al. 2000.

[41] See for some exceptions Faÿ 2007a, b; Puyou and Faÿ 2013; Letiche 2009; Perezts et al. 2015.

[42] "This is why the invisible is not the antithetical, formal and empty concept of phenomenality, but its realisation in the effectiveness of feeling", Henry 2003: 50.

[43] In this respect, however, let us note the recent warnings of the CNIL: "Insofar as these practices contribute to the continuous redefinition of performance and enjoyment objectives so as to place individuals in processes of improvement, the objective of which recedes as they progress, the risk is obviously, for the followers, to fall into a form of 'normopathy' [...]: language, thought and behaviour normalised for performance and efficiency would lose all power of contestation once life itself becomes a programme, itself integrated into that of an immense headless machinery", Gueguen 2015: 35.

[44] "Bonjour-regard-attention-sourire-merci-au revoir" in French.

[45] Gueguen 2015: 32.

[46] Supiot 2015: 257.

Introduction   xvii

Business Administration with a Henryian Lens

In this essay[47] I endeavour to present the working individual in a completely differ-ent way. The importance of adopting a new perspective is amply demonstrated by one of the most pressing, and also tragic, phenomena of the modern economy, gen-erally referred to as burn-out.[48] In a book entitled *Global Burnout*, Pascal Chabot defines this condition as first and foremost "the illness of the 'good American', if by this term we mean the American who dreams in line with the dominant values of work, money, inventiveness, discovery, industrialisation, surpassing oneself and, finally, imposing democratic values of freedom and trade practices on the rest of the world".[49]

This issue is one of the major symptoms of the malaise afflicting contemporary societies and provides a lightning rod for criticisms of the legitimacy of manage-ment. The effectiveness of traditional forms of management and the techniques stemming from the general paradigm of performance are now subject to increasing scrutiny (management by objectives, *downsizing*, *empowerment*, and a host of oth-ers, including recent reports of bonuses dependent on the number of redundancies posted). There seems to have been a sudden realisation of the suffering specific to the contemporary world of work; it is worth noting, moreover, that management professionals are often the first to realise this, as they are the first witnesses, and sometimes also the first victims. They have therefore begun to question the effec-tiveness of their own methods, describing a growing sense of demotivation, cata-strophic for economic development, particularly in Western countries.

According to a study quoted by Peter Fleming,[50] almost half of workers in the United States and Europe consider themselves to be detached from their jobs. A sign of the times: a 2011 report based on the work of the Institut de l'Entreprise/Cercle de l'Entreprise et du Management/FNEGE[51] stressed "the need for critical skills and 'intellectual training' in the education of managers, which has until now, in both schools and universities, been too exclusively concerned with technical training".

In an attempt to approach management from a perspective other than "calculat-ing impersonality",[52] I draw particularly on the phenomenology of life proposed by Michel Henry,[53] a philosopher whose international influence is steadily growing in two separate fields of research, namely phenomenology and management. Henry has resolutely opposed exclusive objectivism, rooting his thought in lived, and

---

[47] Which is an updated and expanded version of the text initially published in French under the title *Critique de la condition managériale* (PUF, 2016).

[48] Dejours 2009.

[49] Chabot 2013: 28.

[50] Fleming 2014: 4.

[51] French management institutions.

[52] *Ibid*, 62.

[53] And with a chapter also devoted to the philosophy of Bernard Stiegler.

xviii   Introduction

therefore experienced, interiority. For Henry, "the activities of work, 'professional activities', do not cease to be personal and are part of the flow of individual life".[54]

Indeed for Henry the social, biological, cultural and economic parameters associated with an individual tell us nothing, show us nothing of what really constitutes her essence, namely the sensation of living experienced by each living individual. Accustomed as we are to perceiving others at work on the basis of "visible" determinations, a parametric compound in a way, we neglect the universal characteristic that unites us all: the fact that we are, first and foremost, living beings.[55] And a living being, a self, necessarily pre-exists any relationships with others (a central theme of all currents of management research, whether critical or not). It should surely go without saying that social relationships can never predate the individuals involved. Yet such is the primordial error committed by many managerial theories, both mainstream and critical (post-structuralist, psychoanalytical, etc.), leading them to concern themselves with "ghost relationships", confusing the parametric and mundane "I" with the constitution of a Self, and forgetting that each individual has a life and an existence before entering into relationships with others.[56] It is this *subjective body* that has been forgotten by managerial theories, in favour of a parametric one that says nothing of the original pathos that constitutes our individual lived experiences.[57] Michel Henry's material phenomenology invites us to adopt a perspective as radical as the words he uses to present his quasi-Copernican project:

> So we philosophers make an effort of rectification to think what is anterior to thought, whereas the human sciences naively take the individual at this empirical stage. Moreover, they have always confused an already objectified individual with what we are in reality, i.e. the original event which is always non-objective. This is why what they say about man is false! And the more they affirm and give a scientific allure to their assertions, the more they go astray and become pseudo-sciences![58]

The criticism made here may seem unfair, or its statement is abrupt to say the least. It is worth noting, however, that it receives an echo today, even in the social sciences themselves. For the historian and sociologist Pierre Rosanvallon, for example, we have entered a new age, that of the *individualism of singularity*, which highlights the permanent superposition of "objective realities and subjective apprehensions of what we experience".[59] This new age can be illustrated, according to him, both by the #MeToo movement, in terms of attacks on individual integrity, and by the Black Lives Matter movement. Rosanvallon adds his reading of the crisis of the Yellow Vests protests in France, one of the main characteristics of which, in addition to bringing together people with a wide range of social, economic and political

---

[54] Henry 1976: 244.

[55] Faÿ and Deslandes 2022.

[56] T. Berlanda, *"La violence du désir ressortit-elle radicalement au désir de violence?"*, in *Le désir de l'autre*, René Girard & Michel Henry, eds. Benoît Chantre and Thierry Berlanda, Edition Petra, p. 43–58, 2016.

[57] Painter et al. 2020.

[58] Henry 2004b: 79.

[59] Rosanvallon 2021: 69.

Introduction   xix

profiles, is that it refuses to be symbolised by a dedicated body (political or trade union), or any leader or delegate accepted by all, thus challenging a representation in the usual sociological form of an objective "class".

According to the author, the significance for traditional sociology is considerable: it means that the classification of statistical data and the establishment of correlations are no longer sufficient, and that it is from the angle of "individual tests" (the term test ("épreuve") giving its title to his book), distinct from structural tests, that it is now appropriate to study the circuit of affects.[60] Everything happens as if, in the end, it is under the affective mode that the world is always revealed to the person who works, manages or is managed. To put it like Dejours: "surprise, annoyance, irritation, disappointment, anger, feelings of powerlessness, etc. These feelings All these feelings are an integral part of the work. They are the fundamental raw material of knowledge of the world."[61] It is as if, in the end, it were no longer only the material history of exploitation that became the object of study – the author notes that it was not so much the differences in income and wealth that drove people into the streets as an individual feeling of indignation – but first and foremost the subjective appreciation of the injustices felt, which is finally better apprehended by "literary documents" (pamphlets or songs) than the measurable character of the evolution of salaries and purchasing power.[62]

Rather than studying songs, perhaps we should take this disobliging Henryian remark seriously, and try to pose the question of human and social relations, particularly in the context of work, on a completely different plane, one that refuses on principle to objectify empirical bodies and instead tries to take their full phenomenological account. Indeed, this book takes this phenomenological perspective as its point of origin to rethink and to rebuild managerial thinking. This viewpoint in fact allows us to make the place for postcritical philosophical investigations to radically call its foundations into question to and to renew its goals.

Forgetting Taylor

But is another definition of management even possible? Adopting a different perspective on management from that proposed by Taylor requires us to take a historical diversion. In order to forget Taylor we must first reacquaint ourselves with a distant past, exploring the history and origins of the word management. We must also apply the resources of philosophy to a field of science where they have rarely been employed in the last century. It is a regrettable fact that philosophers are too often inclined to reject the world of economics out of hand. This attitude can even

---

[60] "Resentment, indignation, anger, bitterness, anxiety and mistrust", cited on page 13.

[61] Dejours 2021, p. 102.

[62] In doing so, he drew on the insights and work of Edward Palmer Thompson, *La Formation de la classe ouvrière anglaise*, translation by G. Dauvé, M. Golaszewski et M-N. Thibault, Paris: Gallimard, 1963.

be found among those who claim to be part of the *critical management studies* movement, although several authors have clearly highlighted the futility of such a posture.[63] If the actors of economic life are supposed to be "in favour of" management, the community of philosophers, and intellectuals, in general, are assumed to be "against"[64] it. We are thus asked to choose between cynicism and despair (or shame),[65] between the operative and the cerebral, between adherence to the values of managerialism and the perpetual denunciation of the power relations at play in the organizational phenomenon. Finally, and perhaps most worryingly, those who are not actively "against" management may simply be indifferent to economic and managerial issues. Bernard Stiegler observes:

> As for the political discourse of philosophers, in France they say almost nothing about the economy. They talk about immigration, Europe or democracy, but they don't talk about capital, labour, industry or marketing. As for those who speak philosophically about labour, and there are some, and they are very interesting and important, they are not generally philosophers.[66]

This book would also like to respond to the long-standing concern expressed here by Stiegler. It thus takes as its starting point the weight of business management in our lives, a weight that has been mainly recognised, and by no means neglected, in the (albeit ancient) history of ideas. The Greeks were the first to question household management and its corollaries, *hubris* and *pleonexia*, the propensity to want more than everyone else in everything. Yet it is precisely the characteristic of modern management, from Fayol and Taylor, to claim an axiological neutrality of management that would have horrified the thinkers of Antiquity, and to which the phenomenological approach developed by Michel Henry in particular responds with new terms and a new ontological resolution. The ambition is to think about management beyond a strictly technical and behaviourist vision, and through a rediscovered ethical purpose, glimpsed by the Ancients.

The first part, entitled From Proto-management to Contemporary Functional Stupidity, highlights the curious reciprocal ignorance of management and philosophy during the industrial era, paradoxically showing how management has historically constituted a major subject of philosophical investigation (notably in Xenophon, then in Aristotle). Nowadays, only a managerial ethics proper could allow us to revive this glorious history while adapting to the economic and political conditions of the present, and trying to revive the idea that economic choices are never made without a moral underpinning. However, today the discipline has been

---

[63] Alvesson et al. 2009.

[64] You only need to take a few moments and go to an online bookstore to realise one thing: there is little critical thinking there. Alain Berkeley Thomas (2003: 5) even notes that management can be considered "as one of the 'non-thinking professions'".

[65] One can think here of the text by Michael Brocklehurst, Christopher Grey and Andrew Sturdy, "Management: the work that dares not speak its name", *Management Learning*, 41, p. 7–19, 2010. Managers prefer to present themselves as professionals, entrepreneurs or project leaders rather than managers: there would be a specific shame in proclaiming themselves as such.

[66] Stiegler 2009: 31.

Introduction xxi

divided into several areas which are developing in parallel: management as a set of techniques, as a science ("management science"), as a (professional) practice, as an ethic ("Business Ethics") and finally as a way of exercising political power (critically examined by the CMS). I investigate each of these aspects here to show that, unfortunately, what should constitute management as such, that is the analysis of the points of contamination between these different meanings, is most often reduced to the constitution of competing "chapels" which hardly ever speak to each other (management ethicists versus technicians of management, critical thinkers versus practitioners, management scientists versus business ethicists, etc.). From this point on, we can see that nothing seems to be able to halt the progression of what we must call the systemic stupidity of organizations, which I attempt to describe and analyse, before emphasising the need to rethink management from top to bottom.

This point is the subject of the second part, and concerns not the representations or figures through which organizational phenomena are generally studied, but bodies, or more precisely according to the terminology proposed by Michel Henry, subjective bodies. Taking a phenomenology of life as a starting point, and thus returning to the real subjectivity of individuals at work, means replacing the traditional "resources management" by relationships between living people understood as both the principles and the end of any organization. This bias, however, prompts us to proceed with a genealogy of the "self" in management studies in order to show the originality of the Henryian proposal to renew a praxis described here as *affectio societatis*, the ultimate modality of motivation and self-realisation in the circuit of affects. A praxis in which each individual experiences herself more and in which the Other is the one with whom I can develop a real cooperation. A cooperation between individuals who certainly have a social role, but who are first capable of deploying their properly affective dimension, which is the origin of all successful work in common. In the last two chapters of this part, I question the conditions of possibility of this overcoming of Taylorism: both from another conception of *productive time*, in particular in the face of generalised social acceleration and short-term logics which constantly influence decisions, and from a posture which critically questions *recognition*, understood as the unique and unsurpassable principle of justice in organizations.

The third and final part is devoted to a reconstruction of both our definitions and our imaginary. The aim here is to try to draw all the consequences when managerial facts are finally no longer grasped as processes without a subject, but as a matter of the manager's power to act (a power clearly distinguished from an alleged power behind which lies a denied vulnerability). From a series of observations on the powerlessness of the "powerful", in an attempt to perceive another figure of the manager on the horizon, and from a series of remarks on the question of the suffering of managers, in order to glimpse the alternative possibility of "work with joy", particularly at a time of teleworking and the crisis of COVID-19, it is finally to another definition of management to which these investigations invite us. I try to formulate this proposal by highlighting the "powers" of constraint and imitation of management, and finally note the crucial importance of its exploratory, transgressive and imaginative virtues in order to limit its most negative impacts. The conclusion invites the reader to conceive of managerial thought in the guise of a *pharmakon*, and opens up postcritical prospects for combating the tyranny of numbers by taking into account the more informal and affective aspects of human relations, and supports the development of a "weak" management, the only one likely to "effectively" combat the systemic, and doubtless algorithmic, stupidity of contemporary organizations.

*

As a matter of fact, some philosophical investigations of management should not hesitate to enlighten one discipline with the lessons learned from others, finally pulling management out of its splendid isolation, reconnecting with its origins and ends.[67] Forgetting Taylor is thus a matter of overcoming, exceeding, pushing beyond the limits, narrow and localised to say the least, of technique and the Taylorian definition of management. Forgetting Taylor will also mean reintroducing the history of philosophical ideas into our understanding of management. The hypothetical imperatives of science must be reconciled with the categorical imperatives of ethics. How then can we confront "what is" (factual findings) with "what must be"? To answer this question, we will also have to forget Taylor.

References

Alvesson, Mats. 2010. Self-doubters, strugglers, storytellers, surfers and others: Images of self-identities in organization studies. *Human Relations* 63 (2).

Alvesson, Mats, and Hugh Willmott. 1992. *Critical management studies*. Londres: Sage.

Alvesson, Mats, André Spicer, and Dan Kärreman. 2009. Critical performativity: The unfinished business of critical management studies. *Human Relations* 62 (4).

Aristotle. 2003. *Economic*, tr. fr. Bernard Abraham van Groningen and André Wartelle. Paris: Les Belles Lettres.

Aubert, Nicole, and Claudine Haroche. 2011. *Les Tyrannies de la visibilité. To be visible in order to exist?* Toulouse: Érès.

Boltanski, Luc, and Ève Chiapello. 1999. *Le Nouvel Esprit du capitalisme*. Paris: Gallimard.

Bouilloud, Jean-Philippe, and Bernard-Pierre Lécuyer. 1994. *L'Invention de la gestion. Histoires et pratiques*. Paris: L'Harmattan.

Cassin, Barbara. 2014. *Derrières les grilles. Sortons du tout-évaluation*. Paris: Mille et une nuits.

Chabot, Pascal. 2013. *Global burn-out*. Paris: PUF.

Chanlat, Jean-François. 1990. *L'individu dans les organisations. Les dimensions oubliées*. Paris: Eska.

de Gaulejac, Vincent. 2005. *La Société malade de la gestion. Idéologie gestionnaire, pouvoir managérial et harcèlement social*. Paris: Seuil.

———. 2012. *La Recherche malade du management*. Quae: Versailles.

De Sutter, Laurent (dir). 2019. *Postcritique*. Paris: PUF.

Dejours, Christophe. 2009. *Live work. Travail et émancipations*. Vol. 2. Paris: Payot.

———. 2021. *Ce qu'il y a de meilleur en nous travailler et honorer la vie*. Paris: Payot.

---

[67] Deslandes 2013, 2023.

Introduction

Deslandes, Ghislain. 2013. *Essai sur les données philosophiques du management*. Paris: PUF.

———. 2014. Management in Xenophon's Philosophy: A retrospective analysis. In *Proceedings of the Philosophy of Management conference*. Chicago: De Paul University.

———. 2020. *A propos du management et d'un problème plus général*. Paris: PUF.

———. 2023. *Erotique de l'administration*. Paris: PUF.

Faÿ, Éric. 2007a. A critical and phenomenological genealogy of the question of the real in western economics and management. *Society and Business Review* 2 (2): 193–203.

———. 2007b. Phenomenological approaches to Work, life and responsibility. *Society and Business Review* 2 (2): 145–152.

Faÿ, Éric, and Ghislain Deslandes. 2022. Extending and discontinuiting phenomenology with Michel Henry. In *The Oxford handbook of phenomenologies and organizations studies*, ed. François-Xavier de Vaujany, Jérémy Arolès, and Mar Perézts, 194–214. Oxford University Press.

Fayol, Henri. 1916. *Administration industrielle et générale*. Paris: Dunod.

Fleming, Peter. 2014. *Resisting work. The corporatization of life and its discontents*. Philadelphia: Temple University Press.

Grey, Christopher. 1996. Towards a Critique of Managerialism: The Contribution of Simone Weil. *Jounal of Management Studies* 5 (33).

Gueguen, Marie. 2015. Les damnés de l'hyper. *Philosophie Magazine* 90.

Hassard, John, Ruth Holliday, and Hugh Willmott. 2000. *Body and organization*. Londres: Sage.

Hendry, John. 2006. Educating managers for post-bureaucracy: The role of the humanities. *Management Learning* 37 (3): 267–281.

Henry, Michel. 1976. *Marx, I & II, Une philosophie de l'économie*. Paris: Gallimard. English version. Michel Henry, *Marx. A philosophy of human reality* (K. McLaughlin, trans.). Bloomington, IN: Indiana University Press, 1983.

———. 2003. *Phenoménologie de la vie, I. De la phénoménologie*. Paris: PUF.

———. 2004. *Auto-donation*. 2nd ed. Paris: Beauchesne.

Illouz, Eva. (dir). 2019. *Les marchandises émotionnelles. L'authenticité au temps du capitalisme*. Introduction by Axel Honneth. Translated from english by Frédéric Joly. Paris: Premiers parallèles.

Le Texier, Thibault. 2011. *La Rationalité managériale. De l'administration domestique à la gouvernance*. PhD thesis in economics, under the supervision of Joël-Thomas Ravix, Nice, Sophia-Antipolis University.

Legendre, Pierre. 2007. *Dominium mundi. L'empire du management*. Paris: Mille et une nuits.

Letiche, Hugo. 2009. Reflexivity and affectivity. *Culture and Organization* 15 (3–4): 291–306.

Painter, Mollie, Mar Pérezts, and Ghislain Deslandes. 2020. Understanding the human in stakeholder Theory: A phenomenological approach to affect-based learning. *Management Learning* 52 (2): 203–223.

Parker, Martin. 2002. *Against management organization in the age of Managerialism*. Cambridge: Polity.

Perezts, Mar, Éric Faÿ, and Sébastien Picard. 2015. Ethics, embodied life and 'Esprit de corps': An ethnographic study with anti-money laundering analysts. *Organization* 22 (2): 217–234.

Perrons, Diane, Colette Fagan, Linda Mc Dowell, Kath Ray, and Kevin Ward. 2005. Work, life and time in the new economy. *Time & Society* 14 (1): 51–64.

Puyou, François-Régis, and Éric Faÿ. 2013. Cogs in the wheel or spanners in the works? A phenomenological approach to the difficulty and meaning of ethical work for financial controllers. *Journal of Business Ethics* 128 (4): 863–876.

Rappin, Baptiste. 2014. *Au fondement du management. Théologie de l'organisation*. Vol. 1. Nice, Ovadia.

Rhodes, Carl, and Edward Wray-Bliss. 2013. The ethical difference of organization. *Organization* 20 (1): 39–50.

Rosanvallon, Pierre. 2021. *Les épreuves de la vie: Comprendre autrement les Français*. Paris: Le Seuil.

Seyler, Frédéric. 2010. *Barbarism or Culture. L'éthique de l'affectivité dans la phénoménologie by Michel Henry*. Paris: Kimé.

Stiegler, Bernard. 2009. *Pour une nouvelle critique de l'économie politique*. Paris: Galilée. English version. Bernard Stiegler, (2010) For a New Critique of Political Economy, Cambridge: Polity Press.

Supiot, Alain. 2015. *La Gouvernance par les nombres*. Paris: Fayard.

Taylor, Frederick Winslow. 1971. *La Direction scientifique des entreprises (1911)*. Paris: Dunod.

Thomas, Alain Berkeley. 2003. *Controversies in management. Issues, debates, answers*. Londres: Routledge.

Virilio, Paul. 1977. *Speed and politics. Essai de dromologie*. Paris: Galilée.

———. 1984. *The negative horizon. Essai de dromoscopie*. Paris: Galilée.

Contents

1 From Proto-Management to Contemporary Functional Stupidity ..   1
  1.1 Management as a Philosophical Problem   1
      1.1.1 Socratic Variations on the Question of Management.   2
      1.1.2 Continental Philosophy and Post-management   6
  1.2 Ethics and Organization(s).   9
      1.2.1 Ethics Versus ROI   9
      1.2.2 Managerial Ethics as Such.   11
  1.3 The Five Senses of Management.   14
      1.3.1 Management as a Technique   14
      1.3.2 Management as a Science   15
      1.3.3 Management as Practice   17
      1.3.4 Management as Ethics.   19
      1.3.5 Management as Politics.   21
  1.4 On Organizational Stupidity   23
      1.4.1 What Is Stupidity?   26
      1.4.2 Philosophical Stupidity and Technological Issues.   28
      1.4.3 Facing a New "banality of evil"?.   31
  References.   33

2 Rethinking Management   39
  2.1 Organizations and the Subjective Body.   40
      2.1.1 Genealogy of the Self in *CMS*.   42
      2.1.2 Michel Henry's Phenomenology of Life   44
      2.1.3 Subjective Bodies.   45
      2.1.4 Praxis and Capabilities   48
  2.2 Desaffectio Societatis   52
      2.2.1 From *Affectio Societatis* to Individual Disaffection.   53
      2.2.2 The Concept of Affectivity from the Henryian
             Perspective.   54
      2.2.3 "Societatis:" Collective Action and Social Roles   56
      2.2.4 Political and Ethical Implications   59

xxv

2.3		Individual Experience at a Time of Social Acceleration	61
	2.3.1	Individual Experience and Acceleration	63
	2.3.2	World-as-Organization	66
	2.3.3	Acceleration and Forgetting about Life	67
	2.3.4	Phenomenology of Life and Management Issues	69
2.4		Beyond Recognition?	72
	2.4.1	Recognition Between Acknowledgment and Claim	73
	2.4.2	Recognition as a Philosophical Question	75
	2.4.3	The Ethics of Recognition: A Critique	77
	2.4.4	Towards a Post-recognition Ethics	80
	2.4.5	Recognition, Hope and Capabilities	82
References			84

3 Rebuilding Management 91

3.1		Leadership or the Powerlessness of the Powerful	91
	3.1.1	The Paradox of Excellence	92
	3.1.2	Activity or Burden: Managerial Polarities	93
	3.1.3	Reign and Charges	95
	3.1.4	Management as a Charge	96
	3.1.5	Between Capacities and Incapacities	99
3.2		Working Without Joy?	100
	3.2.1	Work, Suffering and Joy	102
	3.2.2	Management and the Being of Work	106
	3.2.3	The Dialectic of Suffering and Joy at Work	107
	3.2.4	Joy and Cooperation	109
3.3		Dialectics of Containment	111
	3.3.1	"Feeling the Void" in Times of Lockdowns	112
	3.3.2	Contemporaneity of 'Too Much'	113
	3.3.3	De-intensification Strategies	114
3.4		Redefining "Management"	116
	3.4.1	A Strength	116
	3.4.2	A Vulnerable Force	117
	3.4.3	A Triple Power of Constraint, Imitation and Imagination	119
	3.4.4	Subjective, Interpersonal, Institutional and Environmental Levels	120
References			121

Conclusion: Postcritical Perspectives 127

References 147

Index 157

About the Author

Ghislain Deslandes is Professor at ESCP Business School where his teaching and research activities focus on continental philosophy and management studies. His recent research has been published in *Journal of Business Ethics, Leadership, Management Learning, Organization* and *Organization Studies*. He has published various essays on philosophy such as *Antiphilosopy of Christianity* (Springer, 2021) and *The Idea of Beginning in Jules Lequier's Philosophy* (Lexington Books, 2023), and other essays in the field of management such as *Essai sur les données philosophiques du management* (PUF, 2013) and *A propos du management et d'un problème plus général* (PUF, 2020). He is also a former Program Director at the *Collège International de Philosophie*.

Chapter 1
From Proto-Management
to Contemporary Functional Stupidity

Abstract Xenophon's *Economics* can be considered the first treatise to systematically discuss the scientific and moral character of household management. The industrial era, on the other hand, seems to undermine this moral aspect in favour of the sole objective of efficiency, and the work of Fayol and Taylor, with their objectivist and functionalist paradigm, is emblematic of this view. However, if business administration nowadays refers to a set of techniques and certain scientific theories, is it not only a set of practices, but also a field of application of professional ethics and political relations between managers and subordinates? In the first chapter of this book, the field of continental philosophy is reinvested in order to examine these five 'meanings' of management. I then note the fragmentation of the field management and its difficulty in responding to the contemporary challenges, such as the loss of motivation, the dissipation of knowledge to machines, and more generally the rise of systemic stupidity in organizations. This chapter concludes with a new understanding of intelligence in organizations, as proposed by Bernard Stiegler, and likely to reconnect with management as 'caring'.

Keywords Banality of evil · Continental philosophy · Erotic turn · Managerial ethics · Organizational stupidity · Proletarianisation · Protomanagement · Symbolic poverty

1.1 Management as a Philosophical Problem

If it is true that "philosophy is a form of reflection for which all foreign material is good," as per the elegant definition of doctor and epistemologist Georges Canguilhem,[1] then management as a material could hardly be more foreign or strange. Canguilhem adds: "and we might even say for which all good material *must*

---

[1] Canguilhem 1990.

© The Author(s), under exclusive license to Springer Nature
Switzerland AG 2023
G. Deslandes, *Postcritical Management Studies*, Ethical Economy 65,
https://doi.org/10.1007/978-3-031-29404-4_1

be foreign."[2] From this point of view, the very least we can say is that management is a good subject for philosophy insofar as it has been presented, constituted and institutionalised throughout the twentieth century as a field of knowledge virtually immune to philosophical curiosity (Rendtorff 2014, 2017). But the problem, as we have seen, is that while management has little interest in philosophy, philosophy seems even less interested in management. Surely the time has come for philosophy to address questions of management and the conditions which make it possible.

1.1.1 Socratic Variations on the Question of Management

Probing the etymological roots of management leads us to the French words *mesnagement* and *manège,* which themselves come from the Italian term *maneggiare* (to handle), linked to the Latin term *manus* (hand). *Mesnagement*[3] is at the root of the words used both by Joachim du Bellay, the famous sixteenth century poet who was also the secretary of the Cardinal Jean Du Bellay, in *Les Regrets* ("I was born for the muse, they make me a *mesnager*") and Olivier de Serres, a leading agronomist of the seventeenth century, in his *Théâtre d'agriculture et mesnage des champs*[4]. Furetière's *Dictionnaire,* published a few decades later (1690), defines *Œconomie* as "the prudent management of one's property, or that of others. *Œconomie* is the second part of morality, which teaches how to govern a family, a community in a positive manner."[5]

In the philosophical tradition, critical analysis of management actually goes back to the Greeks, and in particular to Xenophon, whose famous dialogue between Ischomachus and Socrates includes reflections on the role of philosophy in the administration of goods, people and private wealth. This text, traditionally translated into French as *La Mesnagerie,*[6] is one of Xenophon's most widely-read works. It was translated into English in the sixteenth century and into German in the seventeenth century, and was highly-regarded throughout Europe until the advent of modern political economy. Today it is known only to specialists.[7] The framing dialogue between Socrates and Critobulus includes a discussion of the practical management skills of the "experienced businessman:"[8]

---

[2] *Ibid.*

[3] Fréry 2010; Mispelblom Bayer 1996.

[4] "It should be noted here that the human aptitude for planning and accounting in agriculture goes back several tens of thousands of years," Le Texier 2011: 191.

[5] *Universal dictionary containing all the French words both old and modern, & the terms of all sciences and arts,* by A. Furetière, 1690, volume I.

[6] Oeconomicus in Latin, economics in English.

[7] Natali 2001: 265.

[8] Xenophon 1933: 346.

1.1 Management as a Philosophical Problem

> "If I show you first of all people who build inconvenient houses at great expense," explains Socrates, "and then others who, spending a lot less, build houses with all the comforts, don't you think that in this I will show you one of the parts of [management]?"[9]

According to Socrates, one can only consider as assets (*chrêmata*) those things that one knows how to use. A useful asset is one that we know how to take advantage of. An asset that is badly used is no asset at all to its possessor, but rather a kind of enslavement. This is why Socrates, who was not concerned with "increasing the size of his house," was pleased to have so few possessions himself. In the second part of the dialogue, between Ischomacus and Socrates, the former embodies this good manager who honours his debts, makes a profit and cares about the city. According to Socrates'conversational-partner, the good management of a property is akin to a form of virtue, especially when practised with self-control (*sôphrosunê*).[10] Managerial activity is thus understood and defined with reference to the moral conduct of the individual as a citizen of the city; knowing how to be concerned about wealth and one's property is indeed a talent that is inseparable from virtue. Socrates was clearly interested in questions of management in so far as they concern the ethical foundations of human relations. By this token, management is essentially a political and ethical art based on economic reality. Work and production are thus to be considered from the perspective of social morality.[11]

It is curious to note that several of the major themes of contemporary management research are already problematised in this text, including leadership, the subject of so much contemporary management research. We find in Ischomacus' contributions a fascination with the "talent to command,"[12] "instruction and great natural gifts,"[13] but also an "inspiration from above," which has long been a feature of reflections on authority (cf. Max Weber). The dialogue also provides an opportunity to discuss gender issues and the role of women in business administration, examining their closely-controlled and sometimes ambiguous scope of action.[14] But is a detailed analysis of the social trends of the fourth century BC really a prerequisite for understanding management? At the very least it can help us to reconsider, in the Socratic manner, the credibility of one of the fundamental paradigms of contemporary managerial theories, namely agency theory.[15]

Agency theory is a central topic of discussion in contemporary management studies. It stipulates the existence of an asymmetry of information and conflicting interests between the "agent" (the manager or principal) and the "principal" (the

---

[9] *Ibid*, 348.

[10] Murnaghan 1988: 10.

[11] Placido Domingo Suarez 2001.

[12] Xenophon 1933: 419.

[13] *Ibid.*, 421.

[14] Murnaghan 1988.

[15] Jensen 1986; Jensen and Meckling 1976.

owners or agents),[16] advocating the limitation of managerial power in favour of shareholder power. This theory is informed by the idea that management must be accountable to shareholders first and foremost, in a so-called fiduciary relationship. Managers are merely the agents of those they represent: the shareholders' meeting (it should be noted here that *line managers* and *middle managers are* not the only ones who are by definition always managed, since *senior managers* also answer to superiors). This theory appears to be a determining factor in *corporate governance, i.e.* in the composition of supervisory bodies and the distribution of power within organizations, as well as in matters of executive pay.

The relationship between the foreman and the owner is actually a central theme of Xenophon's *Oeconomicus*. While Ischomachus is eager to convince Socrates that management is a subject that can be taught,[17] the latter is sceptical: "Without devotion, what use, is the science of a foreman, whatever that may be?"[18] For Ischomachus, it is enough to align the interests of one and the other: "if a man stands to gain from the preservation of assets, and lose from their depreciation, then he has an interest in watching over them."[19] This reply is very similar to the answer given by agency theory to the problem of asymmetry it observes, namely incentives such as *stock options,* which are supposed to put an end to the divergence of interests between managers and owners. However, for Socrates, the problem remains how to teach this disposition, which he considers a prerequisite for any management science, to those who "are in love with greed," (to which Ischomachus suggests "showing them the profit they will get from it") but also to those who are "not especially sensitive to it."[20,21] Socrates still wonders about how to inspire such a sense of justice in an "experienced manager."[22]

In a famous article in the field of management studies, Sumentra Ghoshal[23] criticises the influence that agency theory has had on management as it is practised, and above all as it is taught in specialised institutions. According to him, the influence of ideas has been neglected for too long by research in management, with the result that theories that have been established for 30 years or more, such as game theory

---

[16] "The agency or mandate theory is therefore an attempt to bring financial theory and organizational theory into parallel. This relationship is problematic because of the divergence of interests and the asymmetry of information between the two parties, which give rise to a whole set of cost categories, referred to as agency costs: *monitoring costs to* avoid deviant behaviour on the part of agents, incentive costs, *bonding costs to* convince principals that their actions are in line with their interests, opportunity cost (the difference between the result of the action for the principal and the optimal behaviour for the principal)," Barabel et al. 2013, p. 63.

[17] "For does he who must be able to keep watch for me when I am not there need to know anything other than what I know myself? If I am capable of directing the work, I can, can't I? teach another what I know myself," Xenophon 1933: 388.

[18] *Ibid.*

[19] *Ibid:* 378.

[20] *Ibid,* 390.

[21] *Ibid.,* 396.

[22] *Ibid.,* 395.

[23] Ghoshal 2005.

1.1 Management as a Philosophical Problem

or transaction cost theory, are seldom contradicted. Managerial practices have their point of origin in doctrines, chief among them being agency theory,[24] which prescribe a strengthening of control and surveillance techniques. What Ghoshal seeks to denounce in particular is the worldwide spread of a supposedly morally-neutral (*value-free*) managerial ideology which has gradually deprived managers of their sense of responsibility. The almost obsessive maximisation of value for *shareholders* has been to the detriment of the many *stakeholders* 'affected'[25] by the activities of organizations.[26] He also urges management schools to rethink their educational models with regard to other disciplines from the humanities and social sciences. Ghoshal bemoans the counter-productivity of the dominant model, with its extreme pragmatism and veneration of the omnipotent investor, as well as the "supposedly positive conception of the nature of man" on which reasoning and recommendations are based.[27]

Friedland[28] extends this analysis by showing that management research pretends to forget the normative and philosophical origin of its content. Management is always concerned with "empirically testing and measuring," *a posteriori*, the theories in play. In medicine or law, for example, journals such as the *Journal of Medical Ethics* or *Legal Theory*, largely devoted to conceptual and philosophical analyses, enjoy great reputations in their respective fields.[29] The most influential international journals in management, such as the *Administrative Science Quarterly* or *Strategic Management Journal*, do not leave any room for philosophical reflection, prioritising an essentially deductive approach based on empirical data gathered in the field. However, to borrow an example highlighted by Friedland, the Supreme Court of the United States defines insider trading as a harmful practice that destroys trust on the basis of logical-formal reasoning, without recourse to any empirical study, since such a study would in fact be almost impossible to conduct.[30] In short, management studies are in urgent need of conceptual and philosophical reflection.

---

[24] The author notes that Michaël Jensen himself acknowledges the flaws in an article published in *The Economist* (16/11/2002). The system of *stock options* or the separation between the shareholder power and the executive power in two distinct *boards* has indeed failed to deliver the expected beneficial effects.

[25] "An issue holder in an organization is by definition a group or individual who has the power to affect or be affected by the achievement of the organization's objectives," Freeman 1984: 46. See also Freeman et al. 2010.

[26] Painter et al. 2020.

[27] Denis and Martinet 2012: 33.

[28] J. Friedland 2012.

[29] The same cannot be said of journals concerned with ethical issues in management, such as *Business Ethics: A European Review*, *Business Ethics Quarterly*, *Journal of Business Ethics* and *Business and Professional Ethics Journal*, which do exist but do not enjoy the same recognition in their own field.

[30] How could such a study be possible? Insider trading would have to be allowed for some and not for others in order to then compare the results, going far beyond the Court's remit.

1.1.2 Continental Philosophy and Post-management

In the previous chapter we observed the tension between the "irreducibly philosophical dimension"[31] of management and its "empirical pretentions."[32] While the former aspect appears to have dominated during Antiquity, it is the latter that has prevailed since the days of Fayol and Taylor. Consequently, in the face of intensified economic pressure and obsessive focus on financial performance, how can we rediscover this lost political and ethical art, the connection between economic activity and individual and social morality which embodied the origins of management?

In recent years, particularly in the American academic context, a steady stream of research has been devoted to questioning management from an ethical point of view. As Alain Anquetil explains, the "separation thesis" has been one of the main questions faced by the authors of this field of research in business ethics.[33] The thesis formulated by Carr, in an article entitled, with reference to poker, *"Is Bluffing Ethical?"*,[34] posits that deception has become a weapon of choice in the pursuit of success. For the author, managers cannot be blamed for simply doing what they are mandated to do, namely focusing on the success of the company, and ethics must therefore remain in the private sphere. Others have argued that, to an extent, ethics may be instrumentalized for the sake of entrepreneurial success (see Hugh Willmott's study of the Enron case).[35] For Edward Freeman, on the contrary, any separation between moral and economic issues is fallacious because moral considerations are always involved in the economic decision-making process.[36]

Let me add an other point: these debates do not seem to concern the other social sciences, such as sociology or economics, which seem in many respects indifferent to the debates that drive management research. While many social scientists readily acknowledge that the contemporary world can only be conceived in terms of organization,[37] it is nevertheless clear that, as a discipline, the administrative sciences (to use a term more frequently employed in the USA than across the Atlantic), despite the steady quantitative increase in their scientific output, have not had quite the impact they might have hoped for, either within the academic and intellectual world or among observers and decision-makers in the economic and social spheres.[38] For many, management remains the domain of techniques associated with the idea of organizational performance. Rare indeed are those who feel that it has become, as Armand Hatchuel presents it, "the fundamental and transversal discipline - the

---

[31] J. Derrida, "Coups d'envoi," 1998: 97.

[32] Châtelet 2000: 14.

[33] Anquetil 2008.

[34] Carr 1968.

[35] In Painter-Morland and Ten Bos 2011.

[36] Freeman 2000.

[37] Morin 1990, Saussois 2007.

[38] Ghoshal 2005; Alvensson and Gabriel 2013.

1.1 Management as a Philosophical Problem

infra-discipline - of the social sciences."[39] It is almost as if "management science consoles itself by providing 'mobility,' leaving to other disciplines such as economics and sociology... the privilege of getting to grips with the 'readability' of the world."[40]

Asked to explain the reasons for this lack of influence in the field of social sciences, management researchers are not lacking in imagination and have put forward several hypotheses: to quote one of the most widely-discussed theories,[41] the problem is not the lack of impact of research on managerial practices, as many previously believed, but instead the ethically questionable nature of the managerial theories conveyed in management research and teaching institutions. According to Ghoshal indeed, the discipline has been built on a certain number of erroneous assumptions that are too rarely called into question, and from which the most influential theories, such as agency theory, have emerged. For Mats Alvesson and Yiannis Gabriel, who highlight the problem of homogenisation in the modes of production and selection of scientific research, this lack of impact is primarily due to the extreme specialisation and conservatism of the contributions, which are intended to be read only by a small community of researchers, generally committed to the same mainstream theories.[42] These contributions generally employ the same overall structure, devoting considerable attention to literature reviews and the elaboration of a consequent research question, before identifying an essentially rhetorical "gap" which the rest of the study then attempts to fill.[43]

How can philosophy help us here? In the opening pages of the dossier "Philosophy and Economy" in Issue 28 of *Rue Descartes,* we read, by way of an introduction to the issue:

> [...] neither two distinct discourses, nor a single discourse, therefore, but discourses that are mutually involved in each other, in tension with each other. Circulation that does not necessarily result in immediately perceptible conflicts or aporias, but which can bring them out in the most stimulating manner when representatives of these two fields cross paths and collaborate.[44]

Authentic philosophical discourse is not, and cannot be, a management tool, much less an intellectual guarantee. Tension is somehow indispensable. Philosophical discourse has its own register which never makes it a "convenient"[45] partner. However,

---

[39] Martinet and Pesqueux 2013, chap. 1, 19.

[40] *Ibid,* chap. 8, 253.

[41] Ghoshal 2005.

[42] Alvensson and Gabriel 2013.

[43] *Id.* The authors propose replacing these more or less institutionalized (we might even say formulaic) forms of academic contribution, which leave no room whatsoever for ambiguity or surprise, with a *"polymorphic"* approach research. In this type of research, the surprising, captivating and/or innovative aspects would at last take precedence over the supposed scientific and methodological "rigour" that is socially constructed and, as such, usually placed at the top of the scale of values among the *reviewers* solicited by the most reputable publications.

[44] Dossier "Philosophie et économie," *Rue Descartes,* 2000, n° 28: 8.

[45] Bevan 2008a, b.

if it succeeds in holding up a sometimes disturbing mirror to management for the "smooth running of business,"[46] then this reciprocal involvement can make it possible to fight back against the "systemic stupidity" of organizations.[47] For his part, Georges Canguilhem specified:

> Once the media clichés about employers, trade unions, social security and foreign competition have been dispelled, the fact remains that a company is an initiative, an adventure and a risk, a collective effort and therefore open to conflict. Insofar as it is not only an object for technicians and economists, but also a place of tasks and conduct, both individual and collective, that are subject to mandatory rules, it is possible and important to subject it to a critical and normative, and therefore authentically philosophical examination. Business should be welcomed into philosophy, which is not a temple, but a building site.[48]

Without being able to say for sure whether the image of the building site is addressed to the company or to the philosophy, it is probably fair to say that both are in the construction phase, in the process of being built; this is precisely where they meet. Yet, until recently as we have already seen, management studies systematically favoured an empirical and positivist epistemological approach, rather than a concern for conceptual argumentation. By introducing philosophical doubt, by relying on philosophical reasoning, management research can no longer conceive of management as an instruction manual for puppets, an algorithm for making the right strategic decisions whatever the context (especially the cultural context), a codified knowledge which chimes with plain common sense. We must instead consider what management entails: an actor, a worker, a manager, acting and being acted upon.

At the same time, management offers an exciting subject for philosophy insofar as it can no longer be assimilated to the mere relationship of means and ends stemming from its Taylorian heritage.[49] We suddenly lose all trace of the all-too famous "*one best way*." As for the terms of management, performance, excellence, vision, authority – in short, the "very strong language" of the discipline – they can finally become the subject of critical analyses, discourses and practices. Philosophy is beginning at last to take a keen interest in management, addressing the complexity and plurality of the values it embodies, to the benefit, I believe, of this "foreign material," which is a beginning to re-examine its canonical texts and authors. Management can thus be opened up to new horizons, new references and new cultural and philosophical perspectives, as witnessed by many recent publications.

I propose to take this as my starting point, specifically our all too common concern about the *lack of influence* of management research outside its own register. I also share the ethical concern expressed by Sumantra Ghoshal with regard to managerial theories that are questionable in practice, as well as the more political concern of Mats Alvesson and Yiannis Gabriel that the standardisation of scientific

---

[46] "In each era, humanism must modify its struggles. It seems that today it has a clear task: to put economic and technical logics back in their secondary place, so that they may serve more interesting, metaphysical and gentle purposes." Chabot 2013: 18.

[47] Stiegler 2004, and 2009.

[48] Canguilhem 1990.

[49] I. Huault 2008: 322; Deslandes 2013.

1.2 Ethics and Organization(s)

production processes in management is essentially a *"pointless game"* which stifles innovation, as well as another key requirement for fruitful and fertile scientific research: doubt. We are indeed currently witnessing a crisis of legitimacy in management, a conviction broadly shared by the critical literature. Questioning has suddenly entered the equation. In these circumstances, philosophy can be a precious assistance when it comes to re-examining the complexity of the issues, especially the ethical issues, that organizations have to face; it can inspire managers to question their practices, to question the way they comprehend the many dilemmas they are faced with, and to constantly reflect on the societal role of the organizations they lead.

I also believe, however, that the supposed 'irrelevance' of management science as a discipline, and its lack of legitimacy and esteem, have their roots in an even more worrying problem: is there still any real agreement as to the meaning of the word management? There no longer seems to be any real consensus, a state of affairs which both Sumantra Goshal and Mats Alvesson, each in their own way, unintentionally highlight. Is it a set of endogenous techniques? A devalued science? A practice, or even an "art"? Or a possible field for the application of ethics or politics?

As Christopher Grey noted as far back as 1996,[50] management is a fragmented field, which has since become more and more fragmented, to the point that the object of research itself now seems uncertain. I will venture into this uncertain realm in the next chapter, attempting to define the conflicting territories on which managerial thought has been built. But before doing so, let us try to take advantage of the Socratic warning, soon extended by Aristotle, aimed at shedding light on management in a double light, strategic and ethical, where the decidable and the undecidable co-exist. This illumination seems to me to be a prerequisite for a better understanding of the deployment in five directions ("The Five Senses of Management" cf. p. 14).

1.2 Ethics and Organization(s)

1.2.1 Ethics Versus ROI

There are two traditional ways of discussing ethics and management.[51] The first is that which would make ethics a discipline of management, i.e. a kind of objective knowledge of management, which has been called "éthique des affaires" in France (an expression that could be translated by "business case for ethics" in english). This is how the notion was introduced in France by Octave Gélinier,[52] with the idea that ethics "pays off", that ethics is by and large a formidable management tool, which allows other management techniques to be valued in society's eyes. There is

---

[50] Ch. Grey 1996.

[51] The following paragraphs reproduce some of the elements published in French in: . Deslandes (2020). Ethiques et Organizations, In: *La recherche et l'enseignement en éthique: un état des lieux,* Rude-Antoine E. Piévic, M. Paris: L'Harmattan.

[52] (1916–2004) French economist, author, director and then president of Cegos from 1950 to 1992.

a risk, however, as Jean-Pierre Dupuy recounts in his 2012 essay, that this is just a way of reducing ethics to the rank of 'economic lubricant'.[53]

Another direction puts management and ethics in tension and, in a way, aims to transform management itself, in relation to ethical and philosophical questions, with the contribution of philosophical curiosity; I would specify with Cartesian doubt and Platonic wonder. From this point of view, the approach that we can have to management is radically transformed and can put us on the path of a *managerial ethics*. This path is marked by the features of a double orientation: on the one hand, the strictly philosophical concern to give content to ethics. As Ricoeur explains: 'The only way to give visibility and legibility to the primordial content of ethics is to project it onto the post-moral plane of applied ethics' (2004, p. 692). In order to avoid ethics being constituted as a wisdom without content, by confining itself "to the reassuring world of concepts and discourse", the field of management offers us the opportunity to explore ethical issues in the particular context of organizations.[54] On the other hand, it is a question of encouraging a fertilisation in the opposite direction, in which the social sciences would be stimulated by the human sciences,[55] in this case management by philosophy. This encounter between management sciences and philosophy thus renews management by offering it the opportunity to multiply the fields of investigation and to mobilise new methodological and conceptual resources.[56] A managerial ethics therefore always participates in this effort to decompartmentalise, in order to avoid, as Chanlat points out, 'the disciplinary mindset obscuring other aspects of reality, thereby leading to those well-known intellectual voids of reductionism and imperialism which reduce any effort at true understanding'.[57]

It should be noted that this particular effort, at the meeting point of two worlds of knowledge, is generally part of an interdisciplinary institutional field recognised since the 1980s in the United States under the name of "business ethics". This field of research exists thanks to academic associations (*Society for Business Ethics, European Business Academic Network*, etc.) or specialised academic journals (*Journal of Business Ethics, Business Ethics Quarterly, Business and Professional Ethics Journal, Business Ethics: a European Review*, etc.), which have highlighted the need for this decompartmentalisation of disciplines in the face of recurring phenomena in contemporary organizations, such as the suffering of managers, or the loss of legitimacy of management.

Any reflection on business ethics is therefore part of a framework in which many debates are taking place in society as a whole. The proof is an article published in an edition of Le *Monde*, written by Valérie Segond, entitled "Faced with the Anglo-Saxon model, business schools are looking for meaning[58]". This is a real question which is being discussed in many circles, and which has been the subject of several

---

[53] J-P. Dupuy, *The Future of the Economy. Sortir de l'écomystification*, Paris: Flammarion, 2012.

[54] Hadot 2002: 371.

[55] Gusdorf 1962.

[56] Jardat 2011.

[57] Chanlat 1998, p. 79.

[58] Cf. *Le Monde* of Wednesday 8 November 2017.

1.2 Ethics and Organization(s) 11

reports (e.g. FNEGE/Cercle de l'entreprise) which tend to show that management schools have focused exclusively on technical education and that it was time to offer other perspectives - particularly historical, philosophical and humanistic - to management learning. A number of essays were then published, including one entitled *J'ai fait HEC et je m'en excuse (I went to HEC and I apologise),*[59] which also caused a stir in French public opinion. Many observers then turned to the management schools and asked them: "What else do you bring to the table, in addition to the strictly management courses?

One of the reasons for this is the increasingly deplorable image of business leaders in society. For example, almost a third of the criminal characters in the major American TV series,[60] which form part of the core of world culture today, are businessmen or businesswomen. Their negative image is regularly portrayed: for example, in the film *Inside Jobs,* which won the Best Documentary Award in 2011 at the Oscars and which recounts the *subprime* crisis in 2007, and in the series *Mad Men* or the two parts of *the Bernie Madoff Affair.*[61] In the meantime, we should note the rise of algorithmic intelligence in organizations, which tends to relieve managers of their responsibility. A recent article by Gary Marcus and Ernest Davies, "Eight problems with Big Data"[62], shows that *Big Data* functions as a kind of cash register, which archives our behaviour and gradually, in a way, disqualifies human discernment. I also draw on the work of Dominique Cardon, who has published a fascinating essay (*À quoi rêvent les algorithmes?*[63]), explaining that algorithms are incapable of imagining that human beings are likely to make bifurcations, to display authority, or even moral sense. He writes the following important thing to think about: "They [the algorithms] cannot conceive that a society can sometimes break out of the hierarchies that haunt it".

1.2.2 Managerial Ethics as Such

So how can we try to define what a managerial ethics would be? It cannot, of course, be an implacable method for applying ethical rules; nor is it the fact that a firm claims to be a "good citizen" because it respects the law by paying taxes; nor is it an algorithm that would enable us to make the right ethical decision, still less a way of reducing transaction costs. Managerial ethics is mostly a way of organising life together among people who meet in the workplace and whose individual ethics differ. More generally, it could be said that this is a discourse opposed to the essentially

---

[59] Florence Noiville, Paris, Stock éd, Coll. "Parti-pris", 2009.

[60] Of course, it cannot be said that this figure has anything to do with the reality of the situation.

[61] On 12 December 2008, Bernard Madoff was arrested by the FBI, revealing to the public what is probably the biggest fraud of all time.

[62] *The New York Times,* 6 April 2014.

[63] Dominique Cardon, *À quoi rêvent les algorithmes,* Paris, Le Seuil, 2015, Coll. "République des Idées".

mechanistic view of management, which is only interested in logistical issues (which, by the way, does not prevent some logistics and *supply chain* researchers from taking a deliberate interest in ethical issues, and increasingly so).

In short, an ethical reflection on management seems to generate a more general questioning, particularly from a metaphysics of the subject (Rappin 2011).[64] Indeed, even if the field of business ethics seems to be primarily concerned with a macro level of analysis ("Business and Society") and a meso level of analysis (concerning in particular compliance and inter-individual behaviour in organizations), the essential character of the "micro" analysis, i.e. at the level of individual moral awareness, should not be overlooked. As Hirèche-Baïada reminds us,[65] there is always a risk that an exclusively social conception of ethics will lead to a certain 'strategic' use of ethical rules by actors at the individual level.

However, most efforts, both by practitioners and business ethics researchers, tend to focus on the "compliance" issue, which include all the management tools that make it possible to align ethical purposes with the organization's day-to-day operations (this may involve codes of ethics, codes of conduct, the appointment of an ethics officer, an audit or an ethics committee, or the warning procedures that may be put in place, etc.). On this subject, Amartya Sen,[66] the man of *capabilities*, explains very well that ethics in organizations most often appears in the form of a *grey area*, i.e. a conflict of values. He uses the example, which is astute for the management of organizations, of a judge who is faced with three children who want it for themselves. The first child wants it because it can play music, the second because he made it, and finally, the third wants the instrument for herself because he has no toy. It is a choice between talent, merit or need, a choice that is found in the dilemmas of day-to-day business.

To define this managerial ethics we could also refer, as is commonly the case, to the somewhat frontal opposition between the work of Friedman, just mentioned, and the work of Freeman on stakeholders.[67] Milton Friedman's idea is that the manager should maximise shareholder value, the goal of 'management by loyalty' to those who employ them. In other words, as the title "The Only Business of business is business"[68] clearly sums up, a company is socially responsible if it respects a moral minimum while seeking profit. However, this language is no longer tenable today, since it is in fact in a very concrete way that ethical questions appear in organizations, especially the largest ones, whose power of action is sometimes greater than that of the States themselves. According to the various management disciplines, whether in finance, human resources management or marketing, problems of environmental policy, employee safety, harassment, particularly moral harassment, safety standards to be respected, discrimination in hiring to be avoided, fair

---

[64] The following paragraphs partly repeat the theses defended in my previous work. See Deslandes (2013), Essai sur les données philosophiques du management, PUF, 2013.

[65] Hirèche Baïada 2007.

[66] Sen 1985, 1987, 2008.

[67] Alain Anquetil is a professor of business ethics and the author of "What is business ethics? (Anquetil, 2008) and "Key texts on business ethics" (Anquetil, 2011).

[68] *The New York Times*, 13 September 1970.

1.2 Ethics and Organization(s)

remuneration policy, etc., are noted, so that ethics is at the heart of management, whether we like it or not, and is in fact, as we have shown above, a major focus. Surveys conducted by BVA[69] for the *Cercle d'éthique des affaires* question the reasons why managers are sensitive to it. To the question: "Is your company concerned (a great deal, fairly, little or not at all) with issues of sustainable development, management integrity, prevention of conflicts of interest, respect for employees and the fight against corruption? the answer is overwhelmingly "yes", from 75% to 80%. On sustainable development, it is almost 85%. This is good news. The bad one, however, seems to be that the motivations for taking an interest in ethical issues are not necessarily the right ones, morally speaking. In fact, we can see that the strictly managerial and pragmatic orientation, the one proposed by Gélinier in the early to late 1980s, has gained a decisive advantage over the second conception. The motivations of companies for ethics are primarily appreciated from a strategic point of view: to give themselves a good image, to avoid legal risks, to improve customer confidence, to better meet customer expectations, to improve economic results, etc. The result is very clear: people are interested in ethical concerns for financial reasons and strategic ones. This position has been stable over time: the criteria have remained the same for the last 10 years, despite some variations here and there.

Should we then try to redefine management, so that the motivational system that these studies show is finally transformed? To try and answer this, we need to bear in mind that we all have a system of constraints, depending on where we are, our idiosyncrasies, our situation in the world, our culture etc. As a result, management can be seen in different ways: either as a physical science of sorts, in which we rely on the search for causes. This would be a position that could be described as naturalist, in a way objectivist, even scientistic, and in this case we find the words of, for example, one of the founders of cybernetics, Norbert Wiener[70] when he said that "words like *life, ends, soul* are grossly useless for expressing scientific thought." This is more or less the choice made in France when management studies were called, during the 70 s, "sciences de gestion".

Or we could put in a little philosophy and ethics... which is certainly a marginal point of view: if we look at the composition of management faculties we see that, for the most part, they include statisticians, economists, computer scientists, anthropologists, marketing researchers, financiers, mathematicians, and very few philosophers, and in the majority of cases none. Let's imagine that a second way, an alternative, is possible. It might be the one outlined by Jean-Pierre Dupuy - here based on Adam Smith - when he writes: "I began this book[71] by recalling that Adam Smith made the economy into an immense theatre where society tells stories about itself". This is obviously another position, rather humanistic, more subjectivist and purpose-driven. In other words - and here we join Aristotle - we could put

---

[69] BVA is a research and consulting company, expert in behavioural science.

[70] American mathematician, theorist and researcher in applied mathematics, best known as the founding father of cybernetics.

[71] The 2012 essay, see *above*.

14 1 From Proto-Management to Contemporary Functional Stupidity

management in the order of practical wisdom, *sophrosunê*, a form of virtue, in short, a human and social skill. This is the path that this book explores, this overcoming of Taylorism already mentioned, of an "ontology of the non-immediately measurable", where solidarity between beings, the singularity of people and joy at work, which means nothing in terms of figures and numbers, find a central place in the ethical concerns of managers, and therefore in any definition of a *managerial ethics* worthy of the name.

1.3 The Five Senses of Management

1.3.1 Management as a Technique

It seems necessary to start from this central idea, that management is presented above all as a technique whose aim is productive performance. Management is therefore not defined by its fundamental nature, which remains undefined, nor even by its goals, established in advance – to fight inefficiency, to defend and expand productivity, etc. - but rather by the techniques used to achieve these goals. Moreover, as Armand Hatchuel pertinently reminds us:

> It is too often forgotten that Taylor's greatest successes were first and foremost advances that today we would call technical. The discovery of tungsten steels for machining, Taylor's and Barth's formulas for setting up lathes, and the study of belts are all important results that had an immense impact in the world of mechanics.[72]

Indeed, it is hard to deny the contributions of Taylorism to productivity. And one may be inclined to agree with Pascal Chabot when he writes that "economic development is first and foremost a struggle against poverty, which has contributed to greater dignity. It would be a simplistic mistake to think that humanity is sick of its tools and means; on the contrary, we need them now more than ever, since there will soon be eight billion of us on earth."[73]

The assimilation of management to a set of techniques, however, seems to me beset by several insurmountable difficulties.[74] The logical conclusion of this technical and logistical conception of management is that we lose sight of what is sometimes referred to as the "human factor." This system puts in place techniques for evaluating results and performances, phenomena which are, by their very nature, ephemeral. But management aims to keep as far away as possible from the subjectivity of desire; as Eric Faÿ suggests, it offers no intelligence, no analysis of "the effort, creativity and solidarity received or deployed to achieve this result by facing all sorts of difficulties and unforeseen events."[75]

---

[72] Hatchuel 1994: 55.

[73] Chabot 2013: 134.

[74] de Gaulejac 2005.

[75] Faÿ 2014: 28.

1.3 The Five Senses of Management 15

By proceeding in this way, by following Taylor and putting the "system first," management as a set of techniques takes the risk, flagged by Socrates, of working in a way that negates the levels of ethical and societal responsibility that its exercise and practice entail. At the risk of witnessing what Dominique Bessire and Hervé Mesure call "a self-fulfilling prophecy",[76] a sense of frustration, of *desaffectio societatis,* which is ultimately detrimental to both the quality and volume of output.

1.3.2 Management as a Science

The second vision of management is what we might call the scientific orientation.[77] Management in the technical sense is certainly "intuitively" scientific (Taylor argues for a "scientific" management, which would have the pomp and influence of science), but it has neither the conceptual means for this self-affirmation, nor the capacity to demonstrate its theory. As Thibault Le Texier explains:

> Nor can management as it was developed in the 20th century be considered as a science [...]. Beneath the veneer provided by the compulsive use of scientific vocabulary by American industrialists at the beginning of the 20th century, their management was much more a matter of rationalising practices than of scrupulously applying methods derived from the mathematical and physical sciences to human realities. In the majority of cases, science is simply about obtaining accurate information and applying it. In doing so, industrialists built *systems* rather than a science. Taylor may have been a good engineer, but he was no physiologist, a charge frequently levelled against him by European labour analysts.[78]

It is, however, on a scientific basis that management and its teaching continue to develop today. And it is, we must confess, primarily management professors who most forcefully assert the scientific credentials of management, not consultants or management professionals. For example, management sciences ("*sciences de gestion*"), is now recognised in France with its own dedicated section ("06") at the National Council of Universities.[79] Moreover, management involves many scientific disciplines and can be presented as multi-paradigmatic since it encompasses wide variety of interdisciplinary connections. Indeed, no one discipline can claim to cover all aspects of the cooperative human experience at work; management sciences therefore necessarily combine several disciplinary matrices made up of different concepts, postulates and laws, invoked by researchers in these academic disciplines. Psychology may be called upon to study behaviour or to enlighten managers on human diversity, while political sciences will be called upon to explain the dynamics of negotiation and power; as for economics, they will be called upon to better discern changes in the economic situation and decisions concerning the

---

[76] Bessire and Mesure 2009.

[77] Willmott 1997.

[78] Le Texier 2011: 99.

[79] Martinet and Pesqueux 2013.

allocation of resources; sociology will convey its understanding of institutions and the dynamics of multicultural groups, etc.

Moreover, it was a sociologist, Max Weber, who first laid the groundwork for a theory of authority in bureaucratic environments. In Weber's view, bureaucracy is the appropriate form of organization for a society whose foundations are no longer the Sacred or Tradition but Law and Reason.[80] And it was an economist, Herbert Simon, who first highlighted the principle of bounded rationality, a fundamental principle in management.[81] In this model, decision-makers build solutions by adopting the most satisfactory option available to them, generally within the simplified schema of reality by which they are constrained. The information available to managers is necessarily imperfect, their control is illusory and the best they can do is to search for a solution which satisfies their existing preferences.

The so-called 'social' approach to management, in which choices are dictated less by reason than by social coalitions and power relations, is based on the scientific experiments of George Elton Mayo (1880–1949) at Western Electric (1924–1932). He noted the importance of the social climate in a working group, including the observation that productivity continues to improve even when working conditions deteriorate (lower light levels). Workers are motivated above all by their membership of a social group and feel the need to relate and belong to that group.[82] Mayo's work was extended by Abraham Maslow and his theory of needs,[83] but other examples of his influence can be found closer to home: the field of strategic analysis developed by Michel Crozier,[84] for example, or Edgar Schein's model of organizational culture.[85] All are united by a scientific approach to understanding organizations and their actors.

Nowadays, it is through the scientific output published in academic journals that 'management science' is deployed and promoted. Mats Alvesson and Jörgen Sandberg, however, have raised questions about the increase in scientific output in the field of management, despite its waning influence on managerial practices.[86] Who in the business world cares about the theories developed in the leading journals in the field? Are there not management gurus and essayists (the authors cite Naomi Klein's essay *No Logo* as a case in point) whose influence on the life of organizations, and on the ability of managers to reflect on their own practices, has been greater than the combined sum of 30 years of scientific production?

---

[80] Weber 1921/1971.

[81] Simon 1955.

[82] Fritz Roethlisberger and William Dickson, *Management and the Worker*, Cambridge (Mass.), Harvard University Press, 1939.

[83] Maslow, 1943.

[84] Crozier and Friedberg 1977.

[85] Schein 2010.

[86] Alvesson and Sandberg 2013.

1.3 The Five Senses of Management

Sumantra Ghoshal also shares this concern over the lack of conceptual and critical thinking among management research professionals. They are more often than not unable to recognise that the theories they produce and transmit may actually be harmful to the practice of management itself. He uses the example of Michael Porter's "Five Forces," a theory taught worldwide, arguing that it undermines company's ability to work with regulators, employees, customers and suppliers by viewing them all as competitors,[87] as the model of maximising shareholder value also assumes. This determination to make management a science, a body of established knowledge, perhaps even scientifically validated and institutionalised, brings with it certain societal risks, particularly on the environmental front, which the management research community paradoxically tends to underestimate.[88]

Finally, Romain Laufer (1994) argues that management as a science plays a role in the legitimacy of managerial decisions; within organizations, science may be invoked to legitimise management.[89] This is precisely what worries Sumantra Ghoshal: as long as they fail to analyse the concrete consequences of 'official' theories in terms of practice (and also, we might add, to conduct a critical conceptual examination of those same theories), and continue to neglect the ideas and conceptual analysis in management, managers, while believing themselves to be free of any intellectual influence, will always be, in Keynes'words, "the plaything of a dead economist."[90]

1.3.3 Management as Practice

The third major vision of management is that which concerns itself primarily with managerial practice,[91] or the "art of management."[92] In this tradition, management is no longer seen as (technical) know-how or knowledge (science) but, in a very general way, as a way of knowing-how-to-be that we sometimes called "soft skills." From this point of view, "management is a 'praxeology', i.e. a science of action which is only meaningful and unfolds in practice."[93] Thibault Le Texier explains:

> "The forms "managing," "to manage," "managed," "manager," "manageable" and "management" have been attested since the second half of the 16th century. They refer mainly to the conduct of public or private affairs with skill, tact or care [...] Since the 16th century, the term "management" has been commonly associated with dressage and driving and riding horses, probably due to the lexical proximity of the English verb "manage" and the French noun "manège."[94]

---

[87] Ghoshal 2005: 75.

[88] *Ibid.*, 88–89.

[89] Laufer 1994.

[90] Ghoshal 2005: 75.

[91] Deslandes 2011a; Drucker 2010; Johnson et al. 2007; Miettinen et al. 2009.

[92] Strati 1992.

[93] Bouilloud and Lecuyer 1994: 15.

[94] Le Texier 2011: 15–16.

By the sixteenth century, somewhat more than half way between Xenophon and Taylor, the crucial derivation from the word "manège" (riding school) had been established, leading us to the common idea of driving. Here, therefore, reference is made not to a principle of efficiency, but to a behavioural imperative ("tact," "care," etc.). It is a question of acting with mastery, notably thanks to accumulated practical experience. With the notion of conduct, it is finally the figure of the manager that appears more clearly than in the two previous levels of analysis. The manager is the one who "takes care," who adapts to the situation. It is the manager who "leads," who shows the way, who "steers" or "pilots" (today we talk about project management, steering and decision-making tools, etc.).

It is obviously this vision of management which is most widely encountered today, particularly among observers of economic life (especially the press). Indeed, management is often define in terms of "best practices," a principle which seems rather close to the Taylorian *one best way*," but which, because of its adaptability to different contexts, differs from it irremediably. The modern "art of management" does not aspire to universality, being more concerned with the capacity for permanent adjustment, in ever-changing professional contexts. As Sumantra Ghoshal further explains,[95] management as an art is fundamentally opposed, in principle, to the very possibility of so-called 'scientific management.' The great strength of managerial practices is their ability to adapt to significantly different professional environments, hence the success of specialised teaching in many fields such as *public management*, *luxury management*, *energy management* or *media management*.

However, the "art of managing" organizations in specific sectors entails two major difficulties: the first is having to transform practices to keep pace with the ever-increasing number and speed of professional changes, without being able to give a conceptual or scientific justification for this; the second is not being able to grasp the societal concerns, particularly the environmental risks, which weigh on the activity of contemporary organizations. Nevertheless, today's managers require a broader vision, in a world plagued with uncertainty over how best to "protect the perishable."[96] The relationship between our actions and the world, and the way we understand people's responsibility towards the planet, have changed considerably in this era of globalisation.[97]

Above and beyond "practices," it is in fact the ethical and political legitimacy of management that is up for evaluation. To put it succinctly, with help from Paul Ricœur, the task of today's teachers is to "make apparent the ethical significance of choices which appear to be economic in nature."[98]

---

[95] Ghoshal 2005: 76.

[96] Ricoeur 1991: 285.

[97] Deslandes 2012a, b.

[98] Ricoeur 1991: 250.

1.3.4 *Management as Ethics*

'Scientific management' has always presented itself as axiologically neutral (this is the position of many theorists, e.g. Milton Friedman),[99] claiming to have no time for the expression of individual and subjective standards. But, as I tried to show in the former section and as Philippe Chanial insightfully notes, "the principle of axiological neutrality is not axiologically neutral."[100] Conflicts of interest, employee security, moral harassment or corruption may exist in organizations, as may joy, friendship or justice. Indeed, management and organizations do not belong to the realm of amorality. On an ethical level, what interests us is not the practices and conduct of managers taken as abstract objects of study, but rather the way that managers actually conduct themselves, eschewing the mechanistic vision of management and assuming that managers, as actors, are capable of ethical judgement.[101] Without a minimum of honesty, integrity and a spirit of cooperation, there is no management. Consider the following quotation from philosopher and psychoanalyst Cornelius Castoriadis:

> It [capitalism] has only been able to function because it has inherited a series of anthropological types that it did not create, and could not have created, by itself: incorruptible judges, honest civil servants, educators dedicated to their vocation, workers with a minimum of professional conscience.[102]

As Amartya Sen also explains: "the purely economic man is a social moron. Economic theory has been very much concerned with this rational idiot."[103] It is time to reintroduce ethics into managerial thinking.

However, business ethics raises many questions. Though it is surely fundamental to understanding the deep issues at stake in management, it may also be interpreted as a managerial tool liable to prevent the free and authentic expression of individuals within organizations. Is it not merely an instrument implemented by managers to better protect themselves, in the legal sense? A management technique like any other, especially when the emphasis is placed on a system of strict and established rules and standards to which employees and managers are expected to refer for all decision-making (*compliance with* its codes, best practices, ethics committees, *compliance* officers etc.)?

---

[99] Friedman 1970.

[100] Quoted by Martinet and Pesqueux 2013: 249.

[101] G. Deslandes 2012b.

[102] Castoriadis 1996, p. 68: "It is because there are different registers on which the role of manager is played and because these registers are constantly evolving in line with organizational changes and performance standards that it is necessary to regularly revisit the foundations of management," explain Barabel et al. 2013: XVI.

[103] Sen 2008, p. 107, and also p. 18: "Why should the pursuit of self-interest, to the exclusion of all other goals, be solely rational? Of course, it is not absurd to assert that the maximisation of self-interest is not irrational, but it seems to me quite extraordinary that anyone could argue that any attitude other than the maximisation of self-interest is necessarily irrational."

Of course, the organizational universe needs codes so that the actors can know the rules of the game, but these codes are not without dangers. Can we really say that formal respect for the rules, ensured by the compliance function, amounts to a genuine sense of ethical concern? Surely the primary objective of such rules is simply to control the behaviour of managers. Codes of behaviour may remain silent on certain subjects, at the risk of implying that "if it's not explicitly forbidden, then it's allowed."[104] From this point of view, moral imagination, as Patricia Werhane[105] (2002, 2006) has applied the concept to management, *i.e.* the ability to visualise and explore new possibilities of responses to the dilemmas generated by life in organizations, seems to me to be an avenue worthy of further exploration.

Ultimately, this is a question of approach: do we want to set up a rigorous system of ethical control, or do we prefer a vision inspired by the group's common values, to which each member adheres informally? Here again, there are some difficulties: a value, such as "loyalty" for example, can be understood very differently depending on nationality, gender, religion, academic and professional background, culture[106] etc.[107] The example of Enron is striking here because, as Ferrell and Ferrell have showed, it was the culture of the company that was failing - the cult of short-term financial performance, "virility" in human relationships, misunderstood individualism - and not its compliance. Indeed, it is worth bearing in mind that Enron was considered a model of compliance in the United States.

Another form of scepticism is also apparent in the work carried out by Robert Jackall. "The emerging moral *ethos of* managerial circles is particularly remarkable for its lack of stability," he argues in *Moral Mazes,*[108] a book in which he examines the situational character of morality as practised in organizations. Incidentally, Paul Ricoeur notes that there is an inevitable tension here between individual ethics, that of the good life and "personal growth," and the financial purpose of an organization, guided by the objectives of productivist growth.[109] The danger for all kind of business ethics would therefore be the temptation of irenicism, a temptation which the political approach to management attempts to dispel.

---

[104] Babeau and Chanlat 2008.

[105] Werhane 2002, 2006.

[106] For example, ethnic subcultures (Westerners and locals in a Qatari company) or professional subcultures (creatives and computer specialists in an interactive communication agency).

[107] Ferrell and Ferrell 2010.

[108] Jackall and Mazes 1988: 101.

[109] Deslandes 2012a.

1.3.5 Management as Politics

"Against management"[110] is the title of an invigorating book by Martin Parker, former editor-in-chief of *Organization* and *Theory & Society*. According to Parker, while management was long considered a natural activity – in the sense of "getting by," of "managing the more or less inextricable nature of everyday business," finding solutions to everyday worries – its status has now changed. Resourcefulness has become an ideology, allegedly an apolitical ideology, based on a set of control techniques whose influence has extended into our hospitals, governments and schools.

Martin Parker goes further: the field of *business* ethics, considered as the intrusion of the question of responsibility into the field of micro-economics, and the organizational sphere more broadly, is in reality a way for the proponents of managerial ideology to save face in the eyes of society. In this view, ethics specialists are handmaidens of economic power (and CSR is mere "*window-dressing*"):

> ... the ethics of philosophy has little to say to someone who needs to get something done by Friday afternoon, and anyway already believes that 'wealth is good'.[111]

The 'managerialisation' of the world and its downsides have also been discussed by sociologist Vincent de Gaulejac in *La Société malade* de la *gestion,*[112] and by epistemologist and philosopher Jean-Pierre Dupuy with his denunciation of the mystification of politics by economics, a humiliation which he describes as "political power being surrendered to stewards."

However, this position is not new. While the first critical journals were created at the end of the 1960s (Critical *Sociology* or *Radical Political Economics*) or at the beginning of the 1970s (*Critique* in 1973, Critical *Inquiry in* 1974), the first critical management journal did not appear until 1994 (*Organization*), even if at the beginning of the 1980s, the work of Michel Crozier and Erhard Friedberg[113] had already highlighted the political games played by actors in organizations.[114] However, this relatively late appearance should not detract from the recent and global development of this stream of research,[115] which opposes the naturalistic, casuistic and objective approaches to the management sciences just as much as the humanist vision. Researchers affiliated with this current of thought have sought to demonstrate that management belongs, perhaps exclusively, to the political field. Their goal is essentially to "think of management as a political science."[116] Why should management be a field of research distinct from political science? Is management only to be considered a research object for political science, and nothing else?

---

[110] *Against Management*, by Parker 1999.

[111] *Ibid.*: 100.

[112] de Gaulejac 2005.

[113] Crozier and Friedberg 1977.

[114] Bessire and Mesure 2009.

[115] Alvesson and Willmott 2012a, b; Golsorkhi et al. 2009.

[116] Huault and Perret 2011: 300.

This is not my point of view, for at least three reasons. The first is that it is reasonable to wonder what would happen to the other dimensions of management, which I believe to be just as essential. Comparing the contrasting positions of Machiavelli and Pascal on this point, I have argued that while for Machiavelli the political order is superior to all the others in that it dominates the main aspects of economic and social existence, for Pascal this absolutism is merely a pretence which in no way removes the possibility of living an ethical life.[117] Quite the contrary, in fact. The manager does not see her responsibility emptied of all substance in the face of the circumstances of power, the system or force alone. Pascalian anthropology, particularly as set out in the *Three Discourses on the Condition of the Great*, shows how it is clearly possible to identify a personal ethical responsibility even among the demands of political and social life.

The second reason is evoked by sociologist Jean-Philippe Bouilloud as he explains that politics cannot be the only concern of the "managerial tradition," which is primarily concerned with "the competitive game." He argues that it is important to push back against this view, and to resist the idea that management represents a new, and perhaps the only (along with Chinese communism, he suggests), political theory.[118] By the same token, the frames of reference of management cannot be relied upon as the only means of thinking about the *polis*, adopting the "ethically dubious model of lobbying."[119]

The third reason is the following: to think of management as a political science would mostly consist of reducing the aim of management to the sole necessities of politics in its most trivial sense, i.e. its partisan ideological orientations. The study of management would then risk becoming beholden to the political disputes stirring within it, producing what Jacques Bouveresse calls "provocative diagnoses" without proposing any kind of therapy.[120]

Excluding political reflection from the management sciences does not seem to me to be either probable or desirable, as it is indeed one of its essential dimensions and contributes to its enrichment. But politics alone will not suffice to encompass the whole sphere of management, its epistemology, its techniques, its practice, or its ethics.

*

Faced with these paradoxical orientations, should we simply lose hope? In management, in addition to the categorical imperatives of ethics, we must also contend with the hypothetical imperatives of science. And the necessities of practice should at the same time be analysed with regard to the categories of politics. Management thus confronts the reality of the facts with axiological considerations. And it must be said

---

[117] Deslandes 2011b.

[118] Bouilloud 2012: 167.

[119] *Ibid.*

[120] Bouveresse 2001.

that no economic activity can henceforth dodge the test of evaluative judgements, neither press giants (e.g. News Corp and the *News of the World* affair) nor telephone operators (the social malaise at France Telecom). The "scientific" temptation of management and the lure of the *one best way* would have us believe that a world without plural values is possible. A pluralistic vision of management must account for the different personal, institutional and societal points of view of the players involved.

It is therefore the managerial condition that needs to be rethought in a realistic way, based on the five components whose contours and limitations I have sought to define above. There is surely room enough for each of these facets, and I have no intention of favouring one approach over another. The technical approach, whose importance I have sought to diminish because of its supremacy in many fields (including teaching), is nevertheless deserving of particular attention. What I hope to demonstrate, however, is that this technical dimension also requires ethical and political analysis by those involved. Management is as much a technical problem as it is an existential problem, it confronts the "hard" and the "soft," the quantifiable and the immeasurable.

As Aristotle would have it, we must endeavour to reconcile household management (*oikonomia*), which is the fact of managing one's house well, and *"chrematics,"* something akin to an art of commerce and finance. And yet, contemporary management appears to be highly fragmented, with its *tracks,* schools of thought and chapels. Is there not a risk that even eminent management experts will one day have nothing more to say to each other, that the ambition to embrace the complexity of management, the source of its scientific and philosophical interest, might melt away as the field continues to give the outward appearance of growth?

1.4   On Organizational Stupidity

If the discipline of management seems to be so fragmented, can it form a fair idea of the complexity to which contemporary organizations invite us? It is doubtful, just as it is doubtful that it has a precise and accurate idea of the 'intelligence'which it claims to have. For many years indeed, studies in business ethics have taken a keen interest in intelligence in all its forms, from corporate intelligence[121] to emotional intelligence,[122] business intelligence,[123] and, more recently, artificial intelligence,[124] omitting each time to refer to its opposite, stupidity, which is no less present in the organizational enrvironment. Yet, participating in the intelligence of organizations

---

[121] Cohen and Czepiec 1988.

[122] Angelidis and Ibrahim 2011; Hartman 1998; Segon and Booth 2015.

[123] Schultz et al. 1994.

[124] Martin, 2019.

seems to be a noble objective for managerial action, both to apprehend its complexity and to try to respond to ethical issues.

Indeed, without intelligence (whatever form it may take), how can we have a meaningful discussion about agency? Indeed, it would make little sense to talk of "ethical deliberation" between actors or agents entirely devoid of any kind of intelligence. By the same token, at the more practical level of actual management, a "best practice" is acknowledged as such when it is applied intelligently, to the extent that it makes the organization itself more intelligent.[125] Once again, we should not be overly surprised to learn that a best practice is essentially an example of intelligent managerial practice, or at least one broadly assumed to be something of the sort. The development and appropriate use of technological tools, including tools based on artificial intelligence, are also held up as means of enhancing the wisdom of managers and decisions-makers.[126]

And yet, it seems hardly necessary to point out that the relationship between organizations and intelligence is not always a smooth one. Mass unemployment and suffering in the workplace, economic despair and the ecological crisis are just a few of the complex issues which the West must face in this generation, and which organizations must confront. But when management is confronted with these extremely complex and urgent situations, a strange thing happens: it appears to be stunned, dazed, stupefied, incapable of taking action or even comprehending the scale of what is at stake. In fact, this situation could be considered the defining feature of our present *condition*. "Stupefied" comes, via French, from the Latin verb *stupere*, "to be stunned or numbed", and shares a root with "stupid". Perhaps, then, the pre-eminent characteristic of the modern human condition, existing within organizations, is stupidity. It's almost as if the "good, flexible, 'applied', conformist, managerial and multilingual technicians" described by Spurk – in his preface to one of Jaspers' books on higher education[127] – have turned out to be totally incapable of understanding and transforming the world they are faced with. This unprecedented situation should be encouraging business ethicists and management scholars to take a closer interest in stupidity than they have previously done.

The root of the problem is the simple fact that stupidity is present in organizations, in spite of all the promises of all the many forms of organizational intelligences. Such is the central tenet and major attraction of the much remarked-upon paper published by Alvesson and Spicer in 2012. In their article the authors highlight the scale of the stupidity phenomenon, even among those organizations which claim to be the most "innovative" and among those highly trained managers generally supposed to be the most ethical and smart. Through the power of mimetism and imitation of competitors, the influence of brands and trends, various members of the organizations studied then in Alvesson and Spicer's book (2016) bear witness to the rise of stupidity. Meanwhile, perhaps precisely because of a rise of stupidity, the

---

[125] Fried 2004.

[126] Moore 2019.

[127] 1946/2008: 8.

1.4 On Organizational Stupidity

organizations in question waste no opportunity to proclaim their commitment to a culture of innovation and strategic intelligence. In Alvesson and Spicer's view it is just when these organizations begin to take pride in their excessive intelligence, for example when they begin recruiting overqualified graduates, that they somehow seem to slip a little further into the morass of systemic "functional stupidity."

At this juncture it is worth noting that, in the authors' opinion, this "stupidification," this process of industrially-organised stupidity, arrives in phases: the first is typified by an inability to challenge the dominant *doxa,* the assumptions apparently taken for granted by all concerned.[128] The second is the incapacity to rethink (bad) organizational habits.[129] The third and final phase is when the managers are leaders in name only, i.e. they have become completely incapable of analysing the consequences of their decisions beyond the scope of their functions.[130] It is nonetheless curious to note that, for these two authors and many others whom they cite[131] a certain amount of incompetence, "mindlessness" or even "foolishness" should not prevent organizations, wherein a certain degree of ambiguity always exists, from obtaining satisfactory results. Indeed, they argue, somewhat surprisingly, that "functional stupidity contributes to maintaining and strengthening organizational order. It can also motivate people, help them to cultivate their careers, and subordinate them to socially acceptable forms of management and leadership.".[132] Organizational stupidity appears to have two sides to it: an obvious negative side, but also a positive one. However, although the work of Alvesson and Spicer does succeed in identifying and convincingly describing a thoroughly striking paradox, it barely touches upon the fact that stupidity, while rarely studied in management or business ethics compared with "intelligence" in all its forms, has received an astonishing amount of attention in other social sciences and philosophy.[133]

This section is intended to serve as a contribution to the question of stupidity and its philosophical scope in the context of business studies. Its primary source of inspiration is the philosophical work of Bernard Stiegler,[134] to which it also serves as a primer. His thought is becoming increasingly influential in the social sciences, on an international level, and yet discussion of his work is almost entirely absent from this particular field of research.[135] Stiegler's philosophical output, which in recent years has focused particularly on the emergence of new technologies and their consequences for human organizations, identifies two important developments which are currently reshaping the contemporary condition of knowledge: the

---

[128] Alvesson and Sköldberg 2009; Jackall and Mazes 1988.

[129] Boltanski and Thévenot 2006.

[130] Alvesson and Spicer 2016a, b; Butler 2016.

[131] Particularly Ashforth and Fried 1988; Cohen et al. 1972; March 2006.

[132] Alvesson and Spicer 2016a, b: 1196.

[133] Although they do include a short and recurring reference to the works of Ronell 2006 and Ten Bos 2007.

[134] Stiegler 2012; Deslandes and Paltrinieri 2017.

[135] Deslandes 2021a, b.

26 1 From Proto-Management to Contemporary Functional Stupidity

transformation of desires into impulses, essentially a critique of consumerism, and the "proletarianisation" of elites, those who occupy the upper rungs of the organizational hierarchy, a symptom of the dispossession of knowledge at the hands of automated machines.[136]

The next sections look at the situation in the wake of Alvesson and Spicer, focusing on the conditions required to escape the bottleneck of functional stupidity, with a view to constructing a new vision of political economy itself.[137] This new vision is to be founded upon *noetisation*, which is to express a new understanding of "corporate" intelligence.

1.4.1 What Is Stupidity?

The notion of stupidity, while not frequently evoked in the field of management studies and business ethics, has been extensively debated in contemporary continental philosophy. For instance, it crops up in the works of Deleuze, and certainly Derrida, one of whose final seminars was entitled "The beast and the sovereign",[138] as well as a host of other authors. But they all avoid directly addressing the organizational aspects of the phenomenon. This is certainly true of some of Derrida's disciples, such as Ronell[139] and Ferraris.[140]

Ronell's position consists largely of a demonstration that the fight against stupidity is always a lost cause. Derrida himself commented on the fact that the English word stupidity does not accurately capture the essence of the French term *bêtise*, derived from *bête* or beast. For Ferraris, who prefers the term imbecility, Humanity can thus be defined first and foremost with the help of this word, that is to say a form of unintelligence which is a primal characteristic of the human condition, echoing the traditional belief, relayed by the Italian philosopher, that the etymological root of the Latin word "imbecile" corresponds to "without a stick," i.e. stripped of all tools and assistance - man as savage, man in his "natural" state.

This goes some way to explaining the second point raised by Alvesson and Spicer, namely that if managers and employees in the business world behave like imbeciles, they do so primarily out of habit, automatically and without really thinking about it, as if it were an integral part of their character. It is worth noting Ferraris' view that social media have inflated what he calls the "burden of civilisation"[141] to a hitherto unprecedented scale, allowing it to spread further and more rapidly. "Imbecility," he explains, "is inherent to modernity because, with all the

---

[136] Johnson 2015.

[137] Stiegler 2009.

[138] Derrida 2008, 2010.

[139] Ronell 2006.

[140] Ferraris 2017.

[141] *Id.,*: 119.

1.4 On Organizational Stupidity

potentialities offered by the modern world, stupidity reveals itself in a manner which would not have been possible in a more thoughtful, more silent age."[142] It is also worth noting that Ferraris' vision of imbecility spares nobody, least of all great minds and philosophers.

Meanwhile, another disciple of Derrida, or at the very least a thinker whose doctoral thesis was supervised by Derrida and who credits his former tutor with a towering influence on the direction of his own philosophical career, has addressed this issue and defined it as a turning point in his work. The thinker in question is Stiegler[143], who has certainly been one of the most dogged explorers of systemic stupidity over the past decade and more.

In these circumstances, and in an environment which Stiegler insists is increasingly shaped by technological developments, our tricky relationship to knowledge and stupidity can only be partially resolved by adopting an approach which he defines as "pharmacological." On this important point his analysis appears to coincide with that of Alvesson and Spicer, but he expands the scope of the argument by insisting that management is not the only force to blame for this situation. Alvesson and Spicer are always quick to point the finger at "stupidity management," invoking the Foucauldian tradition[144] whereas Stiegler contends that this stupidity has a systemic quality which is inherent to the human *condition* when it comes to work, arguing that in the modern age "knowledge is falling into abeyance due to the failure to establish a general understanding of the processes at play".[145]

His view of the contemporary situation is that the *pharmaka* have all turned toxic, to the extent that stupidity has now become a fatality on a scale which he describes as systemic, an inevitable fate which awaits all members of all organizations. He identifies the new system of knowledge, now reduced to the status of "informational merchandise," as the source of the various forms of systemic and organizational idiocy which inundate the modern world and which prevent us from making full and judicious use of our intellectual capacities. The pharmacological analysis which he proposes nevertheless requires us to understand the relationship between knowledge and stupidity both as a form of toxicity and a potential source of redemption, i.e. at once poison and cure. Because in his view intelligence is not a form of science, since stupidity can also be found in abundance in scientific discourse. It is in fact a struggle, which need not always result in defeat, against our own stupidity. It is possible to overcome stupidity. Because, ultimately, it is stupidity which prompts us to think, which serves as a constant admonishment to be more discerning.

In the age of all-conquering technology, which Stiegler defines as "technologies of the mind and spirit," the relationship between knowledge and stupidity needs to be studied pharmacologically, i.e. taking into account the sometimes devastating

---

[142] *Ibid.*: 38.

[143] Stiegler 2009, 2015.

[144] Clegg et al. 2006; Knights et al. 1993.

[145] Stiegler 2018: 766.

28   1   From Proto-Management to Contemporary Functional Stupidity

nature of knowledge, without losing sight of its capacity for salvation, and thus the need to *take care* of it. In this analysis of stupidity, he also insists upon a number of important nuances: the first is that stupidity is not a form of original sin, as Ferraris would have it, but rather the consequence of a psychopower, specifically that exercised by mass media. The notion of psychopower goes beyond the Foucauldian biopower in the sense that, according to the author, it is the cultural industries and the so-called "economy of attention" (via marketing and big data) that have partially taken over the machine-like control of minds and the chain of affects (so as to finally render individuals 'disaffected'). In fact, "Metaphysical stupidity" can always be explained by the psycho-social environment, particularly in relation to technics and the way they constitute, our "milieu."[146] Stupidity exists in relation to our environment, and the same is true of intelligence. Unlike Ronell, Stiegler believes in the possibility of fighting back against stupidity and even escaping its clutches.

It is therefore our responsibility to find reasons to take stupidity seriously, in order to remain aware of it, as part of our contemporary condition, but above all to seek a treatment for this toxic force which appears to be polluting our individual as well as our collective and organizational lives, and to attempt to find a cure.

1.4.2   *Philosophical Stupidity and Technological Issues*

Stiegler's work is closely tied up with a reflection on our current "technological condition" and its implications. As Martin et al.[147] rightly observe, "we should understand the contours of what firms owe society as the rate of technological development accelerates". The rise of digital technologies "can undermine the autonomy of consumers or users. For example, many games and online platforms are designed to encourage a dopamine response that makes users want to come back for more".[148] The authors go on to explain how these manipulation techniques are constantly being fine-tuned, with consumers directly in the firing line. Aggregated data on user behaviour is subsequently used to influence their tastes and choices, particularly by tailoring the advertising to which they are exposed, to an extent which seriously affects their ability to make reasoned purchasing decisions.

As Grinbaum points out, while we often associate technology with ideas of progress and improvement, for example in the fields of healthcare and transportation, the reality is often quite different. As he puts it, "household assistants have become spies, autonomous cars are killing people, chat bots are insulting users. Information systems participate in human conflicts, and sometimes even cause them."[149] In Grinbaum's view, the supposed intelligence of machines should make it an absolute

---

[146] Cf. http://arsindustrialis.org/vocabulaire

[147] Martin et al. 2019: 307.

[148] *Id.*: 311.

[149] Grinbaum 2018: 81.

1.4 On Organizational Stupidity

priority for us to clearly define the values that managers for instance seek to defend with the help of these tools, for therein lies the essence of their own responsibility.

As a matter of fact, we appear to have entered into an era of "emotional capitalism,"[150] and the question which now presents itself is whether or not we as individuals have the capacity to resist the invasion of our sensibility by industrial, artistic and medical marketing. In the fields of management studies and business ethics – particularly in response to the growing influence of artificial intelligence in the business world, and the eerie feeling that it knows us better than we know ourselves – the question is whether or not we are still capable of choosing our own actions and exercising our own responsibility. It is a dilemma which Johnson defines as the "responsibility gap".[151] But how can we resist the (often unconscious) temptation to treat technological developments as being entirely separate from the ethical questions raised by such developments? The question is one which researchers in business ethics have raised repeatedly. On some level, the premises of a "pharmacological" approach to this problem have already been established: perhaps, in ethical terms at least, new collaborative and predictive technologies create as many risks as they do opportunities, even when used in a reasoned, contextual manner,[152] not to mention the possibilities opened up by datamining and new, more elaborate techniques of data processing.[153] This is precisely where Stiegler focuses his attention, in an attempt to rethink the relationship between ethics and technology from a pharmacological and philosophical perspective.

The roots of this analysis are to be found partly in his radical opposition to the positions advanced by some other contemporary thinkers, particularly Alain Badiou. In his polemical (and popular) 2007 essay *What does Sarkozy mean?*, Badiou contends that "technics, which some acclaim as the highest meaning and novelty – splendid or catastrophic – of our future, are almost always to be found in the service of more ancient procedures".[154] Stiegler regards this dismissal of technics, particularly digital technical objects, by one of Europe's most influential thinkers as another instance of philosophical stupidity, typifying the stupidity of contemporary philosophy in general.[155]

In Stiegler's view, we would be rash not to "acknowledge the prominent role played by engineers, since the management of this technical system shapes economic and social transformations much more profoundly than those actors who the people are supposed to choose, i.e., political organizations and managers in the usual sense".[156] In light of which Stiegler prefers to talk not in terms of phylogenesis but instead of *epiphylogenesis*, a term he coins to describe the "mnemotechnic evo-

---

[150] Illouz 2019.

[151] Johnson 2015, p. 714.

[152] Buchholz and Rosenthal 2002.

[153] Martin and Freeman 2004; Gouvea et al. 2012.

[154] Badiou 2007: 16; Stiegler 2013: 267–268).

[155] Stiegler 2013: 271.

[156] Stiegler 2018: 63.

lution resulting from the merger between the industries responsible for calculation, the production of symbols and their telecommunications".[157] To put it more simply, our evolution, and particularly the evolution of our memory, is no longer simply genetic or biological, but has become *epiphylogenetic*, which is to say governed by technical prostheses "external" to the human body.

Alongside with Simondon,[158] Stiegler views declarations of the kind made by Badiou as symptomatic of the sterile separation between the evolution of knowledge and the changes reshaping the real world, particularly the industrial world. In his view it is high time for philosophy and ethics to get to grips with this reality, acknowledging at last that "industrial machines are the ultimate creations of the human spirit. An immanent spirit. Our contention is that *thinking about the spirit means thinking about industry*".[159]

As if to offer some sort of reassurance as to the potentially surprising use of this word in this context, Stiegle reminds us that the term "spirit" was used by Max Weber ("Protestantism and the Spirit of Capitalism") as well as Boltanski and Chiapello ("The New Spirit of Capitalism"), and is thus far from new. What is new, however, and looks set to expand further still, is the long-term decline of this value in contemporary capitalism. We are living in an age of increasingly obvious "denoetization," where intellectual elevation in the field of work seems inaccessible.

Indeed, for Stiegler a pharmakon of the "mode of existence of technical objects"[160] is a necessary condition for any attempt to construct a fair vision of the business world. Because technics function in the same manner as a *pharmakon,* according to the principle of inherent ambiguity: technical objects allow for externalisation of the processes of hominization, providing countless services for humanity at large (particularly with tasks such as storage, archiving, recalling information, etc.). But, and at the same time, the performance of these tasks may prove to be toxic, as automation sees the machines relieve every one of us of certain capacities and forms of knowledge. Only a critical *pharmacology* could possibly equip us to fight back against stupidity.

As we have seen, the ancient Greek notion of *pharmakon* encompasses both remedy and poison. Technics, by their very ambivalence, can thus be a means of domination or of liberation. Take the example of big data, a forecasting tool which can be highly efficient yet still incapable of foreseeing an actual "event," which by its very nature is unpredictable. Or the proliferation of algorithmic intelligence, which has usefully augmented our calculation capacities in many sectors of activity (medicine, tourism, electronics etc.), but in doing so has restricted our scope for autonomous judgement: everything seems to be decided in advance, since processed data "speaks for itself," with no need for our human capacities of judgement.[161]

---

[157] *Id.*, 747.

[158] Simondon 2012.

[159] Neyrat and Stiegler 2006: 94; Deslandes and Paltrinieri 2017.

[160] An expression borrowed from Simondon.

[161] Martin, 2019.

1.4 On Organizational Stupidity

In reality, the digital technology which he sees as the ultimate incarnation of writing is not solely a dangerous phenomenon, threatening our working memory and capacity to recall information. It also provides an opportunity for extending knowledge beyond our selves, exchanging and sharing knowledge, and also preserving it. Digital technologies pose a risk to our attention spans and capacity for memory (hence the importance of reading), but they also provide an opportunity for the diffusion of knowledge, paradoxically helping to protect and preserve the thoughts we all experience internally.

1.4.3 Facing a New "banality of evil"?

In further clarifying his point, it is interesting to note that Stiegler himself draws upon studies in management science to evoke some of the negative aspects of digital automation and expand his analysis beyond the realm of functional stupidity. He sees the role of automation as being to:

> "Short-circuit the deliberative functions of the spirit." This is how "the systemic stupidity that had crept in between consumers and speculators, who became functionally impulsive as soon as ultraliberalism began to promote speculation and discourage investment, now broke through a new threshold far beyond the phenomenon which Mats Alvesson and André Spicer have defined as 'functional stupidity.'"[162]

Functional stupidity has extended its pernicious influence into the very bodies of employees, shareholders and managers, to the extent that nobody seems capable of attenuating its nefarious consequences for economic development, something of which Stiegler never loses sight. We may well hold skilled – or even highly-skilled – jobs, but this changes nothing because full automation targets our very impulses, infiltrating our nervous system itself. In doing so it acts as a "psychopower" which nobody seems capable of escaping. The result is what Stiegler calls "symbolic poverty," a general inability to produce new symbols which express the diversity of our sensibilities and intelligence.

This automation affects all levels of society and is aggravated by consumerism. This latter force acts as a catalyst to the loss of knowledge by imposing modes of existence which are the product of marketing, a system of which he offers his own critique. In doing so he does not limit himself to a critique of consumption in and of itself, or even the act of consuming, which is not inherently problematic. Since entering general parlance in the eighteenth century, the term has simply been used to refer to the way we use goods to meet our (often vital) needs. The true problem of absolute consumerism is that it prevents us from doing anything else. While marketing techniques are constantly being perfected and refined, users of these products and services have not noticed the loss of knowledge and the loss of sensitivity they entail. Marketing and the cultural industries, which have monopolised the majority

---

[162] Stiegler 2015: 43.

of our attention, have nurtured our impulses and short-term instincts but failed to connect us with our true desires (idealisation of the object and sublimation, which require a longer timeframe). Over time, marketing has become the most advanced technic in terms of its sway over consumer behaviour, through pure incitement to buy. But it has not enabled consumers to do anything more than participate in the standardisation of modes of being, and the universal normalisation of our leisure experiences.

The problem here is the system designed to capture our attention and pander to our impulses, at the expense of what Aristotle calls *noesis*, a concept which Stiegler defines as our longing for individual and collective elevation on both the spiritual and intellectual planes, which only sublimation can make possible. He does not deny that new forms of intelligence exist within contemporary capitalism, but he finds that they are generally associated with *mètis*[163] i.e. that category of intelligence devoted to problem solving, particularly logistical problems, and which might also be described as strategic, opportunist or calculating intelligence. But the consumerist imperative, of which neuromarketing is the ultimate expression and the bastion of its propaganda power, works to destroy desire, engendering a quasi-Orwellian process of deindividuation which makes systemic stupidity inevitable.

This critique of marketing, and particularly neuromarketing, might actually seem rather conventional. But what most interests Stiegler here is not the destruction itself, but rather the risk that it represents to the economy by systematising the impulsive character of consumption to such an extent that it becomes impossible to formulate new desires. He makes a fundamental distinction between our reflexes and instincts, which cannot be changed so easily, and desire, which he defines as a capacity for symbolic projection essential to the creation of knowledge, at work and elsewhere (a reference to Freud's *Civilisation and Its Discontents,* which explores the depredation of desire in favour of satisfying base impulses).

Our capitalist economies are thus under threat from two worrying phenomena: the "long-term decline in libidinal energy"[164] and its logical consequence, the extinction of desire and thus of investment in the long term. This is the first meaning that should be given to the paradigm shift mentioned in the introduction towards an 'erotic'[165] turn in management. Desire itself is in need of saving, and this can only come from a form of elevation which sets individual humans on a level apart from animals, who are guided only by their instincts. This is the level defined by Aristotle as the *noetic level,* which consists of taking care of oneself and projecting oneself into the future on the artistic, intellectual and spiritual planes (in the sense intended by the "technologies of the mind and spirit" evoked above).

Denoetisation is intensely problematic, not only because of the threat it poses to our capacity to think about the future, a particularly important subject for business education but also and above all for what it reveals about the decline in our ability

---

[163] Mackay et al. 2014.

[164] Stiegler 2005: 112.

[165] Marion 2006; Deslandes 2023.

to live together, and the ways in which we coexist. "Denoetisation is the new banality of evil, manifested first as a sense of unease".[166] The root of this evil is the fact that the *machines have taken over responsibility for our life choices*. Industrial automation, with its tendency to result in functional stupidity, destroys our capacities as well as our understanding of how to live together (Sen 1985),[167] or, more importantly, how to live together with dignity.

*

To conclude this first chapter, let's remember that stupidity, and especially functional stupidity, has become endemic, systemic even, to the extent that it is feeding the risk of planetary destruction, the breakdown of our society and our faith in its institutions. Stupidity is no longer a laughing matter (as it has been for generations of readers of Molière's *Bourgeois Gentilhomme* or Flaubert's *Bouvard et Pécuchet*, to cite just two examples from French literature); it has become an obstacle to formulating an intelligent response to the numerous, profound ethical issues facing contemporary organizations and their management.

A therapy is from now on needed. The term therapy here reconnects the term management (*mesnagement* in old French) with its original meaning of "taking care" (Le Texier 2011). Stiegler's diagnosis acknowledges the dissipation of our knowledge, in a techno-scientific context where mnemotechnic processes seem better-informed and more capable of resolving contemporary problems than the people who invented them. Technical objects, digital and automated, are also relentlessly dispossessing us of our singularities and capacities of judgement.[168]

In light of all of which, readers may well be asking themselves what such a therapy would look like. How can we reinvent organizations and their management? The next chapter tries to "rethink" our ways of dealing with it.

References

Alvensson, Mats, and Yiannis Gabriel. 2013. Beyond formulaic research. In praise of greater diversity in organizational research and publications. *Journal of Management Studies* 50 (1).

Alvesson, Mats, and Jörgen Sandberg. 2013. Has management studies lost its way? Ideas for more imaginative and innovative research. *Journal of Management Studies* 50 (1).

---

[166] Stiegler 2018: 34–35.

[167] Stiegler compares the average life expectancy in Bangladesh with that in Harlem, New York, i.e. a poor country and a borough of the richest city in the world, and shows that in spite of the disparity in available resources, particularly medical resources, life expectancy is greater in Bangladesh. In his view this is because solidarity and capacitation are alive and well in Bangladesh, but appear to have disappeared north of 43rd Street. He thus warns of the dangers involved in trusting the machines to create knowledge as well as take our decisions for us, since our first priority should be to fight back against the "exhaustion of our human, intellectual, affective, sensitive and artistic resources, which are being wiped out by standardisation" (Stiegler and Riquier 2017, p. 123).

[168] Angelidis and Ibrahim 2011; Holt 2018.

34 1 From Proto-Management to Contemporary Functional Stupidity

Alvesson, Mats, and Kaj Sköldberg. 2009. *Reflexive methodology*. London: Sage.
Alvesson, Mats, and André Spicer. 2016a. A stupidity-based theory of organizations. *Journal of Management Studies* 49 (7): 1194–1220. https://doi.org/10.1111/j.1467-6486.2012.01072.x.
———. 2016b. *The stupidity paradox. The power and Pitfalls of functional stupidity at work*. Profile Book.
Alvesson, Mats, and Hugh Willmott. 2012a. *Making sense of management*. 2nd ed. London: Sage.
———. 2012b. *Making Sens of Management. A critical introduction*. Londres: Sage.
Angelidis, John, and Nabil Ibrahim. 2011. The impact of emotional intelligence on the ethical judgement of managers. *Journal of Business Ethics* 99: 111–119.
Anquetil, Alain. 2008. *Qu'est-ce que l'éthique des affaires ?* Paris: Vrin.
Anquetil, Alain. 2011. *Textes clés de l'éthique des affaires*. Paris: Vrin.
Ashforth, Blake, and Yitzhak Fried. 1988. The mindlessness of organizational behaviour. *Human Relations* 41: 305–329.
Babeau, Olivier, and Jean-François Chanlat. 2008. La transgression, une dimension oubliée des organizations. *Revue Française de Gestion* 183 (3): 201–219.
Barabel, Michel, Olivier Meier, and Thierry Teboul. 2013. *Les Fondamentaux du management*. Paris: Dunod.
Bessire, Dominique, and Hervé Mesure. 2009. Penser l'entreprise comme communauté: fondements, définition et implications. *Management et Avenir* 30 (10): 30–50.
Bernard, Stiegler, and Camille Riquier. 2017. Critique de la raison impure. Entretien avec Camille Riquier. *Esprit* 433 (3): 118–129.
Bevan, David. 2008a. Continental philosophy. A grounded theory approach and the emergence of convenient and inconvenient ethics. In *Cutting-edge issues in business ethics*, ed. Mollie Painter-Morland and Patricia Werhane. New York: Springer.
———. 2008b. Continental philosophy: a grounded theory approach and the emergence of convenient and inconvenient ethics. In *Cutting Edge Issues in Business Ethics: Continental challenges to tradition and practice*, ed. M. Painter-Morland and P. Werhane, 131–152. Springer.
Boltanski, Luc, and Laurent Thévenot. 2006. *On Justification*. Princeton: Princeton University Press.
Bouilloud, Jean-Philippe. 2012. *Entre l'enclume et le marteau*. Paris: Seuil.
Bouilloud, Jean-Philippe, and Bernard-Pierre Lécuyer. 1994. *L'Invention de la gestion. Histoires et pratiques*. Paris: L'Harmattan.
Bouveresse, Jacques. 2001. Les managers peuvent-ils avoir un idéal. In *Essais II. L'époque, la mode, la morale, la satire*, ed. Jacques Bopuveresse. Marseille: Agone (« Banc d'essais »).
Buchholz, Rogene, and Sandra Rosenthal. 2002. Technology and business: Rethinking the moral dilemma. *Journal of Business Ethics* 41: 45–50.
Butler, Nick. 2016. Functional stupidity: A critique. *Ephemera*. 16 (2): 115–123.
Carr, Albert Z. 1968. Is business bluffing ethical? *Harvard Business Review* 46: 143–153.
Castoriadis, Cornélius. 1996. *La Montée de l'insignifiance*. Paris: Seuil.
Chabot, Pascal. 2013. *Global burn-out*. Paris: PUF.
Chanlat, Jean-François. 1998. *Sciences sociales et management – Plaidoyer pour une anthropologie générale*. Canada/France: Les Presses de l'Université de Laval. Editions Eska.
Châtelet, François. 2000. Introduction générale. In *La Philosophie des sciences sociales de 1860 à nos jours*, ed. François Châtelet. Paris: Hachette littératures.
Clegg, Stewart, David Coupasson, and Nelson Philips. 2006. *Power and organizations*. London: Sage.
Cohen, William, and Helena Czepiec. 1988. The role of ethics in gathering corporate intelligence. *Journal of Business Ethics*. 7 (3): 199–203.
Cohen, Michael, James March, and Johan Olsen. 1972. A garbage can model of organizational choice. *Administrative Science Quarterly* 17: 1–25.
Crozier, Michel, and Erhard Friedberg. 1977. *L'Acteur et le Système*. Paris: Seuil.
de Gaulejac, Vincent. 2005. *La Société malade de la gestion. Idéologie gestionnaire, pouvoir managérial et harcèlement social*. Paris: Seuil.

References

Denis, Jean-Philippe, and Alain-Charles Martinet. 2012. Le management, un carré plus que sémantique. *Revue Française de Gestion* 38: 228–229.

Derrida, Jacques. 2008. *La bête et le souverain (2001–2002)*. Vol. I. Paris: Galilée.

———. 2010. *La bête et le souverain (2002–2003)*. Vol. II. Paris: Galilée.

Deslandes, Ghislain. 2011a. Wittgenstein and the practical turn in business ethic. *Electronic Journal of Business Ethics and Organizational Studies* 16 (1)., online available.

———. 2011b. In search of individual responsibility. The dark side of organizations in the light of Jansenist ethics. *Journal of Business Ethics* 101 (1): 61–70.

———. 2012a. *Le Management éthique*. Paris: Dunod.

———. 2012b. Power, profits, and practical wisdom: Ricœur's perspectives on the possibility of an ethics in institutions. *Business and Professional Ethics Journal* 31 (1): 1–24.

———. 2013. *Essai sur les données philosophiques du management*. Paris: PUF.

———. 2021a. Branching off in the Anthropocene era. *Organization Studies* 43 (3): 468–471.

———. 2021b. *Antiphilosophy of Christianity*. Springer.

———. 2023. *Érotique de l'administration*. Paris: PUF.

Deslandes, Ghislain, and Luca Paltrinieri. 2017. Entretien avec Bernard Stiegler. *Rue Descartes* 91: 119–140. https://doi.org/10.3917/rdes.091.0119.

Drucker, Peter. 2010. *The practice of management*. New York: Harper Collins.

Faÿ, Éric. 2014. Affects (situations stratégiques). In Franck Tannery (dir.), *Encyclopédie de la stratégie*. Paris: Vuibert,.

Ferraris, Maurizio. 2017. *L'imbécillité est une chose sérieuse*. Paris: PUF.

Ferrell, O.C., and Linda Ferrell. 2010. The responsibility and accountability of CEOs: The last interview with Ken Lay. *Journal of Business Ethic* 100 (2).

Freeman, Edward. 1984. *Strategic Management a stakeholder approach*. Boston: Pitman.

———. 2000. Business ethics at the millennium. *Business Ethics Quarterly* 10 (1): 169–180.

Freeman, Edward, Jeffrey Harrison, Bidhan Parmar, Simone De Colle, and Stakeholder Theory. 2010. *The state of the art*. New York: Cambridge University Press.

Fréry, Frédéric. 2010. Management 2.0 or the end of the company? *L'Expansion Management Review* 137 (2).

Fried, Andrea. 2004. Corporate knowledge. Theory and practice of intelligent organizations (Book). *Management* 15 (1): 155–158.

Friedland, Julian. 2012. Beyond empiricism: Realizing the ethical Mission of Management. *Business and Society Review* 117 (3): 329–356.

Friedman, Milton. 1970. The social responsibility of business is to increase profits. *New York Times Magazine*, 13 September 1970.

Georges, Canguilhem. 1990. *"What is a philosopher in France today?", speech delivered on 10 March 1990 at the École normale supérieure, at the request of the Société des amis de Jean Cavaillès*. Online: http://www.paris8philo.com/article-4085356.html

Ghoshal, Sumantra. 2005. Bad Management theories are destroying good Management practices. *Academy of Management Learning and Education* 4 (1): 75–91.

Golsorkhi, Damon, Isabelle Huault, and Bernard Leca. 2009. *Les Études critiques en management. Une perspective française*. Laval: Presses de l'Université de Laval.

Gouvea, Raul, Jonathan Linton, Manuel Montoya, and Steven Walsh. 2012. Emerging technologies and ethics: A race-to-the-bottom or the top? *Journal of Business Ethics* 109: 553–567.

Grey, Christopher. 1996. Towards a Critique of Managerialism: The Contribution of Simone Weil. *Jounal of Management Studies* 5 (33).

Grinbaum, Alexei. 2018. *Les robots et le mal*. Paris: Desclée de Brouwer.

Gusdorf, Georges. 1962. Compte-rendu de la séance du 24 Novembre 1962 de la Société Française de Philosophie. *Bulletin de la Société Française de Philosophie*: 67–109.

Hadot, Pierre. 2002. *Exercices spirituels et philosophie antique*. Paris: Albin Michel.

Hartman, Edwin. 1998. The role of character in business ethics. *Business Ethics Quarterly* 8 (3): 547–559.

Hatchuel, Armand. 1994. Frédéric Taylor: an epistemological reading. L'expert, le théoricien, le doctrinaire. In *L'Invention de la gestion. Histoires et pratiques*, ed. Jean-Philippe Bouilloud and Bernard-Pierre Lecuyer. Paris: L'Harmattan.

Herbert, Simon. 1955. A behavioral model of rational choice. *The Quarterly Journal of Economics* 69 (1): 99–118.

Hirèche Baïada, Loréa. 2007. Ethique et gestion des ressources humaines: une revue critique de la littérature théorique et empirique. *Revue de l'organisation responsable* 1: 51–70.

Holt, Robin. 2018. *Judgment and strategy*. Oxford: Oxford University Press.

Huault, Isabelle. 2008. Les approches critiques en management. In *Le Management. Fondements et renouvellements*, ed. Géraldine Schmidt. Paris: Éditions Sciences Humaines.

Huault, Isabelle, and Véronique Perret. 2011. L'enseignement critique du management comme espace d'émancipation. Une réflexion autour de la pensée de Jacques Rancière. *Management* 14 (2): 282–309.

Illouz, Eva. (dir). 2019. *Les marchandises émotionnelles. L'authenticité au temps du capitalisme*. Introduction by Axel Honneth. Translated from english by Frédéric Joly. Paris: Premiers parallèles.

Jackall, Robert, and Moral Mazes. 1988. *The world of corporate managers*. New York: Oxford University Press.

Jardat, Rémi. 2011. Comment étudier le matériau de gestion ? Propositions méthodologiques. *Management et Avenir* 43 (3): 318–353.

Jensen, Michael. 1986. Agency cost of free cash flow, corporate finance, and takeovers. *American Economic Review* 76 (2): 323–329.

Jensen, Michael, and William Meckling. 1976. Theory of the firm. Managerial behavior, agency cost and ownership structure. *Financial Economics Journal* 3 (4): 305–360.

Johnson, Deborah. 2015. Technology with no human responsibility? *Journal of Business Ethics* 127 (4): 707–715.

Johnson, Gerry, Ann Langley, Leif Melin, and Richard Whittington. 2007. *Strategy as practice. Research, directions and resources*. Cambridge: Cambridge University Press.

Knights, David, Fergus Murray, and Hugh Willmott. 1993. Networking as knowledge work: a study of strategic interorganizational development in the financial services industry. *Journal of Management Studies* 30: 975–995.

Laufer, Romain. 1994. Le gestionnaire et la science. Histoire d'une relation. In *L'Invention de la gestion*, ed. Jean-Philippe Bouilloud and Bernard-Pierre Lécuyer. Paris: L'Harmattan.

Le Texier, Thibault. 2011. *La Rationalité managériale. De l'administration domestique à la gouvernance*. PhD thesis in economics, under the supervision of Joël-Thomas Ravix, Nice, Sophia-Antipolis University.

Mackay, David, Mike Zundel, and Marzin Alkirwi. 2014. Exploring the practical wisdom of mētis for management learning. *Management Learning* 45 (4): 418–436.

March, James. 2006. Rationality, foolishness, and adaptive intelligence. *Strategic Management Journal* 27: 201–214.

Martin, Kirsten. 2019. Ethical implications and accountability of algorithms. *Journal of Business Ethics* 160 (4): 835–850.

Martin, Kirsten, and Edward Freeman. 2004. The separation of technology and ethics in business ethics. *Journal of Business Ethics* 53: 353–364.

Martinet, Alain-Charles, and Yvon Pesqueux. 2013. *Épistémologie des sciences de gestion*. Paris: Vuibert/FNEGE.

Maslow, Abraham. 1943. A theory of human motivation. *Psychological Review* 50 (4): 370–396. https://doi.org/10.1037/h0054346.

Miettinen, Reijo, Dalvir Samra-Fredericks, and Dvora Yanow. 2009. Re-turn to practice: An introductory essay. *Organization Studies* 30 (12): 1309–1327.

Mispelblom Bayer, Frederik. 1996. Le management entre science politique et méthodologie d'encadrement. *Les Cahiers d'Évry* 1.

References

Moore, Phoebe. 2019. Artificial Intelligence: What everyone needs to know. *Organization Studies* 40 (3): 466–470.

Morin, Edgar. 1990. *Introduction à la pensée complexe*. Paris: ESF.

Murnaghan, Sheila. 1988. How a woman can be more like a man: The dialogue between Ischomachus and his wife in Xenophon's Œconomicus. *Helios* 15 (1): 9–22.

Natali, Carlo. 2001. Socrates in the *Economics of* Xenophon. In *Socrates and the Socratics*, ed. Gilbert Romeyer and Jean-François Gourinat. Paris: Vrin.

Neyrat, Frédéric, and Bernard Stiegler. 2006. De l'économie libidinale à l'écologie de l'esprit. Entretien avec Frédéric Neyrat. *Multitudes* 1 (24): 85–95. https://doi.org/10.3917/mult.024.0085.

Painter, Mollie, Mar Pérezts, and Ghislain Deslandes. 2020. Understanding the human in stakeholder Theory: A phenomenological approach to affect-based learning. *Management Learning* 52 (2): 203–223.

Painter-Morland, Mollie, and René Ten Bos. 2011. *Business ethics and continental Philosophy*. Cambridge: Cambridge University Press.

Parker, Martin. 1999. Capitalism, subjectivity and ethics: Debating labour process analysis. *Organization Studies* 20 (1): 25–45.

Placido Domingo Suarez. 2001. *Esclaves et affranchis en Grèce in the Economics of Xenophon*. Besançon: Presses Universitaires de Franche-Comté.

Rappin, Baptiste. 2011. De l'unité ontologique des épistémologies gestionnaires et de ses conséquences. *Management & Avenir* 43 (3): 476–489.

Rendtorff, Jacob. 2014. *French philosophy and social theory: A perspective for ethics and philosophy of management*. Vol. 49. Springer, Ethical Economy.

———., ed. 2017. *Perspectives on philosophy of management and business ethics: Including a special section on business and human rights*. Vol. 51. Springer, Ethical Economy.

Ricoeur, Paul. 1991. *Lectures 1: Autour du politique*. Paris: Seuil.

Ronell, Avital. 2006. *Stupidity*. Paris: Stock.

Saussois, Jean-Michel. 2007. *Théorie des organisations*. Paris: La Découverte.

Schein, Edgar. 2010. *Organizational culture and leadership*. 4th ed. San Francisco: Wiley.

Schultz, Norman, Allison Collins, and Michael McCulloch. 1994. The Ethics of Business Intelligence. *Journal of business ethics*. 13 (4): 305–314.

Segon, Michael, and Chris Booth. 2015. Virtue: The missing ethics element in emotion intelligence. *Journal of Business Ethics* 28 (4): 789–802.

Sen, Amartya. 1985. *Commodities and capabilities*. North-Holland.

———. 1987. *On ethics and economics*. Oxford: Basil Blackwell.

———. 2008. *Ethique et économie*. Paris: PUF.

Simondon, Gilbert. 2012. *Du mode d'existence des objets techniques*. Paris: Aubier.

Stiegler, Bernard. 2004. *Mécréance et Discrédit, t. I, La Décadence des démocraties industrielles*. Paris: Galilée. English version. Bernard Stiegler, (2011) *The Decadence of Industrial Democracies: Disbelief and Discredit*, 1, Cambridge: Polity Press.

———. 2005. *Constituer l'Europe. 2. Le motif européen. En collaboration avec Jean-Paul Basquiat et Alain Didier-Weil*. Paris: Galilée.

———. 2009. *Pour une nouvelle critique de l'économie politique*. Paris: Galilée. English version. Bernard Stiegler, (2010) For a New Critique of Political Economy, Cambridge: Polity Press.

———. 2012. *Etats de choc – Bêtise et savoir au XXIème siècle*. Paris: Mille et une nuits. English version. Bernard, Stiegler, *States of Shock: Stupidity and Knowledge in the 21st Century*, Cambridge: Polity Press, 2015.

———. 2013. *Pharmacologie du Front National*. Paris.

———. 2015. *La société automatique – 1. L'avenir du travail*. Paris: Fayard. English version. Bernard Stiegler, *Automatic Society, Volume 1: The Future of Work*, Cambridge: Polity Press, 2016.

———. 2018. *La technique et le temps*. Paris: Fayard. English version. Bernard Stiegler, *Technics and Time, 1: The Fault of Epimetheus*, Stanford: Stanford University Press.

Strati, Antonio. 1992. Aesthetic understanding of organizational life. *The Academy of Management Review* 17 (3): 568–581.

Ten Bos, René. 2007. The vitality of stupidity. *Social Epistemology* 21: 139–150.

Werhane, Patricia. 2002. Moral imagination and systems thinking. *Journal of Business Ethics* 38: 33–42.

———. 2006. A place for philosophers in applied ethics and the role of moral reasoning in moral imagination: A response to Richard Rorty. *Business Ethics Quarterly* 16 (3): 401–408.

Willmott, Hugh. 1997. Management and organization studies as science? *Organization* 4 (3): 309–344.

Xenophon. 1933. *Economique. Notice par Pierre Chambry.* Paris: Garnier.

Chapter 2
Rethinking Management

Abstract The second chapter of this essay is about rethinking management from a phenomenological approach and the notion of the subjective body. The aim is to reconsider work relations from an approach inspired by Michel Henry's radical phenomenology of life. Two subjects are then discussed: demotivation at work, called here *desaffectio societatis*, a sign of the disintegration of the affective and living link within an organization. And the question of social acceleration, where managers and employees find themselves victims of suffering as a result of the logic of the short term, so prevalent in the business world today. In the last section, I question whether recognition can be a basis for an ethical review of management. The chapter ends with an analysis which shows that, while recognition is necessary, it cannot be the last word in this challenge. It concludes with the prospect of a post-recognition ethics around the notion of "beau geste".

Keywords Beyond recognition · *Affectio societatis* · Affectivity · Business ethics · Material phenomenology · Michel Henry · Phenomenology of life · Praxis · Social roles · Social acceleration · Subjective bodies · World-as-organization

Thinking about organizations from the standpoint of a phenomenology of life or an ontology of vital[1] *praxis* is ultimately a matter of questioning all the representationalist presumptions of 'production' and social relations, so prevalent in the managerial literature. It is a question of turning them on their head, restoring the real, sensitive, pathetic subjectivity of individuals, managers or employees, to the detriment of the "pure" objective and traditional modes of representation, especially visual ones, of contemporary organizations.

In the Galilean objectivity of the most classical forms of management science, where human resources are managed like natural resources, "anything can take the place of anything: individuals are as interchangeable as objects."[2] The object of

---

[1] É. Faÿ 2007, 2009.

[2] M. Henry 2000: 315.

© The Author(s), under exclusive license to Springer Nature Switzerland AG 2023
G. Deslandes, *Postcritical Management Studies*, Ethical Economy 65, https://doi.org/10.1007/978-3-031-29404-4_2

39

these management sciences then becomes a gigantic abstraction that no longer has anything in common with the efforts of the living beings who make management and collaboration possible. More to the point, what does "human resources management" actually mean? Are we talking about actors within the system, or agents, or talents? It seems fair to say that the existence of living human individuals is a necessary prerequisite for management to exist.[3] In any case, we must not forget that living individuals, as Paul Ricoeur explains,[4] represent the guiding principle and end of all organizations and institutions.

Nevertheless, management studies still abound with postulates on 'human resources,' without always questioning the conditions which allow such resources to exist. "Giving a scientific and abstract turn to management makes it possible to side-step encounters or painful negotiations between actors who might struggle to reach intersubjective agreement," Éric Faÿ astutely notes.[5] In this respect, management must be reconsidered as an opportunity to assert our shared existence: not in the more or less functional repetition of a certain social and political order determined in advance ("Social existence placed under the seal of ambient pragmatism is characterised by organizational schemes and collective routines from which life as such has almost disappeared," as Hugo Letiche would have it),[6] but rather by trying to anchor it in the vital process of subjective activity, understood as the one and only true activity.

Let us now attempt to free management of its objectivist and scientific pretentions, instead connecting its main categories – resources, power, development and so on – to subjective bodies, and to life.

2.1 Organizations and the Subjective Body[7]

Holly Martins – Have you ever seen one of your victims?

> Harry Lime – Victims? Don't be dramatic. Look down there. Would you really feel any pity if one of those dots stopped moving forever? If I offered you 20,000 pounds for every dot that stopped, would you really, old man, tell me to keep my money, or would you calculate how many dots you could afford to spare?. *The Third Man*, dir. Carol Reed, 1949, Screenplay by Graham Greene.

Suspected by Holly of being the mastermind of a traffic of adulterated penicillin in post-war Vienna, Harry Lime, surveying the ruins of the Austrian capital from atop the *Prater* ferris wheel, looks down on the people below as unimportant little dots. Linguist Raffaele Simone derives the following moral lesson from this classic of

---

[3] Here we quote Michel Henry quoting Marx: 1976a: 193.

[4] D. Bessire and H. Mesure 2009.

[5] É. Faÿ 2014: 23–24.

[6] H. Letiche 2009: 301.

[7] A version of this chapter was previously published in G. Deslandes, G. (2017), To Be or not to Be a Dot? Philosophy of Management and the Subjective Body, in: Rendtorff, Jacob Dahl (Ed.), *Perspectives on Philosophy of Management and Business Ethics*, Springer, p. 47–60.

2.1 Organizations and the Subjective Body

film noir: "Vision is not empathetic. If we consider others as mere images, then cynicism is almost obligatory."[8]

In the world of contemporary organizations, are human beings not considered primarily as images? From the top of his or her control tower, the newly appointed CEO takes pleasure in contemplating the map of the organization's stakeholders, the organizational diagram representing the senior management team, and the staff photo taken at the end of an internal executive education seminar. But what does she really think about the people she manages? How does she see them? How would she define them if asked? 'Selves',[9] "followers",[10] resources',[11] 'talents'[12] maybe, or even objective "bodies" (lest we forget, *corporate* has its roots in the Latin word for body, *corpus*).[13] She would no doubt reply that they are employees, from whom she expects the highest possible level of performance.

Management research has quite naturally taken up this question of identity and self.[14] In fact, an immense literature has developed, particularly in the field of social psychology and its behaviourist tradition,[15] but also in the field of critical studies in management, primarily under the influence of Michel Foucault's work on the theme of subjectivity. To discuss this point, Mats Alvesson uses images and metaphors (*self-doubters, strugglers, storytellers, surfers*, etc.) in order to propose the most accurate representation of the process of identity construction at work.[16] This use of imagery, in what is an important article, does not indicate a desire to collect all the (too numerous) images which characterise research on personal identity, but rather to select the most pertinent among them. This research is ultimately intended to help researchers finally answer the question posed in the previous paragraph: how do we conceive of the people we encounter in our working lives?

In this chapter, I propose to re-examine the way in which the issue of the subject has been approached in *organization studies* in recent years, following the lead of Campbell Jones and André Spicer – for whom debates around the issue of the subject in management have become "self-satisfied and repetitive"[17] – albeit from a different perspective. I will first attempt to establish a genealogy of the self within critical management studies. I will then present Michel Henry's material phenomenology as a primary philosophy before delving deeper into his conception of the self as a *subjective body*. Finally, I will underline the opposition between Foucauldian and Henryan self-concern.

---

[8] R. Simone 2012: 60.

[9] M. P. Follet 1919.

[10] Ch. Thoroughgood et al. 2012.

[11] K. Inkson 2008.

[12] C. Tansley and S. Tietze 2013.

[13] J. Hassard et al. 2000.

[14] C. Rhodes and E. Wray-Bliss 2013.

[15] G. Mead 1934; B. Ashforth and F. Mael 1989; J. Ford and N. Harding 2011: 468.

[16] M. Alvesson 2010.

[17] C. Jones and A. Spicer 2005: 237.

2.1.1 Genealogy of the Self in CMS

It is in the field of *critical management studies* (CMS) that this essential question has been addressed with the greatest acuity and precision: what is hiding behind the term "colleague?" For Mats Alvesson and Hugh Willmott, "the question 'who am I?' or 'what are we?' calls for a response in terms of some dominant or defining identity."[18] This should not come as a surprise: interest in the theme of subjectivity only really develops when management recognises that it is not solely a discipline devoted to the quest for economic performance, but actually remains exposed to issues of identity, politics and ethics.[19] It is only then that the problem of subjectivity becomes "the main issue."[20] Recent developments in contemporary continental philosophy and psychoanalysis have made it possible to develop new ways of defining this *self*, centred around two key points which converge within the field of critical studies: on the one hand, the decline and fall of the sovereign subject, and on the other, the passage from an ontology of interiority to a metaphysics of exteriority.

The end of the sovereignty of the subject can be observed in the contradictory debate between the proponents of the *labour process Marxism approach*[21] and those of the *post-structuralist approach*, a debate in which some of the difficulties concerning individual agency crystallised in the mid-1990s.[22] For the post-structuralist approach, especially the Foucauldian-inspired current of thought, it was a question of disavowing the essentialist conception of human nature that Marxism still contains. For the thinkers associated with this movement, the time had come to discard the humanist and sovereign model of an essential and stable subjectivity, inherited from the early days of philosophical modernity, by proposing an alternative in which the subject would be decentralised, divided, and recognised as determined, but only partially, by different techniques of power. Behind this idea also loomed the destruction of the hero, that is to say the will to destroy the myth of the leader or the *"great man"* theory, so prevalent in management and leadership studies.

Post-dualism, as proposed by Hugh Willmott, thus made it possible to rethink the traditional distinctions of agency and structure, subject and object. With this added claim to "subjectivism," the subject begins to fall off its pedestal and loses the ontological primacy it enjoyed in the modernist tradition. As Parker explains,[23] breaking out of traditional dualisms required a double movement: deconstruction of the self and "dereification" of social relations. Since then, the development of poststructuralist research in management has been particularly attentive to this problematisation of the *self*, both as a project and as a body, the latter always a central concern.[24]

---

[18] M. Alvesson and H. Willmott 2002: 625.

[19] M. Reed 1988; D. Knights and G. Morgan 1991.

[20] M. Parker 1999: 31.

[21] H. Braveman 1974.

[22] Ph. Hancock and M. Tyler 2001; M. Holmer-Nadesan 1996; D. O'Doherty and H. Willmott 2001.

[23] P. Parker 1999: 31.

[24] M. Alvesson and H. Willmott 2002; J. Ford 2006; M. Painter-Morland 2013.

2.1 Organizations and the Subjective Body

This deconstruction of the central and unified subject was taken up enthusiastically by the psychoanalytical tradition. For Marianna Fotaki, Susan Long and Howard Schwartz, psychoanalysis, because of its interest in the study of the psyche, has the clear potential to contribute to a better understanding of managerial issues and human relations at work[25]; it "clearly represents the most advanced conceptualization of human subjectivity, a position that no other theoretical approach can validly claim."[26] For their part, Campbell Jones and André Spicer call for a constructive confrontation between Foucaultian and Lacanian studies. They draw upon their reading of Lacan to examine the identity of the entrepreneur as a figure, arguing that this figure "necessarily indefinable; the entrepreneur is an 'absent centre';"[27] an empty and phantasmatic entity, the figure of the entrepreneur thus becomes, in Slavoj Žižek's words, "the sublime *object*." For Gilles Arnaud, who offers a historical survey of psychoanalytical approaches, this psychoanalytical advance contains an even more radical decentring: "In fact, the psyche is radically external, it is inscribed in social norms," he explains.[28]

This analysis of the subject with specific reference to organizational world is consistent with the work of Peter Fleming and André Spicer, which borrows both from psychoanalytical theory and from post-structuralist advances.[29] They consider subjectivity to be very different from the usual notions of person or personality, which are defined primarily by the importance they accord to that which is "internal" and private. However, this supposed prioritisation of "interiorisation over external reality" is fallacious and, in their view, deserves to be reversed. Referring variously to Slavoj Žižek and Louis Althusser, they do not contest the presence of interiority as such in each individual, preferring instead to focus on the external, objective dimension of the processes by which the identities of employees and managers are forged. We are defined just as much by our actions, practices and rituals, they claim, as our inner certainties. In fact the latter are surely dependent upon the former. "Althusser takes up the advice that Pascal suggests to anyone who wants to believe in God, namely to kneel and move your lips until you believe."[30] But if belief can also be considered an objective phenomenon, then how can we escape, ask André Spicer and Peter Fleming, from the "cultural colonisation" of institutions which, in turn, ask us to kneel and move our lips? Consider, for example, the ritual aspects involved in the celebration of the "values" of a brand or the launch of a new project.

The authors propose an "externalisation of disbelief" as a cynical strategy of resistance, whereby it is sufficient to shift, to reverse – as long as such a thing is

---

[25] M. Fotaki et al. 2012.

[26] *Ibid.*, p. 1105.

[27] C. Jones and A. Spicer 2005: 236.

[28] G. Arnaud 2012: 1178.

[29] P. Fleming and A. Spicer 2003.

[30] *Ibid.*, p. 170. In the *Pensée* referenced here, Pascal certainly advises kneeling to pray, but with the aim "that the outside be joined to the inside [...]. To expect help from the outside is to be superstitious." (br. 250). See G. Deslandes 2011b.

44   2 Rethinking Management

possible or desirable – the internal processes of identification towards the outside, that is to say in a form that is clearly visible, in full view of everyone.

2.1.2   Michel Henry's Phenomenology of Life

For Michel Henry, psychoanalysis could certainly be considered as the apogee of subjectivity,[31] the spectacle of Western philosophy voluntary entangling itself in the naive objectivism of contemporary sciences, and of the human sciences in particular. This is not, however, about forcing the philosophy of the subject into retreat, or making it play a new role. Criticism of the subject, Henry remarks "does not have to be ashamed of its past, but nor should it lean nostalgically towards it."[32] It is, in fact, a challenge to the great continental philosophies of the twentieth century – for which the meaning of being can only be reached by detours – and an assertion of the primacy of *affectivity* as mode of self-knowledge. Affectivity constitutes the only irreducible and infallible source of knowledge available to every human being, specifically the immediate capacity to experience oneself in all aspects of being.

It would be wrong, of course, to suggest that Michel Henry's research was entirely without precedent or precursor in the history of ideas. Indeed, Henry is in constant dialogue with the philosophical tradition, and in particular with Arthur Schopenhauer, who holds a particularly important place in his work.

For Henry, if Arthur Schopenhauer is so decisive in this context, it is because his thought is presented as a primary philosophy,[33] that is to say a philosophy concerned with the origins and foundations of all reality. The priority is to adopt a position from which "one sees everything and understands everything."[34] Now, according to Schopenhauer, nothing that appears to us in a represented form is endowed with any sense of will; on the other hand, will entirely characterises that which is presented to us by means of representation. For Michel Henry, this is what constitutes the heart of the Schopenhauerian message. Representation, which claims to give us access to truth, is unreal. What is real, and thus forms reality, is the other mode of appearing which we might call the will understood as impulse, passion, desire, affection, action. Schopenhauer, an important influence on what would later constitute Freudian psychoanalysis, belongs to the line of thinkers highlighted by Henry, who supports the central thesis of the *Essence of Manifestation*,[35] namely the coexistence of two modes of appearance. *The World as Will and as Representation*, Schopenhauer's central work, attests to the presence of these two perfectly distinct essences, the representation that is without will and the will that is without represen-

---

[31] M. Henry 1985, 2000: 221.

[32] M. Henry, "La critique du sujet," *Phénoménologie de la vie*, t. 2, *De la subjectivité, op. cit.*

[33] P. Guillet de Monthoux 2000.

[34] M. Henry 2011a: 110.

[35] M. Henry 1963.

2.1 Organizations and the Subjective Body   45

tation. His philosophy rejects the claims of representation, and of the world as a combination of phenomena that I represent to myself, revealing the immanent essence of reality. By contradicting the capacity of representation to unveil reality, and by juxtaposing a force, the will, as a constitutive element of it, Schopenhauer's thought opened up fundamentally new philosophical perspectives.

But in Michel Henry's view, Schopenhauer's true discovery did not concern the will, but its very condition, which is to say life, which is irreducibly opposed to representation: "it is the immanence of the will that makes it reality – as long as it does not fall into the rank of a will to live seeking its reality in the world of unreality – and which, at the same time, disqualifies it."[36] In short, will is life, since any movement that comes from life imposes itself on the will.

This commentary on Schopenhauer's work, admirative though it is, nevertheless contains a degree of criticism. Schopenhauer's great limitation, according to Michel Henry, is that he did not see that the body is the totality of the powers ("I can") given to me by and in life: desire cannot come first, since one must first be capable of desiring. So the reappearance of life in European philosophy at the beginning of the nineteenth century, notably thanks to Schopenhauer's will to live, came at the expense of the subject. Schopenhauer's will to live leads to a practical aporia: I cannot want without power, and have power only in and through life… which therefore precedes all will.

2.1.3 Subjective Bodies

"It is always and only as a self-appearance of appearance that subjectivity is constructed internally and unfolds its essence,"[37] writes Michel Henry in *Material Phenomenology*. Since this is the major theme of our investigation, let us now try to define the terms egoity, self and subject, which so frequently appear in his works and which define the figures of individuality.

Egoity, first of all, denotes the interiority of self-presence, one's immediate presence. It is what can be experienced as self. Thus the essence of the ego is *ipse*, that which affects itself. It is self experienced as self. In other words, the ego is not the person as such, but the essence of the person, the structure of her being, which is subjective. Ego is a necessary condition of manifestation, the primary ontological principle.

What this definition suggests is that the primary structure of the human being, her "matter," cannot be understood in an exclusively empirical, psychological, biological or social sense. Michel Henry calls this first "pathos" affectivity,[38] affection

---

[36] M. Henry 1985: 208.

[37] M. Henry 2011a: 25.

[38] H. Letiche 2009.

being the pure manifestation itself. It is from this affectivity that being may emerge, and the two remain inseparable.

For the author, who questions here the presumptions of contemporary psychology, this affectivity as suffering and as joy can in no way be apprehended in a strictly empirical dimension. A person who suffers can neither understand, nor delimit, nor analyse that suffering, but only suffer it as a constituent reality. This suffering has no mirror that can reflect it in its own eyes. She who suffers is made of her suffering:

> Pain is not, therefore, what it has long been assumed to be, an unfortunate accident, a natural peculiarity or the fatality of an incomprehensible destiny. It is the apriorical structure of everything, its most interior possibility and, as Nietzsche might say, echoing Schopenhauer, the Mother of Being.[39]

The lesson we can learn from this is that the auto-affected self can never be separated from itself. This self-affection is not a faculty of the self but constitutes that self considered in itself. Thus, the subject that can never be separated from itself is not the ego as it appears in the history of metaphysics, but the ego that exists only through and in an *ipseity* that gives it to itself to constitute a self.

But then, if each of us is this carnal self, what of corporality? This question is primordial, and in no way repressed in Michel Henry's philosophy. The starting point for his analyses is to be found in his in-depth study of the treatises of the French metaphysicist Maine de Biran (1766–1824), who defines the body as the original movement, experienced in its very fulfilment. It is the seat of all power, the place where all things are revealed, where the intensity of life is revealed. The body is the power that is given to us to accomplish our life and by which we originally take possession of our faculties, our senses, our limbs.[40] If we were not this body, no performance, no action, no collaboration would be possible.

To establish his definition of the body, Michel Henry resorts to an essential distinction, which constitutes his theory of the three bodies. This power of the body as the origin of all power is that of the subjective body (or of the original body, which Michel Henry called "flesh" in his later works). This should not be confused either with the body of representation (the visible one), the one to which management generally refers, or with the biological ("*chosique*") body, i.e. as a physical, chemical, molecular or neuronal entity. By insisting upon the distinction between the constituent body, which is immanent, and the 'worldly' and constituted body, Henry signifies the primacy of the first over the second, because it is here that we live and desire. Here, then, is the ultimate, intimate refuge of our essence.

Is Michel Henry essentially resurrecting the old dualism between body and mind? Quite the contrary: he proposes a means of moving beyond the confused

---

[39] M. Henry 1985: 219.

[40] On the contrary, "is a world and is constituted as such only that which I have a princely possibility of access to, that which I can see or hear, touch or feel as often as I want, and this precisely because I have the possibility of doing so, because each sense is a power and each of its effects is an effect of this power and not an act that comes from who knows where and whose possibility would be forever mysterious if it were not first given to me as this possibility that I am," *ibid.*, 395.

2.1 Organizations and the Subjective Body

conceptions of the past, insisting upon his definition of the human being as a *"living carnal self"* that has nothing to do with the definitions that shape, in diverse forms, this compound of mind and matter, soul and body, 'subject' and 'object' where it is impossible to understand anything whatsoever."[41] Ultimately, what Henry proposes is a unified view of human beings, insofar as it is indeed our flesh that gives us access to material reality, and nothing else.[42]

At this stage, I also feel it is important to compare the living self as Henry defines it with the concern for the *self* which occupied an important position within Michel Foucault's later work. The Foucauldian self is indeed an important element of comparison here insofar as it has served as a point of reference for a whole range of research in the field of *critical management studies*,[43] and continues to inform, directly or indirectly, numerous works on questions of ethics and politics applied to management.[44]

In his final lectures at the Collège de France, Michel Foucault returned to a notion partly forgotten since the Greeks, *epimeleia heautou*.[45] Translated as "care for the self," Foucault used it as the basis of an ethics which aims to achieve, through practice, the transformation of the self itself.[46] To this end, Foucault invoked "techniques of the self," which he defined as "procedures such as there are undoubtedly in any civilisation, which are proposed or prescribed to individuals to fix their identity, maintain it or transform it according to a certain number of ends, and this thanks to relationships of self-control over oneself or self-knowledge by oneself."[47]

In everyday terms, these practices are characterised by the search for self-control over oneself (*egkrateia*) and the setting up of mechanisms to regulate the subject itself. The process of creation of the subject is thus conducted as much through modes of subjectivation as through modes of objectification. The Foucauldian subject experiments with freedom by constructing her own ethics, but without ever encountering her own essence, as this is radically impossible. Only the empirical self, sculpted by daily practice, rejecting all forms of metaphysical hope, interests Foucault. Concern for the self is not given, it is conquered and, like a "work of art," it is constructed in the "courage of truth," by evaluating and re-evaluating oneself.[48]

This brief summary of the self in Michel Foucault's work allows us to compare it with Michel Henry's understanding of the self. According to Henry, the concern for the self described above is essentially a concern for the world. The relationship to the self implied by concern for the self makes reference to the "outside" world,

---

[41] M. Henry 2003: 176.

[42] Ch. Gschwandtner 2012: 124.

[43] G. Burell 1988; A. Crane et al. 2008; Ibarra-Colado et al. 2006; D. Knights and G. Morgan 1991; B. Townley 1993, 1994.

[44] S. Gagnon 2008.

[45] M. Foucault 2001, 2008.

[46] G. Deslandes 2013, 2023.

[47] M. Foucault 2001: 494.

[48] M. Foucault 2008.

making its "shaping" improbable. Indeed, there can be no "relation to self"in the ether of pure exteriority, but only a relation to two external terms, as if they were foreign to each other.[49] As such, the relationship to oneself is always imposed from outside, by life, the ultimate, immemorial and invisible power.

Michel Henry's understanding of the relationship with the self is not a question of activity, as in Foucault, but rather of ontological passivity towards oneself. Life is defined by immediacy to oneself and passivity, which nevertheless endows individuals with all of their constituent powers. This is also at the heart of Henry's critical contribution to phenomenology: it is not thought that gives us access to life, but life that gives us access to ourselves. It is not the self that defines the relationship to oneself, but life, which precedes and constitutes it.

This passivity has very important consequences: what characterises Michel Henry's *ipseity* of the self is the sheer impossibility of freeing ourselves from it: no effort of reflexivity has ever allowed anyone to get rid of her subjective body. Here he comes close to Kierkegaard and his *Practice in Christianity*: "it is superficial to say that the desperate man wants to destroy himself, because that is precisely what, to his great despair, he is incapable of doing."[50] Escape from oneself is, after all, impossible, and this is what causes anxiety: It is not his own suffering that Kierkegaard describes, as a romantic writer or a particularly gifted psychologist would – the young son of an elderly father, the excessively anxious young man and his failed marriage plans, the wounded genius ridiculed by the gutter press for trousers that were too short... He develops an ontology of the ipseity, "that is to say of existence understood as originally monadic, as the individual."[51]

2.1.4 Praxis and Capabilities

Economic analysis must therefore return to the place where reality is located, i.e. the concrete life, action, vital *praxis*. For Michel Henry, who based himself in particular on Marx and the *1844 Manuscripts,* this means "a real action, that of the craftsman or worker, it designates the concrete activity of the person who handles, knocks, lifts, carries, traps, etc."[52] By *praxis,* he means a notion that makes no room for an idealistic and abstract representation of consciousness, but is rather an intimate test that coincides with its doing. It has nothing to do with a process in the third person, like the movement of a piston, which Michel Henry takes as an example, and which therefore has nothing to do with this *praxis* and with the being of work.

In this case, how does the notion of vital *praxis* connect with that of social life? What place for others, or for social roles, in a philosophy that considers reality to be

---

[49] M. Henry 2003.

[50] M. Henry 1996: 11.

[51] *Ibid*: 9.

[52] M. Henry 2004: 30.

2.1 Organizations and the Subjective Body

an intimate affair? According to one of the foremost commentators on Henry's work, Raphaël Gély,[53] the notion of character makes it possible to preserve real action as well as the will to develop in the eyes of others. As François-Régis Puyou and Éric Faÿ put it:

> speaking, listening and acting collectively represent the conjunction of powers and the sharing of life. Collaboration can also be a way to meet and get to know others better, by experiencing the pleasure and dynamism of successful cooperation.[54]

Any potential for growth is amplified by living contact with others and their personhood. Henry thus intends to resist the philosophies of "suspicion," according to the expression generally attributed to Ricoeur, with their propensity to make the human being "the victim of objective processes of which he is unaware."[55,56]. To the objective knowledge of who we are, Michel Henry's ethics opposes the recognition of the affective purpose of our conduct and decisions:

> If I execute my movements without thinking about it, it is not because these movements are mechanical or unconscious, it is because their entire being belongs to the sphere of absolute transparency of subjectivity. There is no intermediary between the soul and the movement, because there is neither distance nor separation between them.[57]

This is an ethics rooted in action, in doing, and not in the order of objective thought or in the interiority of a beautiful soul. Henriyan and Schopenhauerian ethics are united by their disdain for normative conceptions of ethics (so prevalent in *business* ethics research): the will cannot conform to the moral code, only thought can, which cannot act upon the will.[58] In an interview conducted at the end of his life, Henry offered the following explanation:

> My phenomenology of life is not intended to replace the phenomenology of the world. The phenomenology of the world has its own right. Husserl and Heidegger have extraordinary descriptions of this world [...]. I have worked upstream, in another region.[59]

This statement should lead us to further explore the possibilities, if not of reconciliation, at least of dialogue between philosophies where the subject is inseparable from the world (Husserl, Heidegger), and the Henryian model, where the subject is inseparable from her life. The point at which a dialogue is possible is Michel Henry's repeated reminder that the transcendental world of the appearance of the world does exist (even if it is not capable of accounting for reality on its own). Two

---

[53] R. Gély 2007.

[54] Fr.-R. Puyou and É. Faÿ 2013: 11.

[55] M. Henry 1988: 94.

[56] M. Henry 2013: 138.

[57] M. Henry 2011c: 82.

[58] M. Henry 2008b. It is through the determination of affectivity that a representation can in turn be collected, or driven out, from the psyche. For Henry, elation and joy occur only positively, in their affective phenomenality, and not as the satisfaction of a desire, which always occurs only through the suppression of the need, that is, negatively.

[59] M. Henry 2005: 130.

forms of receptivity of being coexist: towards the world and towards oneself. It is therefore not a question of withdrawing into one's inner self, but of being where reality is, in one's heart, that is to say in life. All of which means that the material world should not be denigrated, and that the biological body retains its value as "precisely that ambiguous element that hides, under the determination of the being, the infinity of the subjectivity that secretly inhabits it."[60]

While Michel Henry stood apart from most of his contemporaries in philosophy in terms of his views on the original self, he nevertheless admitted that a mundane self exists and is transformed according to the trials of life, especially cultural and professional[61] ones. The philosopher addresses this mundane self in *C'est moi la Vérité,* where he insists on cultural, functional and sexual identities, all of which are, according to him, linked to habit, that is to say to the concrete modalities of *praxis.*[62] In Henry's view, if we were not defined by what we do, this would imply that a need to be exists independently of appearances. But such a theory would be antithetical to the phenomenological credo he applies throughout his work.

It should be noted that this theme of *praxis* is a central concern of contemporary management research, particularly that based on the work of Michel Foucault, whose decisive influence on research into identity has been noted above. The two approaches of Henry and Foucault seem to me, in spite of their differences and perhaps also for this reason, interesting to compare from the perspective of elaborating strategies of resistance to the "self-monitoring" proposed by the practices of "human resources management."[63] Certainly, in Foucault there is the will, faithful to antiquity, to produce the self, to invent it, whereas in Henry, the self is received in life, giving value to values. But wouldn't building the self, restoring it in the world, paradoxically imply rediscovering the self? For example, Henry's approach could be used to support the Foucauldian argument proposed by Jackie Ford and Nancy Harding[64] on the subject of 'authentic leadership', which they denounce as an injunction to managers to internalise only the interests of their organization (a *quasi-agency-free* subject), while, outside, *followers* are reduced to 'abject objects.'[65]

Finally, Henry's philosophy also deserves to be discussed in the light of the proposals made by Amartya Sen during a lecture given at Stanford University on the concept of capabilities.[66] As a theorist of social choice and welfare economics, Sen views economic development from the perspective of expanding capabilities that enable individuals to make the most of their individual potential, which is by definition unequal. Any development project only makes sense to the extent that account is taken of an individual's capacity to satisfy, or not satisfy, some of her needs, from

---

[60] M. Henry 2011c: 297.

[61] O. Ducharme 2012.

[62] Whether these are elementary (work, need) or more elaborate (art, ethics and religion).

[63] B. Townley 1994.

[64] J. Ford and N. Harding, 2011.

[65] *Ibid.*: 13.

[66] H. Rocha and S. Goshal, 2006; M. Gilardone, 2010.

2.1 Organizations and the Subjective Body

the most basic to the most refined. This theory is based in particular on Aristotelian *eudemonia* and on various currents of analytic philosophy, notably John Rawls, of which the theory of capabilities is a possible extension.

As Benedetta Giovanola notes, the capability approach "shows how people can be happy and ultimately fulfilled, rather than just satisfied, in the sense of personal well-being derived from the classical utilitarian and/or welfare state conceptions."[67] Alexander Bertland and Cécile Renouard have also attempted to translate this theory into the field of business ethics. Alexander Bertland insists in particular on a reinterpretation of *stakeholder theory* based on capabilities, where the manager's responsibility would be precisely to encourage its development among his stakeholders.[68] As for Cécile Renouard, she emphasises the notion of *empowerment*[69] *and* a reading of Amartya Sen which gives priority to what she calls an "atomistic anthropology,"[70] in which each person remains open to her own opportunities, developing her own potential and, in order to achieve this, working closely with others. On the other hand, notes Muriel Gilardone, "those who think they will find in Sen a clear formula for making interpersonal comparisons, or even an algorithm for comparing individual well-being or situations, risk being disappointed."[71] The diversity of human beings needs to be recognised both in terms of their sociological characteristics but also on a more intimate and personal level, which is precisely what the notion of capabilities shows.

In Michel Henry, such an algorithm does not exist, but this focus on self-actualisation right through to professional life is very much present. According to Frédéric Seyler, "the principle of practical competence [in Henry] asserts that the decision is made by the most capable individuals in the field concerned."[72] The only real power is that of the body; and those who would break with the idea of immanence to oneself are dissatisfied with themselves first and foremost.[73] I would argue that Henry's theory of the body echoes the capability approach; it brings to it an ontological and phenomenological level of analysis, providing the connection to the experience of sensibility which it otherwise lacks,[74] potentially allowing it to become more than a simple pragmatic conception of personal contentment and well-being.

---

[67] B. Giovanola, 2005: 253.

[68] A. Bertland, 2009.

[69] C. Renouard, 2011: 85.

[70] *Ibid.*: 87.

[71] M. Gilardone, 2010: *18–19*.

[72] Fr. Seyler, 2009: 374.

[73] "Nietzsche described all the forms that this break might take: doubt about oneself, loss of belief, scepticism, objectivism, scientism, self-criticism in all its forms, one is tempted to write "analysis," all the doctrines of bad faith, of bad conscience, of self-examination, of interpretation, of suspicion, all those that place the truth of life outside of life, making our time this "rotten present"," M. Henry, 1985: 271.

[74] M. Gilardone, 2010; B. Giovanola, 2005, 2009.

2.2 Desaffectio Societatis

The notion of *desaffectio societatis* extends our analysis of the body in many ways. Let me venture to say why and how, not without first giving an overview of what the notion of *affectio societatis* is all about.

There are two main aspects to this: firstly, an aspect linked to French business law, that which enshrines the will when setting up a company. This will is materialised by the acceptance of the partnership contract, which generally underlines a convergence of interests and the desire to collaborate shared by various partners. It is equivalent to the partners accepting the consequences, both positive and negative, of this association.

But *affectio societatis* also covers a second aspect, linked to its common expression, which tends to oppose the legal aspect, or at least to complement it. In what way? By reminding us that there is always a non-contractual side to organizations, a dimension which transcends the contractual. To use the expression *affectio societatis*, in fact, is to say that not everything is procedural in the employment contract, that there is something essential not covered by the legal terms of the contract which binds employers and employees, institutions and staff members, and also employees among themselves.[75]

From this point of view, *affectio societatis* is that which resists quantitative evaluation and makes the supervisory function, which is so important (and costly) in management, uncertain and partly useless: when I have *affectio societatis,* there is no need to evaluate my level of commitment or my fidelity to the company's objectives, since by this very fact I want to affirm that I am ready, if need be, to "go the extra mile," to use a common trope of American managerial literature: the extra step, the extra hour, the effort by which I take it upon myself to advance the interests of the community to which I belong; or the special care I take to make things work, going beyond the simple duty imposed on me by the terms of my contract.

This is why the management is constantly striving to make the company friendly in the eyes of its employees. One could even here recognise managerial activity in its two major functions, which are: (1) recruiting "talent;" assigning functions that are consistent with the skills required; ensuring that skills are deployed where they can best express themselves, and (2) getting the group to adhere to the action undertaken, to the point where a relationship develops and members recognise their attachment to the organization that employs them and/or the mission incumbent upon them. To return to Xenophon: "foremen, stewards or supervisors, can make the workers zealous and diligent, they are the ones who create prosperity and bring wealth into the house [*oikos*[76]]." Dedication, disinterestedness, such are the ultimate rewards of management, and also, for Socrates,[77] the manifestation of its end, which

---

[75] This also means, as we will come back to this later, that not everything in management can be easily calculated.

[76] Xenophon, 1933: 420.

[77] *Ibid.*, 388.

can be understood here in both senses of the term: the manager as an *achiever* of ends, and the manager putting an *"end"* to her own limitations.

To have *affectio societatis* is to recognize in a certain way that our primary and secondary needs, up to our highest expectations, which we might call post-materialistic (recognition of others, self-improvement, joy at work, etc.) are satisfied. *Affectio societatis* places us beyond the "apology of efficient calculation,"[78] which seems to be the unassailable horizon of contemporary organizations. It means accepting, without perhaps realising it, to go beyond the simple language of performance, to recognise the presence of *otium* even in *negotium*,[79] in short, to contradict the etymological definition of work; and thereby to discern an affective dimension in effective work.

2.2.1 *From* Affectio Societatis *to Individual Disaffection*

Hence springs the first ambiguity of the notion. Admittedly, it might initially appear to concern the community, the *societatis*. But, at the same time, it establishes a principle of individualisation of the relationship to work: in fact, two individuals may have the same experience, the same course content, the same students, may teach in the same classrooms, may arrive at the university via the same gate, and breathe the same air, and yet, in the long run, one may be affected for good by this experience, the other for bad. *Affectio societatis* thus recognises a heterogeneity of human experience at work, as if the feelings stemming from collective experience could only be perceived individually, with the result that the intelligibility of the collective depends upon the individual – a counterpoint to sociological approaches to this subject.

With *affectio societatis*, we find ourselves moving away from traditional notions of economics, such as 'opportunity costs', which are based on the assumption of a total homogeneity of human experience.[80] Lecturing in the same auditorium hall filled with the same students, answering the same customers at a bank counter, selling fruit and vegetables in the same markets, is never quite the same experience. We might even propose a connection between *affectio societatis* and the "authentically living work" of Michel Henry:

> When living labour is understood as the unique source of all real and economic wealth, as the action producing use values as well as exchange values, which are merely the quantified representations of this action, one of two scenarios may arise depending on whether the life force invested in this labour is deployed according to its greatest power, or whether it is dissatisfied with itself and the world, renouncing the free and full exercise of its powers,

---

[78] P. Ricœur, 1960: 437.

[79] These concepts will be explored in more detail in the conclusion.

[80] M. Crawford, 2009: 68.

54 2 Rethinking Management

embarking on the dangerous path of refusing to make an effort, content to do as little as possible and, in some situations, to do nothing at all.[81]

Perhaps it is time here to recognise that the issue of motivation at work is not new to management. Socially-minded authors (Abraham Maslow) have written extensively on the subject. So what is different about the terms of this problem today? Why is this issue so topical – or indeed timeless, if we consider it to be recurrent to the point of permanency – but never recognised as such? It is the problem of demotivation and demobilisation, which affects no one as much as managers themselves, who now constitute the population most prone to stress in the workplace. Suffering at work concerns employees, of course, but managers are just as affected, it not more so. Victims of the prevailing short-termism, caught between boards of directors where they are not listened too much and teams that, understandably enough, reject their authority,[82] subject to permanent paradoxical injunctions, managers have ample experience of disaffection, i.e., to use Jean-Philippe Bouilloud's words, "life without affection" but also without "use" or real function.

Examples abound, where exhausted employees (in this case exhausted supervisors) describe themselves in terms of rejection, obsolescence, uselessness, inability to do what they used to do, which was so valuable for them and for the company.[83]

A slow but sure process of de-individuation seems to be taking place, and the author cites some very significant examples, particularly in the banking sector, where systems of contradictory constraints and injunctions are proliferating.

Burn-out is often the result of a total loss of the sense of agency, on the part of managers who feel emotionally, deep down inside themselves, that something is wrong. Hence the phenomena of managers losing faith in their own role, memorably described by American sociologist Robert Jackall as individuals who are dissatisfied with themselves.[84] We therefore need to examine what we really mean by affectivity, and what material phenomenology can reveal about its specificities, and its potentially productive consequences.

2.2.2 The Concept of Affectivity from the Henryian Perspective

Affectivity can be understood in one of three main ways. The first belongs to the pragmatic register. Means have to be allocated in order to achieve a certain result. Even when, for example, the canonical definition of *stakeholder theory* uses the verb 'to affect' ("stakeholders are those who are affected by the activities of the organization'), this is still the case. Moreover, this theory has been developed

---

[81] M. Henry, 2008a: 130.

[82] R. Damien, 2013.

[83] J.-Ph. Bouilloud, 2012: 37.

[84] R. Jackall and Mazes 1988.

2.2 Desaffectio Societatis

essentially in an instrumental mode, where it is a question of allocating resources to each stakeholder according to criteria such as urgency, power or legitimacy.[85] The second interpretation is akin to 'pretending': affecting belief. The third and final interpretation refers to the idea of being deeply affected. This meaning is linked to the Latin *affectus,* which expresses a part of our human sensitivity.

This triple meaning of affectivity, considered in the context of organizations, allows us to propose three possible views of the individual at work:

– the pragmatic view: the human being considered as a resource, a human resource, so to speak.[86] Each player is expected to perform to the highest possible level, to enable business to develop and economic prosperity to grow. The subject is often devoid of her own desiring subjectivity, limited in complexity to what generally constitutes her "technical skills," assessed during the recruitment process and subsequent appraisal interviews;
– the theatrical view, where the individual plays a role in the sense of "pretending"; this is man/woman as representation or image. In the world of contemporary organizations, are human beings not primarily perceived in the form of images?
– the third view attributes to the human being at work emotional and inner qualities, which are neither resources as such nor visible characteristics, and which therefore elude familiar definitions of people at work. This sense is opposed both to the exclusive objectivism of man as a resource (the replacement of vital relations by relations of interest, what Henry calls the "bourgeois illusion")[87] and to the image-becoming of thought, which is very present in critical management research.

Let me now attempt to specify, with reference to the Henryian hypothesis, the object of the dispute: the being of the subject has never been recognised as such by Western philosophy. From the very first moments of the philosophy of the Subject (Descartes/ Kant), and throughout its subsequent critical extensions, Western philosophy has believed subjectivity to be right in front of our eyes, which is to say in a world where it has no chance to appear.[88] Hence Michel Henry's unflagging opposition to the phenomenology of exteriority, preferring an approach in which life as experienced by each person conditions all possible experiences. The strictly Henryian meaning of the word affectivity engenders a conception of human beings in which affective phenomenality is the primary element. This is why Henry and his principal

---

[85] R. Mitchell et al. 1997. Seel also Painter et al., 2020.

[86] K. Inkson, 2008.

[87] "It is precisely political economy which claims to reduce, in spite of their essential heterogeneity, vital relations to the relation of interest, and this is its illusion, the very illusion of the bourgeois," M. Henry 1976: 102.

[88] "Whether we like it or not, it is the philosophy of the subject that has raised the most serious objection against the subject, to the point of making its mere existence problematic. Certainly, Kant did not entirely dismiss the problematicity of the subject, as some of today's charlatans would have it, but he did reduce it to "a mere proposition" which he considered to be, at most, worth mentioning, albeit without providing the slightest reason." M. Henry, 2011a: 12.

56   2 Rethinking Management

commentators prefer to speak of self-affection,[89] in which the subject is passively given to herself/himself in the form of a "body."[90]

As Hugo Letiche notes, Michel Henry's position amounts to a radical transformation of the meaning generally attributed to the term "affection."[91] It is no longer a phenomenal object nor a trait of character, but the ultimate content of our humanity, the original essence of our subjectivity. It is no longer a matter of an affection "perverted by the gaze"[92] of a sensation, of a particular emotion which would be self-sufficient and which we could therefore isolate from the ontological context on which it depends and to which it belongs. The pure affection in question here is not the same as sensitivity or the "naive concept of an ontic causality"[93] which psychologists might analyse.[94] That which experiences and that which is experienced existentially, feeling and sentiment, are identical. From the world we receive nothing but the revelation of our own capacity to feel, of our subjectivity in its own immanent testing of life (which is thus the opposite of anonymity). It is because affectivity is the primary reality, is materiality itself, independent of the world, that we are capable of being truly touched by the world.

2.2.3   "Societatis:" Collective Action and Social Roles

I have thus far limited my discussion largely to the *affectio,* without yet devoting much attention to the status of the *"societatis,"* perhaps at the risk of giving the impression that this *societatis* drifts further and further away as we embrace the principle of self-affection, which seems to be opposed to the idea of community or collective. By emphasising the effort and emotional power of individuals in their living corporeality, their flesh, does Henry's philosophy not risk hampering any efforts towards the political sides of organizations? And by demonstrating that society does not 'do' anything strictly speaking, that it always depends first and

---

[89] "Of course, one will concede to phenomenologists (in general, with the exception of Henry himself) that there are transcendental qualities – the sky is blue, the river is serene – and that I am capable of feeling that my foot hurts. But the quality that extends into the thing – the colour on the coloured surface, the pain in the foot – is only the unreal representation, the ob-jection of a real living impression, which affects and impresses itself in its affectivity and only in it," M. Henry, 1985: 95.

[90] As Giulianno Sansonetti remarks, this definition brings Michel Henry closer to Kierkegaard (see J. Butler, 1993 and N. Hatem, 2006) when he notes that 'the self is a synthesis, that is to say, 'a relationship to oneself posed by another', 2006: 115. In Michel Henry's work, the relationship to oneself (ipseity, self-affection) always depends on this invisible life that we have not chosen but which sets out the modalities of this relationship and constitutes, at its core, its primordial condition.

[91] H. Letiche, 2009: 298.

[92] M. Henry 1963: 800.

[93] M. Henry 1985: 281.

[94] Y. Martin 2011: 67–81.

2.2 Desaffectio Societatis

foremost on individuals who precede any political and social organization, does it not prevent us from thinking about *affectio societatis*? Is there not an unbridgeable gap between the problem of living subjectivity and a proposal for organizing collective action?

We are by now well aware that the phenomenon of *desaffectio societatis,* i.e. reverse *affectio societatis,* the disintegration of the affective link with the organization rather than its strengthening, has a lot to do with a process in which community factors play a dominant role. Following on from Jean-Philippe Bouilloud's remarks,[95] we should add Bernard Stiegler's description of a movement of affective and cognitive saturation which is increasingly frequent in organizations and which resembles a kind of continuous crumbling of affective capacities, a more or less generalised 'disaffection': "This is where ethics comes in [...], whose knowledge is that of the *stay,* the word by which the Greek *ethos is* translated into French, letting me know my place is in the *circuit of affects* by which the process of psychic and collective individuation is constituted."[96] What this analysis reveals is that individual uncertainty (what is my place in the circuit of affects?) corresponds to a difficulty at the level of what Stiegler calls collective individuation, which is indeed the keystone of any community, of any possible "enterprise," their shared assets, in a way. The modern age appears to have been deprived of its sensitive qualities, it no longer knows where it stands emotionally, its original experience is "put out of circulation." The philosopher and journalist André Gorz describes a similar feeling:

> Work has disappeared because life has withdrawn from the universe. There are no more people; only numbers chasing numbers in silence, unquestionable because they are insensitive, mute. At the end of his day, the operator gets up. Nothing remains of what she has done, no visible, measurable material assets: s*he has achieved* nothing. But this nothing has exhausted her.[97]

There are any number of accounts to suggest that this extenuating nothing, this exhaustion that results from the incompleteness of daily life, fairly accurately describes the daily life of an executive who, unlike those bound by emotional and moral attachments to the institutions for which they work, is prey to doubt, deep dissatisfaction and a pervasive sense of uneasiness: weariness, sadness and despondency are terms that we can provisionally group together under the umbrella notion of *desaffectio societatis*.

So, let us ask ourselves the question: if everything that is real is subjective and exists within the sphere of radical immanence, what place remains for society as a whole? To apply that question to management: what becomes of the notion of social roles in this sphere of radical immanence? As the "Notes on the experience of others" in the *Revue Internationale Michel Henry* clearly show, a philosophy of subjectivity is precisely what allows and accounts for the experience of others. Indeed, our encounter with "the other" is made possible by our common attachment to this same

---

[95] J.-Ph. Bouilloud 2012.

[96] B. Stiegler 2006a, b: 19.

[97] A. Gorz 2008: 141–142.

power of being one self. The existence of others is attested by their own self-immanence.[98] This is a matter of protecting oneself from the danger, always present when it comes to others, of wanting to represent them. In this case, in fact, "I make him the object of my representation," so that he "is nothing more than an object, my object."[99] The other is not a product of my observation, but a concrete and individual experience participating of the same life force granted to each of us.[100] As the philosopher Marc Maesschalck puts it:

> faced with a modern tradition in which universality depends on an 'exteriority of recognition' [from which a formal principle of equality derives], Henry conceives universality through 'interiority of belonging' – from which he derives an original principle of equality, which could also be called 'metaphysical equality'.[101]

Ultimately, the other is a person with whom I can develop and increase that creativity which is the wellspring of life. Acting with others is therefore not just a matter of objective and measurable criteria, nor is it about the procedural reciprocity of egos as a basis for the social calculation of justice. Acting with others ultimately means collectively activating the powers of life.

For Henry, the customer, supplier, journalist or landowner never cease to be persons in the sense of a capacity to experience themselves. Individuals live out their social roles endowed with this original affectivity that constitutes them as acting selves. If social roles are lived intensely, it is because they reveal, as Raphaël Gély forcefully puts it, "within the forces of life [...] that the possibilities of others are my own possibilities, that the way life intensifies in them is linked to the way it intensifies in me."[102] The subjectivity of each person is never suspended, the social role is always lived by those who perform it: the image of believing that a person can behave like an automaton within the framework of her social function, precisely in order to avoid alienation, is a delusion. In a phenomenology of life, it is precisely because the person does not fundamentally have the capacity to separate herself from herself, from her affectivity, that she can never really behave as an automated machine; this is the very reason for her suffering in the case of alienation, or for her joy when her social function allows her to intensify her power to act.

---

[98] M. Henry 2011b: 108.

[99] M. Henry 1976: 397–398.

[100] "What matters is not at all the experience of what the other experiences but the experience of the other experiencing this or that thing," M. Henry 2011b: 87.

[101] M. Maesschalck 2000.

[102] R. Gély 2007: 79.

2.2 Desaffectio Societatis

2.2.4 Political and Ethical Implications

Can social and political activity break away from its foundations, which is the reality wherein it finds its origin as well as its destination, the affectivity from which we experience others and the world? If we answer no, then it is because "individual activity, private life, affectivity, sensitivity, sexuality, [which] must themselves be political."[103] The language of fraternity and equality only makes sense if it is based on the recognition of each individual, each citizen, each worker. The principle of individual action is in fact the reference from which any social practice, any organization, any collective enterprise, made public and visible to all, can find its effective reality. Social *praxis*, which is the representation of all the acts accomplished by the managers and employees of a collective enterprise, is necessarily rooted in individual action.

Is this not, ultimately, the very definition of collaboration, a necessary condition of management? All collaboration is based on the existence of a community which is politically accountable but which is neither source nor condition. This is why every institution is first and foremost a mediator, because it can in no way supplant action and change, which always come from acting oneself, without which no institution, no change and no collaboration would be possible. Cooperation, above and beyond organised processes, emerges from a desire to meet and share, which is the desire to feel alive. Observing management controllers in charge of monitoring costs and revenues in airport shops, François-Régis Puyou remarks that:

> it is indeed the search for a feeling of closeness, the desire to experience the joy of mutual aid and to immediately experience a shared praxis that is the driving force behind all collaboration [...] It is in the articulation of the powers of each of the "characters" that an ever-regenerated trust in life is founded.[104]

It is because individuals wish to inscribe their power of action in a living endeavour that they take on a social role, which brings them into contact with others. The notion of "character," implying active communication between an individual and a social role, a concept borrowed from Raphaël Gély,[105] is indispensable because it is the essential condition of mediation, allowing individuals to achieve common goals and experience an emotional solidarity that breaks through the functional and formalistic framework of labour relations, all too often a source of dissatisfaction and self-denial.

The passage from the individual to the common Being is nothing other than the relationship of reciprocal phenomenological interiority in which living beings recognise that they are driven by the same absolute Life, the vessel into which others and myself are poured. Any policy anchored in reality must therefore necessarily concern itself with the original subjectivity of individuals, creating the conditions

---

[103] M. Henry 1976: 57.

[104] Fr.-R. Puyou 2013: 550.

[105] R. Gély 2007.

60   2   Rethinking Management

for the fulfilment and expansion of their respective possibilities, nurturing what can be accurately described as *affectio societatis*. For, as François-Régis Puyou and Éric Faÿ put it:

> Talking, listening and acting collectively is the expression of a conjunction of powers and the sharing of a common life. Having a job is a way of getting to know others better in the pleasant and dynamic experience of working together.[106]

Promoting ethics within an institution sensitive to such matters is a question of enabling employees to take on a *role* that allows them to experience the radical singularity of their lives. More modestly: ethics in organizations concerns the question of whether employees and managers are considered as means, as robots from which automatic objective behaviour is expected, or as living individuals, capable of inhabiting and taking on a 'social role', and not just a function. An ethical analysis of organizations necessarily begins with a critique of representations as much as of a science which, when it wants to try to enter into intelligence with human relations, "knows only objectivity."[107]

This is why Michel Henry's criticism of political economy chimes so clearly with the critique of management in the guise of "management sciences."[108] Over time, these sciences have indeed become a hyper-developed universe of tools, *best practices* and methods that never talk about living individuals as such. The development of research in neurobiology applied to management, "neuro-management," is exemplary in this respect,[109] as is the invasion of the human sciences by statistical methods inspired by biological or physical sciences. In the process, human beings are reduced to their genetic potential.

Nevertheless, in material phenomenology, the world of organizations and its associated models cannot exist independently of their unveiling, which is neither objectifiable nor measurable. No economic theory can fully account for a manager's sense of responsibility towards others: this is beyond calculation. Any general theory in the field of management and economics that aims at the objectivity of positive science will always be missing an essential ingredient: full knowledge and understanding of life. When this knowledge is copied from the natural sciences, as is the case with behaviourism or even behavioural psychology, managerial research turns its back on its very object. When the quality of research is defined by its scientific presuppositions, it loses all value and all possibility of being admissible and credible. It is when management proposes to "manage human resources," or "talents," as we say today, like natural resources, that it loses all connection with what constitutes its very substance.

***

---

[106] Fr.-R. Puyou and É. Faÿ 2013: 11.

[107] M. Henry 2008b: 112.

[108] They are in any case recognised as such in France by a separate section ("06") of the National Council of Universities. See M. Henry 1976: 27.

[109] R. Gilkey and C. Kilts 2007.

2.3 Individual Experience at a Time of Social Acceleration

Affectivity is the source of all work, especially successful collaborative work. Otherwise, frustration prevails, becoming a self-fulfilling prophecy: people do not feel well indeed (bad faith, self-doubt and hatred, bad conscience, etc.), so they behave badly. This is why *affectio societatis*, which replaces, within economic relations, the relationship of interest with a vital one, is irreplaceable. For it is from life that economic processes and political determinations take on their full meaning, and not the other way round. This implies an abandonment of the theories commonly used in the management of the cogeneration of the self by the other, the other without whom I would be nothing (coming from empirical, behaviourist but also phenomenological approaches, as in the case of the philosophers Emmanuel Levinas or Paul Ricœur, for whom our ideas and affects are always mediated by models that come from others). The worldly "I" is not the origin of the living "I" but, on the contrary, stems from it. This is what the notion of the *subjective body* seeks to highlight, in order to allow the community to exist on the basis of the fundamental categories of suffering and joy, need and strength: "These categories are at the heart of every singular affectivity, regardless of whether this singular affectivity is a woman, a man, a poor person or a rich person."[110]

In reality, *affectio societatis* has its roots in the fact that it is in life that living selves are absolutely equal: in the world, on the contrary, they are different, dissonant, discordant or always susceptible to becoming so. *Affectio societatis* is therefore fundamentally, and even transcendentally, an 'incursion of life' into the world, the origin of all possible forms of society and, no doubt, every genuine innovation and every entrepreneurial impulse. Contrary to Jones and Spicer's approach,[111] which views the entrepreneur as an individual inhabited by death, the act entrepreneurship must instead be seen as a desire for life that "gives us the desire and strength to work with others."[112]

2.3 Individual Experience at a Time of Social Acceleration

> If you believed more in life, you would devote yourselves less to the momentary.
> Nietzsche, *Thus spoke Zarathustra.*

The two subsections of this chapter have introduced a phenomenological approach to the notion of the subjective body and the resulting conception of work motivation under the label of 'affectio societatis'. In the following two sections, I want to explore how a phenomenology of life can help us rethink management around two central questions: that of social acceleration, where managers and employees find themselves victims of suffering linked to the logic of the short term, so prevalent in the corporate world today. And that of knowing whether recognition, which is the

---

[110] O. Ducharme 2012, p. 131.

[111] C. Jones and A. Spicer 2005.

[112] É. Faÿ 2014, p. 15.

subject of strong demands from the world of work and the people who are part of it, could serve as a basis for establishing a new managerial ethic.

For the management and administration of human resources, the question of time is neither insignificant nor marginal.[113] It was by analysing increases in production rates and the remuneration system that Taylor determined his entire approach. In this respect, he is indeed the distant precursor of just-in-time organizations.

However, let us ask one question: is productivism (or productivity, the quantified relationship between production and time) the final word, or indeed the only word, on management's understanding of time? Is there not something in the perpetual agitation of organizations, in the progressive acceleration of the capitalist world, something which is in fact of the order of pleasure, excitement, "intensity," in short, tumult and entertainment, which seems to hint at a potential "metaphysics of disenchantment?"[114] Is management, the force that sets the rhythm for collective action, first and foremost a matter of fighting against time, of "managing" it, putting it at a distance, in order to better free oneself from its constraints?

In a recent study examining the effects of acceleration and the ethical risks involved,[115] the editor of a Chicago-based magazine expressed his fascination with this phenomenon:

> I love speed. I particularly appreciate the opportunity it gives me to reinvent the news distribution model, and to use different media to communicate to different audiences. Proposing new and creative ways to deliver messages gives me a special energy.[116]

This particular energy is represented, or even fuelled, by the feeling of speed itself, an impression encountered in many managerial speeches, including former Google CEO Eric Schmidt writing in the columns of *The Economist*: "Make your mistakes quickly – so that you can try again in a hurry."

It is thus between productivism and entertainment, between forced acceleration (working with no timeout) and the force of acceleration (managing without hindrance), between the obsession with time and its lack, between *besogne* and *besoin*, words meaning "work" and "need", which – as Bernard Maris notes in *Houellebecq the Economist*[117] – share an etymological root, that I situate the relationship between management and time. This approach allows us to focus precisely on the individual experience which, together with technical processes and social changes, constitute the three categories of acceleration processes as highlighted by the sociologist Hartmut Rosa.[118] The causes of acceleration are linked to the promise, proffered to all of us, that the multiplication of experiences will allow us to "lead a 'good life', more fulfilled and richer in experiences."[119]

---

[113] This chapter includes the following article: G. Deslandes 2015.

[114] N. Aubert 2003.

[115] Carried out in the form of round-table discussions and in-depth interviews on three continents. See M. Painter-Morland and G. Deslandes 2017.

[116] Quoted in M. Painter-Morland and G. Deslandes 2014: 7.

[117] B. Maris 2014: 57.

[118] H. Rosa 2010, 2012.

[119] *Ibid.*, p. 166.

2.3 Individual Experience at a Time of Social Acceleration 63

In this section I will venture to describe the condition of the modern manager (and those they manage) in several manners, demonstrating that acceleration is simply another term for disembodiment of the world, its devitalisation, while also arguing that management can play a role in revitalising it, provided that certain of its presuppositions are adjusted.

2.3.1 Individual Experience and Acceleration

Sociologist Hartmut Rosa emphasises: "The dynamics of contemporary acceleration not only transform the doing, but also the being (or 'existence'), the identity of the subjects and their relationships to oneself, since it is these actions and relationships that constitute them."[120] As such, it is not only managerial processes that are transformed by speed, as one might expect, but also the relationship that managers and executives have with themselves, and it is this point that will be the focus of our attention.

To evoke the effects of the acceleration of individual experience, let us return to Bernard Maris' *Houellebecq the Economist*. He notably evokes Valérie, "the heroine of *Plateforme*, a brilliant executive in the communication industry." In her own words:

> I am caught up in a system that no longer brings me much, and which I know is useless; but I don't see how to escape from it. We should take the time to think, sometime; but I don't know when we'll be able to take the time to think.[121]

What is supposed to be the privilege of management, imposing its rhythm on the work of others, turns against it, and against the managers themselves. Master of time for others, the manager is for himself the slave of time. Nietzsche's phrase in *Human, all too Human* springs to mind: "Whoever does not have two thirds of his day for himself is a slave, let him be what he wants: politician, merchant, civil servant, scholar." Today, what manager can say that she has even a little time for herself? Here we can see the problem: the manager imposes maximum speed upon others, and suffers the same fate in return. On the one hand, she benefits from the positive effects of speed ("*speed is good*"), from its entertaining character, but on the other hand, she suffers the negative aspects all the more strongly as she is the bearer of this discourse on the necessary acceleration of collaborative processes.[122] In short, time management provides an opportunity for every manager to experience the paradoxical twin polarity of her role.

However, this power/vulnerability bipolarity, which is part of management, seems to have been overlooked by management researchers in their discussions of speed. On closer examination, we can perhaps discern the archetype of the "speed leader" in a short article published in the *Harvard Business Review* by Robert Thomas and Warren Bennis in 2002. They suggest that time is not an obstacle but,

---

[120] H. Rosa 2010: 180.

[121] B. Maris 2014: 80.

[122] J.-Ph. Bouilloud 2012.

64 2 Rethinking Management

on the contrary, a key factor in problem solving. "Speed leaders are quick to build a team around them that can engage in collaborative problem solving," they explain. "At the same time, speed leaders are able to make difficult decisions, interrupt discussions abruptly, and be authoritative when they need to be."[123] They add:

> Like master craftsman, speed leaders exercise their skill with apparent effortlessness and fluidity. Like magicians, they seem capable of transcending physical constraints. And like consummate artists, they use practice to avoid becoming hostage to time: they learn while others are merely watching or unreflectively doing. This attribute is probable the most profound differentiator between those who succeed as speed leaders and those who fails. (...) Like martial arts master, the speed leader is already planning her response to stimuli that others are just encountering. Constant practice has greatly enhanced her ability to anticipate what comes next.[124]

Leaving aside the magical dimension of these proposals, what they somewhat clumsily attempt to demonstrate is that only by transforming into speed leaders can stem the harmful effects of time. It is a question of being stronger than time, of playing with it. Underpinning this reasoning is the idea that managing time is something that can be learned, something[125] that everyone can train for. From this point of view, Alec MacKenzie's seminal work, *The Time Trap,* published in 1972, already opened up new perspectives, describing four groups of time-wasting factors in organizations and proposing some solutions to reduce their negative effects. These time-wasting factors included poor information, procrastination, lack of *feedback,* time spent on the phone, incompetent staff, time spent with visitors (group A), fatigue, lack of procedures, *junk mail* (group B), incompetent subordinates, coffee breaks, poor physical health, *socializing* (group C), chatter, weak moral principles, inconsistent actions, or wanting to do too much at once (group D).[126]

In fact, and with considerable foresight, the author put his finger on three of the main problems associated with the general acceleration of society, which seem insoluble and have only increased since the early 1970s: the physical and moral fatigue of the 'elites', bureaucratisation – the transition from lack of procedures to overflow – and finally our state of constant hyper-connection. With regard to these three major consequences of the acceleration of social[127] and individual time, Alec MacKenzie offers a series of proposals based on this idea, no doubt a little naive, that time always 'organizes' ('Planning time saves time[128]'), plans itself, 'retemporises' itself through the sheer force of human will. Today, very few of us can still share this optimism: the speed leader struggles unsuccessfully against the meanderings of overabundant bureaucratisation, while the individual who shelters behind his function (as manager, leader or *follower*) has a "life experience" that is constantly shrinking.[129]

---

[123] R. Thomas and W. Bennis 2002: 3.

[124] *Id.*

[125] I. Sabelis 2001.

[126] A. MacKenzie 1972: 5.

[127] "Fast food, speed-dating, lightning naps and drive-through funerals," H. Rosa 2012: 17.

[128] A. MacKenzie 1972: 41.

[129] C. Pollmann. Introductory note of the seminar "Acceleration and regulation: the challenges of speed for politics and law," in which the author participated.

2.3 Individual Experience at a Time of Social Acceleration 65

In order to account for and better understand these phenomena of acceleration in the individual experience, perhaps it would be preferable to turn to other fields of research which have attempted to analyse this very theme: the weariness and exhaustion experienced at work. In *The Burnout Society* (2014), Korean philosopher Byung-Chul Han provides an original analysis of acceleration phenomena in their dimensions of personal experience. "The successful subject who imagines himself to be sovereign, *homo liber,* reveals himself to be a *homo sacer*. In a paradoxical logic, the sovereign and the *homo sacer* engender each other in the society of performance."[130] This ambivalence of the relationship to time is close to that described above: as a cause of entertainment, acceleration proves to be the worst form of servitude. Byung-Chul Han describes the busy, *multitasking* man in striking terms, imaging him as a wild beast:

> An animal busy with eating must also attend to other tasks. For example, it must hold rivals away from its prey. It must constantly be on the lookout, lest it be eaten while eating. At the same time, it must guard its young and keep an eye on its sexual partner. In the wild, the animal is forced to divide its attention between various activities. That is why animals are incapable of contemplative immersion [...]. Not just *multitasking* but also activities such as video games produce a broad but flat mode of attention, which is similar to the vigilance of a wild animal[131]

Here we find the portrait of the hyper-connected individual, attentive to everything and nothing in particular, crushed by the weight of the struggle for survival, blurring the boundaries of her personal and professional life (the "fusion of worlds" evoked by Nicole Aubert and Hartmut Rosa) that is enunciated and denounced. The *homo sacer* is the creature of *homo liber,* his double failure. "Failed" is moreover a word used by the author to qualify all the unlucky ones left behind by the performance society contained in the image of the speed leader (and a society prone to doping, too). In the high-performing subject that the manager necessarily constitutes, a "narcissistic relationship with oneself"[132] develops, a sort of personal experience that represents a secondary cause of the exploitation of oneself by oneself. This exploiter/exploited, manager/managed identity, one might say, is the fruit of a "paradoxical freedom[133]" whose psychological consequences for society are endless.

Byung-Chul Han's interpretation of the ultimate causes of this societal burnout is as follows: "such tiredness stems from the redundancy and recurrence of the Ego. I-tiredness, as solitary tiredness, is worldless and world-destroying; it annihilates all reference to the other in favour of narcissistic self-reference."[134] Byung-Chul Han proposes that we must escape from the "I" in order to better find the world, to get out of this incessant and recurrent relationship with ourselves, to better reconnect with what makes up the world, to better win over this world, in order to get out of

---

[130] Byung-Chul Han 2014: 33.

[131] *Ibid.*: 60.

[132] *Ibid.*: 12.

[133] *Ibid*: 57.

[134] *Ibid.*: 8.

society's breathlessness. The solution is therefore no longer to be found in health, but in vigorous tiredness, "where the I makes room for the world," a healthy tiredness "that places its trust in the World" (quoting Peter Handke here).

Before discussing this proposal, let us look more precisely at what is happening in the world of organizations in the age of social acceleration.

2.3.2 World-as-Organization

For Baptiste Rappin, "the organization is not a 'social fact', but the locus, that is to say the necessary condition of our world's coming into being."[135] This thesis requires us to understand phenomena on two levels, ontic and ontological. At the ontological level, it is a question of giving an account of the future organization of the world, hence the title of the book, a 'theology of organization.' Of particular interest is Rappin's discussion of the influence of cybernetics on the modes of thought that define the world-as-organization, "a pantheistic movement ensured by an informational conception of humanity, reducing us to a box whose function is to process messages and signals."[136]

At the ontic level, it falls to organizations to make itself a world, that is to say conquer all the territories of the planet, otherwise they will no longer exist, disappear from the world. This double ontic and ontological movement leaves the individual with no other choice than to "be-in-the-world," i.e. more precisely to "be thrown into organizations" and into management (its corollary). There is no longer any escape route, each individual is caught up in the movement towards the domestication (*domus*, Latin translation of the Greek 'oikos') of the individual, i.e. a process by which the boundaries between the private and public spheres are gradually removed.

In order to "make the world," organizations have recourse to procedures and managerial mechanisms. However, as Béatrice Hibou notes, these bear the hallmark of a continuous process of bureaucratisation. Bureaucratisation means "the requirement [...] and a need for calculability and predictability specific to the industry and adopted by capitalism in increasingly formal and rigorous terms."[137] What appears to be valuable in these organizational systems must be measurable. Nothing that cannot be measured is deemed to have any value. Here the author agrees with Baptiste Rappin: "it is no longer men that need to be looked after, inequalities that need to be reduced, principles that need to be defended, but flows and stocks that need to be managed effectively."[138] Language taken from cybernetics, sprawling *reporting systems*, continuous statistical flows, excessive codification and standardisation are all "operations of abstraction"[139] that are being accumulated at an ever faster rate.

---

[135] B. Rappin 2014: 47.

[136] *Ibid.*: 82.

[137] B. Hibou 2012: 21.

[138] *Ibid.*: 135.

[139] *Ibid.*: 34.

2.3 Individual Experience at a Time of Social Acceleration

This bureaucratic 'fluidity', made up of ebb and flow, is indeed what Robert Jackall describes when he extends the bureaucratic problem to questions of ethics.[140] Managers are beset by the constant emergence of new situations, in which the relationships between individuals are in turn constantly changing. And "as these professional relationships are always multiple, contingent and fluctuating, corporate ethics are always situational and relative."[141] Managers are the first victims of this contingency, this short-term logic in relationships between people: subject to permanent paradoxical injunctions, reduced to an instrumental relationship with themselves, they experience depression, which Hartmut Rosa considers to be the emblematic illness of acceleration.[142] In Rosa's view, acceleration is a central factor in executives' experience of a "decline in the reliability of [their] experiences and expectations."[143]

Nevertheless, in Hartmut Rosa's differentiation between the world of work and life, life for him is still essentially the flipside of work, what he calls "free time" as a source of potential diversity of experience.[144] What most interests him in the late modern age is the deregulation of the temporal organization in relation to the dichotomy of life at work and life outside of work. The 'dedifferentiation' he denounces only concerns the preservation of free time, which he calls 'life', that life which is managed, that life of which we still want to be 'co-authors'.[145] Clearly, if the relationship between individual experience and acceleration must indeed be traced back to its source, life, then it is the ontological perspective that we must prioritise.

2.3.3 Acceleration and Forgetting about Life

Michel Henry's phenomenology does not claim to be interested in all phenomena (an attitude which is appropriate for science, and only for science) but in the way they are given, in their conditions of possibility: in their phenomenality. It is precisely the question of individual experience that lies at the heart of his philosophy. Henry calls it subjectivity, which is not related to the rest of the being (the world, especially the social world) but constitutes its condition. It is therefore necessary to

---

[140] R. Jackall and Mazes 1988.

[141] R. Jackall and Mazes 1988: 101; G. Deslandes 2011b.

[142] H. Rosa 2010.

[143] H. Rosa 2012: 22. "The subjects, in the ultra-rapid environments of late modernity, do not manage to reconcile and align the different temporal horizons of their lives; the models, structures, horizons and expectations that characterise our daily actions, even though we would undoubtedly be able to master them, are becoming increasingly separated from the expectations and horizons we develop for our life taken as a whole, from the temporal perspective of our life project," H. Rosa 2012: 139.

[144] H. Rosa 2010: 208–209.

[145] *Ibid.* He is firmly on the side of sociology when he writes that "the relationships with things and the social relationships of the actors change, because 'relationship to oneself' and 'relationship to the world' are irrevocably intertwined," *ibid.*, 275.

note here Michel Henry's proximity, already mentioned, to Maine de Biran's project, which consists in questioning an internal mode of perception that would precede, as it were, any understanding of the object.[146]

This reasoning obviously has implications for several traditions and disciplines in the social sciences. When Hartmut Rosa explains that "it is therefore a commonplace for sociology to posit the correlation between the structure of society and the structure of the relationship to oneself, so that processes of social modernisation, for example, necessarily have their equivalent in the construction of the subjective relationship to oneself,"[147] one can measure the distance between the two authors: For Michel Henry, in fact, it is not a question of a "relationship to oneself" in the sense of a creation of the self, but of a relationship to oneself in life which is not an active construction but which passively constitutes, in immanence, the unique source of all our powers, even before any process of social modernisation takes place. On the subject of sociology, Henry has these words:

> The sociology of Tarde's fierce opponent, Durkheim, which is based on social laws independent of the individual – and therefore of life, since life exists only in individual form – is an absurdity which has extended a primary scientism to the human domain. It is possible to make a suicide statistic without understanding a word of the angst that every suicide presupposes.[148]

Hence perhaps the need for us to analyse *burn-out*, the fatigue society, the *desaffectio societatis* as defined in the previous chapter, in greater depth than that permitted by quantified inventories.

Let us therefore try to clarify the dispute and to understand what such a philosophical proposition can mean, firstly in the field of management and work, and secondly on the question of time. Michel Henry's philosophical proposal is developed and deployed in the two volumes he devoted to Marx following his PhD thesis (*The Essence of manifestation*), in a resolutely anti-Marxist vein. For the young Marx, it is the fact of being measured that gives real work its socially recognised character as work. This measurement is that of time: a commodity is characterised first of all by the time it took to produce it, which then allows us to compare multiple commodities according to the time needed to produce them. Indeed, in Marx's writings, the unit of measurement for labour is time.[149] The time of watches, spatialised, fragmented and quantified, the *measuring time,* which objectifies work and lends it its "value." But the immanent effort it took to produce a commodity – living labour – is always absent from the temporal, unreal and worldly representations of the time standard.

Michel Henry acknowledges that Marx was able to differentiate between the objective and abstract work on which economic exchanges are based and real and

---

[146] Indeed, "Deprived of its dimension of radical interiority, reduced to a condition of objectivity and representation, constituting instead this structure, the subjectivity of the subject is nothing more than the objectivity of the object," M. Henry 2011a: 70.

[147] H. Rosa 2010: 180.

[148] M. Henry 2005: 76.

[149] M. Henry 1976: 161.

immanent time, which evades any measure. But Henry then proposes a substitution, a replacement of subjective *praxis* by a system of abstract equivalents (e.g. the *Key Performance Indicators* used in human resources management, based on objective and worldly time). For him, the anchoring of work is at the level of individual experience, i.e. at the subjective level where the actual reality of work is situated and re-evaluated and where the very movement of life is expressed as a *need.*[150]

So how in this context can we return to the question of time? With Michel Henry, one should distinguish the presence to oneself from the subjectivity of the consciousness of the present (which has interested philosophy up to him, notably the phenomenology of the consciousness of time in Husserl). This presence to oneself is what "opens" time at each moment and which we experience in the opportunities we have to enjoy and suffer. It is indeed in the self-affection that characterises us that every 'living present[151]' takes place. It is precisely life that confronts us first and foremost with the materiality of time; however, the temporality of life is not the temporality of the world. In a way, this is the order of speed-space in Paul Virilio's work, where motors, machines, light, abstraction reign, an order quite apart from the self-affected presence which reveals to us the reality of conscious acts.

In short, there are two opposing forces at play here: on the one hand, an immanent self-presence, the uninterrupted living present (where there is always time), and on the other, a temporality that signs and structures the disappearance of things, a time that is the internal structure of the world. The world/time is that which disappears, which never ceases to expire, having no power of its own to appear, that is to say, to "bring oneself into life." In short, the less we consider the world to be "the world of life," the more the facts of the world accelerate within it, and the more time extends its dominion.

2.3.4 Phenomenology of Life and Management Issues

Let us now try to draw some lessons for management theory. Shortage of time actually means lack of life, lack of time means lack of attention to life; this can help us to think about the issue of social acceleration in relation to management. How to allow the expression of life in the face of the force and dominating position that time exerts on the lives of managers and executives? In a context of generalised acceleration, the effects of which are never stronger than in the world of organizations, how can we find a way to reconnect with the world of life?

Is it enough (solution 1) for us to "rely more on the world?"[152] We have seen that, since time is the structure of the disappearance of things, relying more on the world means relying on crumbling, unstable ground, and in reality, it means always suffering more and more from the effects, both negative and positive, of acceleration. I

---

[150] G. Deslandes 2015.

[151] G. Jean 2014: 62.

[152] Byung-Chul Han 2014.

say negative and positive: in acceleration there is an ambivalence between, on the one hand, a need to always feel more, to increase, to intensify one's relationship with the world and with oneself, and on the other hand, the desire to forget oneself, to forget one's condition or, to put it in Pascalian terms, to entertain oneself.

Or would it be better to create "oases of deceleration" (solution 2), as suggested by sociologist Hartmut Rosa,[153] in both personal and professional life, by trying to find ways to reduce the speed of social acceleration? But how would such a thing even be possible? Hartmut Rosa says it himself, decelerating is like getting out of the game. Of course, deceleration seems obvious; but at the same time it is a false pretence. Admittedly, the philosopher Éric Hamraoui is right when he speaks of the need for time, "necessary for the acquisition of experience and investment in the life of the City,"[154] as a specific need, requiring special treatment, distinct from monetised relationships, for example. However, can we imagine that this "concern for entertainment" that leads people into ever greater acceleration, in a sort of heterochronic spiral, will simply, suddenly cease? Might we thus achieve an accentuation of the feeling of intensity mentioned above (what is commonly called "living," that is to say, in the end, agitation)? It is curious to note that the "resubjectivisation of work" is not absent from Rosa's preoccupations. Indeed, he evokes what he calls a "'colonisation' of skills and resources from the *world of life,* thanks to the abolition between spheres[155]." But, as we have seen, this world of life of which he speaks is nothing more than time outside work, and not life as a *self-experience,* as a self-affection that defines the content of individual experiences.

So, how can we counter the pangs of speed? In the bid to reconnect management theory to life, at least two perspectives spring to mind, both of which are potential research topics, particularly for educational studies. The first concerns the inclusion of classical culture and aesthetics in the teaching of "management sciences:" what managers and executives suffer most from is the impoverishment of their discourse in bureaucratic formats that stifle their ability to act and think. "The sciences never talk about individuals, or, which amounts to the same thing, they always talk about them as something other than themselves, as atoms, molecules, neurons, acid chains, biological processes, etc." explains Michel Henry. "The 'humanities,' on the contrary, build in their own way, which often seems confused, and of which they are perhaps not always clearly aware, a real knowledge of man in his transcendental humanity."[156] The teaching and learning of the humanities,[157] in the broadest sense – history, geography, literature, philosophy, art but also cinema – still seems to be the

---

[153] H. Rosa 2010: 173.

[154] É. Hamraoui 2013: 69.

[155] H. Rosa 2010: 212.

[156] M. Henry 2008b: 224.

[157] A reminder in this regard: "25% of students worldwide are enrolled in management programmes," A.-C. Martinet and Y. Pesqueux 2013, p. 3. However, as Vincent de Gaulejac notes, "social and human sciences such as philosophy, anthropology, history and sociology have been practically eliminated from the training of managers. Only behavioural psychology is retained" (2013: 72). The situation is not the same everywhere, of course, depending on the level of commitment of institutions to management education linked to the social sciences or which are content with strictly technical courses.

2.3 Individual Experience at a Time of Social Acceleration

best way, perhaps the only way, to re-enchant the world, or at the very least to reconnect it with the world of life and to develop the interpretative capacities of "decision-makers" (whose development is the humanities' stated educational aim), such as the place of beauty judgements in management.[158] On this point I am inclined to agree with Hartmut Rosa:

> in a nationwide US survey of participation in arts events, most respondents explained that the main reason for not going to various cultural venues or museums was lack of time (four times more frequent than 'no money for it') – whereas … it was precisely those with the least time (i.e. the busiest work schedules) who went most frequently.[159]

In other words, when activities make sense for life, lack of time is no longer a problem. Moreover, the humanities remind us of the importance of emphasising the human character of organizations, above their biological dimension,[160] in order to avoid what Clayton Crockett calls the "motorisation of humanity."[161] Yet management sciences, through their predilection for positivism, where human facts are treated as "objects," and through an epistemology modelled on the natural sciences, tend to deny the very existence of that which is neither objectifiable nor measurable.

The second perspective concerns the necessary change of discourse regarding management and its very nature: the position of manager, as the etymology of the word reminds us, is a power (it is management as presented in most management handbooks), but also a burden. There is a managerial difficulty, a managerial fragility, which are at the source of its capacity to act. On the one hand, vulnerability is a characteristic that is often denied to management (which sometimes likes to present itself as akin to 'omniscience,' and therefore 'omnipotence'), and on the other hand, responsibility is 'managed', and therefore denied, thanks to bureaucratic mechanisms that aim to maintain its self-declared omnipotence: "In the name of individual responsibility, everyone must respect the norms, but respecting the norms is akin to failing to take responsibility in the event of a problem."[162] Thus, it is the society of performance transformed into a doping society that ends up catching up with managerial activity itself. However, particularly from an educational point of view, vulnerability should not be seen as an evil, but rather as a necessary condition for action and for "measuring" one's own responsibility.

---

[158] Ch. Dejours 2009; J.-Ph. Bouilloud and G. Deslandes 2015.

[159] H. Rosa 2010: 174.

[160] The performance society, an active society, is slowly evolving towards a doping society. The negative term "mental doping" is being replaced by "neurological reinforcement," Byung-Chul Han 2014: 93.

[161] C. Crockett 2005: 183.

[162] B. Owl 2012: 50.

2.4 Beyond Recognition?

Nowadays, it is an all too common experience to hear people complain about a lack of recognition. People want to be better recognized for who they are, what they do or what they long for – be it within couples, in professional lives or among friends. Not only in academic circles, the subject of recognition has thus become a pivotal concept to all those who strive to comprehend human relations in the workplace and in the social sphere, in the broadest sense of the word. In most cases, the notion of fairness in organizations happens to be related to requests for recognition; it bears fundamentally upon the quest for protection and the urge for self-fulfillment.[163]

Could this notion, which is so prevalent in contemporary social sciences and philosophy, constitute a basis on which to rethink managerial ethics?

The concept of recognition spans contemporary philosophy[164] and sociology[165] where it presents itself as an alternative to the social contract theory or conventional economics.[166] Besides, its influence tends to extend to other disciplines such as management and business ethics.[167] Accordingly, it is not surprising that interest for this notion should be growing. Indeed, employees are thought to achieve better and more durable performance levels precisely because they receive higher recognition, i.e. because their true value is recognized.

Actually, a whole body of management literature shows that recognition is indispensable to "successful" management.[168] This is also observed by Bigi et al.[169] for whom 'human' management takes on its full meaning when attempting to recognize employees' achievements by not relying solely on quantitative methods, but by also exploiting its analytical capabilities:

> Management has a major role to play in compensating for the lack of recognition: it is vested with the responsibility of adequately assessing employees' performance. [...] It must not fulfill this task by resorting to quantitative indicators that remain superficial and do not take into account more important elements. It should instead rely on a brand of human judgment that is capable of correlating, comparing, weighing and differentiating criteria, as well as giving credit where credit is due.[170]

---

[163] This chapter is based on an essay published in French: Deslandes Ghislain & Jean-Philippe Bouilloud, "Pour une éthique d'après la reconnaissance", *Rimhe – Revue Interdisciplinaire Management, Homme et Entreprise* (34): 88–102. I would like to thank my co-author Jean-Philippe Bouilloud for authorising me to include these elements of reflection on recognition in the present work.

[164] C. Taylor 1992; A. Honneth 1995; P. Ricœur 2004; G. Le Blanc 2008.

[165] M. Bigi et al. 2015.

[166] H. Guéguen and G. Malochet 2014: 3.

[167] L. Hilgendorg and B-L. Irving 1978; Brun and Dugas 2005; Brink and Eurich 2016; F. Pierson 2011; Islam 2012; Hancock 2016.

[168] B. Nelson and D. Spietzer 2003; C. Ventrice 2003.

[169] M. Bigi et al. 2015.

[170] M. Bigi et al. 2015: 286–287.

2.4 Beyond Recognition?

In the next section, I would like to attempt to go beyond the limits of such widespread demand for recognition in management since it is a desire that knows no end and cannot possibly be fulfilled[171]: there will, so to speak, never be enough recognition. I shall consequently endeavor to outline the necessary conditions for the advent of what could be dubbed 'a post-recognition ethics' applied to the world of organizations. For that purpose, I shall start with a definition of this notion by relying chiefly on research conducted by Honneth.[172] I then propose a critical analysis of it, on the basis of a 'self-esteem/other-esteem' opposition, stressing at the same time the risk that managerial systems may instrumentalize recognition. Extrapolating from that analysis, I shall try to achieve a third goal by endeavoring to go beyond managerial demands for recognition along two distinct paths: reasserting the crucial importance of a relation to self and exploring the broader subject of capabilities. In doing so, I shall constantly strive to avoid the risks posed by the endless and inextinguishable debt resulting from recognition by resorting to an ethics of the *beau geste* and unadulterated selflessness.

2.4.1 Recognition Between Acknowledgment and Claim

Firstly, three dimensions of recognition come to mind: (1) It is first and foremost a feeling, a perception which may seem disconnected from a reality that is assessed using objective criteria (number of quotations or volume of sales for an academic, pay level for employees…); this gap is likely to cause problems in interpersonal relations, especially among managers. (2) It is an acknowledgment (e.g. "I am recognized as having such and such a quality"). (3) It often presents itself in the form of a *demand* for gratitude, often negative (e.g. "I am not sufficiently recognized…"). In the words of Ricœur, recognition embraces two notions, "identification" and "expectation".[173]

After exploring the different senses of the word in French, Ricœur attained what he termed a semantic "chain" made of the meanings of the word '*reconnaissance*': "to accept, hold as true, admit, acknowledge, confess, be indebted, thank".[174] That chain unfolds between the pole of identification (to accept, hold as true, admit) and that of gratitude (be indebted, thank). The two extremes are bound, the second pole ensuing from the first: as we have identified an action and its intrinsic value, a debt (the feeling of 'being indebted') exists; such extremes make possible or desirable to move to the practical action of thanking, and even to offer a reward which materializes both the acknowledgement of the debt and its clearance. The workplace serves

---

[171] S. Ekman 2013.

[172] A. Honneth 1995, 1997.

[173] P. Ricœur 2004.

[174] P. Ricœur 2004: 28.

as a good illustration of those two dimensions: staff members and people employed at certain levels of responsibility have had to struggle to be recognized as "executives" or "executive-level employees"; blue-collar workers fight to gain recognition of the arduous nature of their jobs; laid-off employees expect legal authorities to acknowledge the moral or financial prejudice they have suffered; employees desire to be recognized by their organizations and managers; managers in turn also want their performance to be acknowledged by top management; chief officers crave recognition from the business community and financial analysts etc...

In this quest for recognition at different levels, one can clearly perceive its structural incompleteness. As a matter of fact, it is difficult to fully recognize merit in proportion to the expectations that people harbor, and one's can fear to be doomed to be structurally plagued with inadequate recognition. If it is predicated on an individual's perception, the difficulty is to reconcile the perceptions of different individuals, and to avoid creating an often-painful gap between expectations and appreciations. The quest for recognition throws people into evaluation processes that differ from more common yardsticks such as qualification or pay levels that may generate more potential disappointment than actual rewards. It stands to reason that individuals deserve to be recognized as persons in their own right.

Yet, the particular virtue of any reward system based on recognition is to distinguish certain employees. Reward systems in organizations are, by definition, selective and accordingly "recognize" only some employees, while excluding others. It appears as if the concept faces a "paradoxical situation", as accurately described by Dubet[175]:

> On the one hand, the language of recognition progressively imposes itself as relations of domination are experienced within a symbolic environment, in a psychological mode. It is also prevalent in 'post-national' societies in which various groups and cultures coexist and claim their specific differences with their own means of expression. On the other hand, as it is endowed with a strong homogeneity, recognition turns out to be a fathomless abyss in which everything is engulfed, given that the demand for recognition can never be totally fulfilled. One may fear that recognition may live on as a subject of compassion and brotherhood, which is to be taken seriously as it most probably defines an essential human and democratic value. Yet, one can hardly view it as the bedrock of a theory of justice and, beyond that, of political action.

At this point, we might add '… of managerial action'. Indeed, how could we strike a balance within organizations between multiple demands supported by a principle of heterogeneity such as that of recognition?

---

[175] F. Dubet 2008: 159.

2.4.2 Recognition as a Philosophical Question

In the field of philosophy, the notion that has been amply studied, notably by prominent philosophers like Hobbes, Hegel[176] or, more recently, Rawls.[177] It was also present in Aristotle's theory of the good life (*eudiamonia*). In that case, it must be considered as an element of life in the sense of an aristocratic ethos in which individuals recognize themselves as potentially capable of self-control and judgment (*phronesis*), which makes them members of the masters' community. It should be noted that in its contemporary definition, this notion is correlated with the history of social sciences according to which recognition is presented as preexisting the construction and expression of individual identities. Mead in particular contended that this relation prevailed over the existence of a self, and that self-evaluation depends directly and constantly upon the vision and appreciation of others.

Nonetheless, the philosopher Axel Honneth whose research is based on critical theory was the first scholar who made it the key notion of his work by ascribing to recognition the status of a concept likely to maintain a link between individuals as well as to provide an evaluation criterion for the legitimacy of their social demands. In this light, the desire for recognition "is nothing but the expression of individuals expecting others to confirm their own capabilities and value."[178] Besides, to the contemporary German philosopher, there are three forms, which Guéguen and Malochet summarize as follows: "primary relations (love), legal relations (law), communities sharing values (social solidarity)".[179] Thanks to the influence of these three levels, all members of a group can shape their own identities, which can also be denied to them: in such a case, Honneth points out contempt as the obstacle

---

[176] "One can argue, at least as a working assumption, that there are three basic forms of recognition that (although they do not comprehensively encompass the wide scope of all acts of recognition) correspond to those which people regard as most important and which they would place on top of the hierarchy of their preferences. These three forms were described in Hegel's earlier works, namely his two publications "Philosophy of Spirit" of 1804 and 1805. They embrace three types of social relations that express essential aspects of human life: social relations involving the distribution of forms of social esteem to individuals (which are merely suggested in *Formal Conceptions of Ethical Life*, legal relations in connection with the status of property and citizenship, and interpersonal relations within families, which Hegel translated into three categories: social ethnicity, law and love. Through such early works, he endeavored to elaborate a theory of recognition predicated on those three types of social relations." (C. Lazzeri and A. Caillé 2004: 91).

[177] H. Guéguen and G. Malochet 2014; C. Lazzari and A. Caillé 2004.

[178] C. Lazzeri and A. Caillé 2004: 90. "This is why" explains Honneth, "in his underlying theory on the subject, he argues: "the formation of individual identity is accomplished at the same pace as the interiorization of appropriate, socially standardized reactions, in accordance with the demand for recognition which individuals are exposed to: individuals learn how to achieve self-awareness, both as being endowed with an intrinsic value and as particular members of the social community. Indeed, they progressively become aware of the specific capabilities and needs that help them exist as persons thanks to the positive reactions that they encounter with all partners involved in interaction." (Honneth 2004: 134).

[179] H. Guéguen and G. Malochet 2014: 49; F. Pierson 2011.

which prevents the strengthening of social ties.[180] Accordingly, recognition (granted not only to individuals, but also to life-styles or values shared in a given cultural context) has dual characteristics: it preexists the formation of identities within social groups, and is also the result of and the condition for the development of social processes and the self-fulfillment of all members in their own fashion.

Voswinkel for instance suggests a differentiation between a form that he describes as "appreciation recognition, based on moral appreciation", and another form named "admiration recognition", which implies distanciation and a verticalization of the relationship between the different stakeholders.[181] The moral connotation of recognition, as approached by Voswinkel through "appreciation" indeed implies that self-esteem is determined by social recognition. Consequently, denying it would likely result in violence. All forms of self-ethics would thus start with overcoming the alienation represented by self-reification attempts[182] resulting from lack of recognition. Accordingly, all pathological forms of social organizations (for example a business firm or a given administration) would forebode the denial of self-respect by the individuals who belong to them: as a matter of fact, failing to provide recognition is tantamount to denying individuals their dignity.

All things considered, Islam relies on the same moral connotation, pursuing the orientations suggested by Honneth when promoting a *recognition-rich work environment* that would complement a work environment predicated on resources, most notably on human resources.[183] Defining work relations this way fosters a critical relationship to practices that tend to reify the human nature of people at work, at the expense of their own dignity.[184] The sort of reification that Islam refers to in fact poses a risk to Honneth's vision: a denial that would necessarily spawn impressions of contempt and depreciation felt by individuals who have a strong influence on the building of their own social identities. This is why other researchers like Taylor have tended to shift the notion from the status of moral duty to that of a quasi-civic right, to be respected while preserving differences.[185]

However, to Honneth, the two aspirations should coexist within a "pact" that also includes the obligation to recognize individuals not only for what they are but also for their achievements. As observed by Pierson, these two facets lie in the arena of a fight for recognition that, within the organizational framework, may extend to

---

[180] A. Honneth 2006.

[181] S. Voswinkel et al. 2007: 65. They further add that, "*appreciation* provides a substitute for prestige; it bestows recognition on players who enjoy little power, success and prestige."

[182] See A. Honneth and S. Haber 2008: 98.

[183] G. Islam 2012.

[184] G. Islam 2012: 45.

[185] C. Taylor 1992; N. Pless and T. Maak 2004.

2.4 Beyond Recognition?

learning collective resistance, as illustrated by middle managers striving to voice their claims even though such resistance is increasingly depreciated and despised.[186]

A different angle such as 'visibility' can be chosen to approach such issues, as analyzed by Le Blanc (2007). According to him, the social visibility conferred by recognition should be interpreted as a major moral stake:

> By contrast, denying recognition socially impairs the lives of individuals by failing to recognize their moral value, i.e. the only attribute that can justify their existence: caught in the web of social contempt, the "self" is then forced into the loss of "self", as it is no longer connected to a positive moral standing whose absence casts them at the limits of social visibility, on the brink of inexistence, insignificance.[187]

In the following section, I tentatively propose a critique of an organizational ethics that would limit itself to this demand. The question here is not to challenge the importance of recognition, but rather to delineate it as the one and only moral principle to understand ethical problems within organizations. Should it be accepted on principle as a foundation of justice, we run the risk of having interactions between individuals work only with respect to a debt. The quest for merit involved in all recognition policies is thus likely to become a new form of competition in which every single individual would be pitted against each other, creating a "struggle for merit", triggering an endless race, likely to partly account for present-day phenomena of suffering and burnout in the workplace.[188] Moreover, this quest would forge a new form of instrumental reason, its consequences would run counter to initial goals.

2.4.3 The Ethics of Recognition: A Critique

This demand in fact poses a problem of temporality: the pact is only valid for a given period of time; it needs to be constantly renewed. Time is not favorable to it, which means that oblivion erases the reward or depreciates the debt. The employee whose performance is commended naturally expects to be "recognized" every time, in the same situation. Otherwise said, it is as if there would be "an eternal return" of the desire for recognition; the recognition expressed today creates an expectation for tomorrow, which will need to be met yet again.

Another difficulty clearly arises here, as a result of a policy based on its dual nature on the one hand, the demand for compensation, in appreciation for efforts made (a request that transactional management systems are themselves fond of and keen on receiving); on the other hand, a "horizon of expectations" that demands the verbalization of apposite words or the carrying out of an appropriate action, which

---

[186] F. Pierson 2011.

[187] G. Le Blanc 2008: 138.

[188] M. Sandel 2020.

need to go beyond the standardized evaluation and the cold logic of return on investment. This race towards recognition poses two problems: first, it contains an inner contradiction, since it calls for recognition for all, whereas only the most deserving can be rewarded; furthermore it involves a risk of confusion, since organizations need to sift through the heterogeneous demands of employees whose individual perceptions are unique.

Undoubtedly, these demands are not always homogeneous. Yet, none of them can claim to be consistently legitimate and equitable in comparison with other demands. Subsequently, these demands cannot be the one and only bedrock for a theory of fairness. Indeed, it is always necessary to determine whether demands for recognition are justified or not.[189] Such demands for social approval are therefore bound to breed unfulfilled expectations that may cause "moral wounds" as described by Lazzeri and Caillé[190]: these are, so to speak, negative forms that inflict on employees a feeling of helplessness in the face of what they consider as a sign of disdain toward themselves.

Here, we should insist on the risks of instrumentalization by management systems (e.g. annual appraisal interviews, "best employee of the month" notices posted in restaurants etc...), which can be regarded as specific forms of distribution of social esteem. From the very moment that managerial logic sets priority goals to be attained, one may fear that intersubjective recognition may actually fall back into second place. In the face of this ceaseless demand, management may be tempted to implement evaluation tools and systems that respond to it in a fictitious manner and, in fact, radically eradicate its moral character.[191] Thus, as managerial techniques are predicated on recognition processes, they subdue individuals instead of liberating them "from the real-life world", as explained by Guéguen and Malochet,[192] all the more so as such techniques breed resentment between employees competing for the same reward.

As a matter of fact, the separation between quantitative goals set by management on the one hand and the collaborative nature of projects developed within organizations on the other hand goes counter to the promises of a recognition policy as outlined by Honneth: to him, the latter must essentially be preserved as a "grammar"[193] that should regulate relations between people in the workplace. Thenceforth, as

---

[189] "There is however a gap, a threshold, between this particular level and that of fairness. Stakeholders bridge such a gap when they wonder why the contempt suffered by some employees is just or unjust and also when they turn into staunch supporters of Kant or Rawls – although they are not metaphysical subjects. Consequently, all forms of recognition are not just and certain claims for recognition can seem unacceptable, let alone ludicrous – a problem that is hardly addressed by Honneth. Lastly, there is a gap between this moral level and the one of collective action? Indeed, the only employees who resolve to take action should not be the victims of unfair treatment". (F. Dubet 2008: 158).

[190] C. Lazzeri and A. Caillé 2004: 104.

[191] S. Voswinkel et al. 2007.

[192] H. Guéguen and G. Malochet 2014; 17.

[193] G. Islam 2012.

2.4 Beyond Recognition?

observed by Honneth himself, the management of human resources is attracted to reification when it strives to translate the alleged "talent" of employees into multiple evaluations, notably cognitive ones; it systematically does so with whatever data may be "exploited", disregarding employees' real-life experience.[194] Wieviorka[195] made the same statement in reference to Jérôme Kerviel,[196] the rogue trader of *Société Générale*, when he underscored the inner contradiction that is contained in the implementation of management tools relying on a recognition-based logic. Such tools indeed "reinforce all types of individuation logic applied to collective problems; employees are expected to act in solidarity [and] comply with a single corporate culture, whenever possible supported by a company's history."

All managerial evaluation systems share a common feature: wresting oneself from them is difficult for any employee, particularly an executive.[197] Indeed, if employees identify with an entrepreneurial dimension as "self-entrepreneurs", if they respond to "the call of subjectivity",[198] they automatically abandon the appraisal system and can no longer claim any form of recognition – which applies even more specifically to "self-entrepreneurs". Since it is impossible to write off the debt resulting from recognition, managers may be faced with a paradoxical injunction, which consists in demanding from them a form of recognition that *in fine* can never be fully established. Furthermore, in the eyes of those who crave it, is not such an expectation similar to a "luring fantasy" on account of its inevitable unattainability? Cohen takes issue more harshly with such organizational forms of recognition, arguing that "an intolerable suspicion is rampant with respect to similar proclamations that are perceived as strategic dissimulations of domination and manipulation."[199] To this author, one should distinguish between the "outraged", who have nothing to offer but their indignation and the "resigned", who are simply maintained in evaluation systems of performance that negate their real-life experience. Cohen further contends that such people express the *"nihilism of the unrecognized"* since, according to him, "they have indeed grown weary of recognition and its illusory promises."

In such a quandary, how could one escape the never-ending claims of employees and the contempt of management? Is it possible to envision a "post-recognition ethics", that is to say an ethics of oneself and of others, which would free itself from the trap described above?

---

[194] *Id.*

[195] M. Wieviorka 2013: 35.

[196] "This is what was said by Jérôme Kerviel, the trader who allegedly caused the loss of billions of euros by *Société Générale* (excerpt from an interview given to *Journal du Dimanche*, quoted by Vincent de Gaulejac 2011: 56): Individualism (at work) is encouraged at all costs. At the same time, you are imparted a corporate culture that tells you that we are a big family." (Wieviorka 2013: 35).

[197] In fact, according to Sennet, economic flexibility is justified by the fact that employees are encouraged to become personally autonomous (Sennett 1998). Those who want to work independently can no longer want to be valued servants. (S. Voswinkel et al. 2007: 76).

[198] M. Wieviorka 2013: 38.

[199] M. Cohen 2013a, b: 166.

2.4.4 Towards a Post-recognition Ethics

In the following discussion, let's attempt to go beyond recognition by drawing on three different sources: a philosophical critique[200]; a theory on the notion of capabilities[201]; the proposal of an ethics of the *beau geste* and selflessness.

Far from providing rough-and-ready answers, pondering over recognition seems to raise primordial questions in connection with a difficult choice: should we favor individuation logic to solve collective problems or rather prefer to act in sole the interest of the community? Should organizations prefer management approaches that benefit individual well-being or collective happiness? Should they give priority to the comfort of each employee or the satisfaction of all? Let us ask the question in a different way: to what extent can we argue that a correlation between well-being and common good exists within organizations? Do they represent two antagonistic orientations that, ultimately, can never be reconciled?

Faced with the difficult nature of such questions, it might be useful to look back at the philosophers who explored in depth the relationship to oneself and to others. In contemporary philosophical research, the phenomenology of Michel Henry's life, as presented before, is likely to help us approach the problem in an original way. According to Henry, the self-relation pertains to ethics whereas moral philosophy focuses on relations with others. It is no wonder that ethics should primarily concern the relation to self: from Wittgenstein's "work on oneself"[202] to Foucault's "self-concern",[203] numerous ethicists share a concurring interest that consists not so much in focusing on individuals, but rather in having them face their relation to themselves. "Whether we recognize it or not, there actually is a pure relation to self that does not include, in its very essence, any relation to others".[204]

Would that imply an improbable revival of selfishness, at least as a positive character trait or, more plausibly, a negative one (self-esteem with Rousseau)? Or should we consider with Schopenhauer that selfishness here is an ontological category akin to our desire for well-being?[205] If we explore the second option, recognising with Henry (1985) that ethics starts from a confrontation with oneself, an explanation with oneself, a stumbling block on oneself, "such that one can always 'hope' not to suffer from oneself, but (that) this is a hopeless prospect."[206] For that very reason, real action is always first of all that of a self that experiences itself as ipseity. It is in this sense, and in this sense only, that ethics precedes any reflection that takes place in the realm of morality, and thus politics.

---

[200] P. Audi 2007; Henry 1985.

[201] P. Ricœur 2004; Sen 1987.

[202] G. Deslandes 2011a.

[203] G. Deslandes 2012.

[204] P. Audi 2007: 32; J-L. Marion 2002.

[205] A. Shopenhauer 2000.

[206] P. Audi 2007: 147; M. Henry 1985.

2.4 Beyond Recognition?

Yet, this does not lessen the importance of politics, quite the opposite. The common good can be a reality only if it endeavors to look into the well-being of members of a community. As concerns the well-being of individuals, is it possible to address this topic without considering issues of fairness and justice toward others? Should not management researchers pay more attention to organizations viewed as places of collective life? Are not such positive notions as philanthropy, transparency, commitment, happiness in the workplace, homeostasis, etc. or negative ones like burnout, corruption, harassment – stemming from either the best or the worst managerial practices – always closely connected to the same dialectic? The good for oneself in contradiction with justice toward others matches with ethical as well as moral issues.

At the beginning of this current chapter, I attempted to show that the recognition theory depended upon the prevalence of the relation to others. Therefore it would seem that this theory partly overshadows the ontological primacy of self-relation for the benefit of a primordial recognition of others by other individuals. Honneth or Pierson in particular uphold this vision: to them "individuals cannot develop specific identities without being recognized, that is to say unless they are understood and deemed legitimate by the people who interact with them. Recognition results from interaction".[207] Before it becomes intersubjective, can we claim that action primarily originates in our own selves and our own bodies,[208] from which we can never extract ourselves? To Henry, real action is first and foremost the result of a person's self that tests its own ipseity or selfhood. There can be no constructive recognition without a positive self-relationship (which implies for instance a form of self-consistency that I owe to others as much as to myself) on the basis of which recognition processes come into play.

The same vision can be traced to Ricœur's analysis of recognition viewed as a debt. To Ricœur, it amounts to "confessing to a debt" since, with recognition, the imperative of duty is never far away: one always "must" do or think something – be it rewarding, identifying or anything else.[209] From such a stance, one can perceive the present-day desire of generalized recognition: it can be found in minorities, employees, or even in individual specificities, as the token of the widespread individualism of a tired society[210] in which all citizens exhaust themselves in building, claiming and gaining recognition of an elusive self.

---

[207] F. Pierson 2011: 357.

[208] Knowledge of the world, which is the prerogative of the body, is 'neither intellectual nor even representative': it results from a subjective movement. So much so that we constantly need to 'place ourselves inside the powers that it unfolds in order to understand the nature of the world experienced by our body'. (...) It is 'indeed inside such powers that we stand.' This is where our abode lies: inside the powers of our body (Audi 2007: 47).

[209] P. Ricoeur 2004.

[210] B-C. Han 2014.

2.4.5 Recognition, Hope and Capabilities

Recognizing oneself already amounts to a fraction of the demand for recognition, since individuals who crave it harbor a prior notion of what they desire or are worth: without such a perception, no demand for recognition would be possible. Any demand from others is grounded in a prior self-assessment, an evaluation of one's feeling of satisfaction or dissatisfaction. As a consequence, not only is "self-esteem one of the expressions of recognition",[211] but more importantly self-recognition is intrinsically primordial and thus necessarily at the core of any other demand for recognition sought from others.

Yet, an assessment is not sufficient: it must be supplemented by a project, a desire supported by specific hope. Individuals who find themselves deprived of consideration, but who resign themselves to such indifference are not inclined to entertain expectations of recognition. To engage oneself in that "struggle", as Honneth rightly refers to it, one first needs to make that prior "self-assessment", evaluate one's initial perception ("Am I recognized or not?"). Besides, one must feel reasonable hope of being able to change the situation, expect that the claim will be met, that the perceived wrong will be righted or that the social order deemed normal or just will be restored. Such hope will surely provide adequate energy to carry on the "struggle".

Reducing recognition to mere social interaction would thus amount to overlooking the primacy of self-assessment. This notion of hope makes it possible to complement Ricœur's stance on the links he established between recognition and capabilities. "Believing that I am able already is enough to endow me with a capability" Ricœur claims. By grounding recognition in capability, in the wake of Amartya Sen, Ricœur grants autonomy to individuals in the ways they shape the various facets of their lives – at work, in their leisure time, their family and social lives, etc. With such attention paid to individual capabilities, his desire is to broaden the scope "not with closed identities, but 'capabilities', that is to say an anthropology of capable and creative humans".[212] Nonetheless, as noted by Giovanola, the capability approach "shows how people can be happy in the sense of 'flourishing', but not in the sense of 'subjective well-being' – as used by the welfarist and utilitarian tradition".[213] This foray into capabilities is somehow equivalent to hooking into the future: recognition is a bet on the future, a way of pledging today what will materialize only tomorrow (e.g. consideration, reward...).

Be that as it may, this capability-based approach does not have much to say on the subjective experience of recognition, nor on the need for hope, should anyone wish to initiate a claim for recognition. Although the disconnection between capabilities and individual perception with respect to recognition was already

---

[211] J. Greisch 2006: 153.

[212] H. Guéguen and G. Malochet 2014: 91.

[213] B. Giovanola 2005: 253.

2.4 Beyond Recognition?

underscored,[214] we might find an anchoring point (namely the human body) by taking an other side-glance at Michel Henry's work. If we consider with Michel Henry that the only real power is that of the body, the immanent "I can" that creates, expands and generates the whole diversity of human capabilities, then we can find in our corporeal experience the source of the hope which allows us to engage in the demand for recognition. Given that the human body is ontologically hope, that is to say a projection into the future, a future that is that of life itself, then the demand for recognition relies on this very reflection in the body to gain strong support. This is how Henry's theory echoes and complements the capability-based approach, an anchoring into "the sensory experience of the humankind" which is very sorely lacking[215] and does not allow it to go beyond a pragmatic conception of well-being.

In the end, when dealing with these issues, we are also lurking in the shadow of others, waiting for them to notice us, which both gives us life and enslaves us. Yet, this shadow is always short-lived. The imperative of recognition is therefore doomed to fail for several reasons: the debt can hardly be measured and cannot be erased since time is fleeting; it unceasingly strives to gather diverging interests or viewpoints, resulting from specific or even antagonistic perceptions; self-relationship is superseded by an alienating domination of the relation to others; it concerns a future that it cannot control. As Bigi et al.[216] rightly observe:

> the managerial revolution" has completely failed to meet all the expectations it had created [...] Recognition concerns less an objective reality than an ideal, a representation entertained by every individual of what work is and what it should be.

For the sake of comparison we could recall that Reason, the liberating principle of the Enlightenment, attempted to struggle against a myth. However, according to Adorno and Horkheimer, it turned out to be "the myth of the modern world". The same goes for managerial theories: while they endeavored to emancipate employees from social injustice, they subjugated them even more to the tyranny of the relationship to others.

This is precisely where a different position may be considered. A "post-recognition ethics" makes it necessary to consider recognition of others as a "pure gift", a "*beau geste*"[217] that precisely cannot be built as part of an illusory symmetry, but rather in the firm proclamation of the self as a gift without any hope of requital. Endorsing this approach demands breaking away from any desire for symmetrical appreciation. It also implies questioning Mauss's symmetrical theory of gifts and counter-gifts, which anyway failed to account for all the aspects and implications of gift-giving.[218]

---

[214] M. Gilardone 2010: 18–19.

[215] M. Gilardone 2010: 3; 2009.

[216] M. Bigi et al. 2015: 14.

[217] J-P. Bouilloud and G. Deslandes 2015.

[218] J-L. Marion 2002.

Yet, as with any bottomless pit, the urge for recognition cannot possibly be satisfied when it is symmetrical. An adequate recognition ethics that avoids the ontological disappointment implied by the imperative of recognition, as found in management, would necessarily rely on a practice that should itself be dissymmetric. It would feature two elements: responding to the recognition desire expressed by others (employees, followers, co-workers or even superiors) and the primacy of a self-relation including a scaled-down degree of recognition. Accordingly, true leaders would only count on self-recognition, on recognition *per se*, while striving to offer others as much recognition as they can.

References

Alvesson, Mats. 2010. Self-doubters, strugglers, storytellers, surfers and others: Images of self-identities in organization studies. *Human Relations* 63 (2).

Alvesson, Mats, and Hugh Willmott. 2002. Identity regulation as organizational control: Producing the appropriate individual. *Journal of Management Studies* 39 (5): 619–644.

Arnaud, Gilles. 2012. The contribution of psychoanalysis to organization studies and management: An overview. *Organization Studies* 33 (9): 1121–1135.

Ashforth, Blake, and Fred Mael. 1989. Social identity theory and the organization. *Academy of Management Review* 14 (1): 20–39.

Aubert, Nicole. 2003. *Le Culte de l'urgence. La société malade du temps.* Paris: Flammarion.

Audi, Paul. 2007. *Supériorité de l'éthique.* Paris: Flammarion.

Bertland, Alexander. 2009. Virtue ethics in business and the capabilities approach. *Journal of Business Ethics* 84 (1): 25–32.

Bessire, Dominique, and Hervé Mesure. 2009. Penser l'entreprise comme communauté: fondements, définition et implications. *Management et Avenir* 30 (10): 30–50.

Bigi, Maëlezig, Olivier Cousin, Dominique Méda, Laetitia Sibaud, and Michel Wieviorka. 2015. *Travailler au XXIème siècle – des salariés en quête de reconnaissance.* Paris: Robert Lafont.

Bouilloud, Jean-Philippe. 2012. *Entre l'enclume et le marteau.* Paris: Seuil.

Bouilloud, Jean-Philippe, and Ghislain Deslandes. 2015. The Æsthetics of Leadership: Beau Geste as Critical Behaviour. *Organization Studies* 36 (8).

Braveman, Harry. 1974. *Labor and monopoly capital: The degradation of Work in the twentieth century.* Londres: Monthly Review Press.

Brink, Alexander, and Johannès Eurich. 2016. Recognition based upon the vitality criterion: A key to sustainable economic success. *Journal of Business Ethics* 67: 155–164.

Brun, Jean-Pierre, and Ninon Dugas. 2005. La reconnaissance au travail: analyse d'un concept riche de sens. *Gestion* 30 (2): 79–88.

Burell, Gibson. 1988. Modernism, postmodernism and organizational analysis 2. The contribution of Michel Foucault. *Organization Studies* 9 (2): 221–235.

Butler, Judith. 1993. Kierkegaard's speculative despair. In *The age of idealism*, ed. Robert Salomon and Kathleen Higgins. Londres: Routledge.

Cohen, Yves. 2013a. *Le siècle des chefs: Une histoire transnationale du commandement et de l'autorité (1890–1940).* Paris: Editions d'Amsterdam.

Cohen, Joseph. 2013b. Force et faiblesse de la reconnaissance. *Cités* 54 (2): 164–166.

Crane, Andrew, David Knights, and Kenneth Starkey. 2008. The conditions of our freedom: Foucault, organization, and ethics. *Business Ethics Quarterly* 18 (3): 299–320.

Crawford, Matthew. 2009. *Éloge du carburateur: essai sur le sens et la valeur du travail.* Paris: La Découverte.

References 85

Damien, Robert. 2013. *Eloge de l'autorité. Généalogie d'une (dé)raison politique.* Paris: Armand Colin.

Dejours, Christophe. 2009. *Live work. Travail et émancipations.* Vol. 2. Paris: Payot.

Deslandes, Ghislain. 2011a. Wittgenstein and the practical turn in business ethic. *Electronic Journal of Business Ethics and Organizational Studies* 16 (1)., online available.

———. 2011b. In search of individual responsibility. The dark side of organizations in the light of Jansenist ethics. *Journal of Business Ethics* 101 (1): 61–70.

———. 2012. The care-of-self ethic with continual reference to Socrates: Towards ethical self-Management. *Business Ethics: A European Review* 21 (4): 325–338.

———. 2013. *Essai sur les données philosophiques du management.* Paris: PUF.

———. 2014. Management in Xenophon's Philosophy: A retrospective analysis. In *Proceedings of the Philosophy of Management conference.* Chicago: De Paul University.

———. 2015. La besogne et le besoin. Réflexions sur le vécu individuel à l'heure de l'accélération sociale. *RIMHE,* 4 (18): 83–96.

———. 2017. To be or not to be a dot? Philosophy of Management and the subjective body. In *Perspectives on Philosophy of Management and business ethics, 51: 47–60,* ed. Jacob Rendtorff. Ethical Economy: Springer.

———. 2023. *Erotique de l'administration.* Paris: PUF.

Dubet, François. 2008. Injustice et reconnaissance. *Esprit, Juillet:* 144–159.

Ducharme, Olivier. 2012. *Michel Henry et le problème de la communauté. Soi, communauté, habitus,* doctoral thesis in philosophy under the supervision of Sophie-Jan Arrien, Laval (Québec), Université de Laval.

Ekman, Suzanne. 2013. Fantasies about work as limitless potential – How managers and employees seduce each other through dynamics of mutual recognition. *Human Relations* 66 (9): 1159–1181.

Faÿ, Éric. 2007. A critical and phenomenological genealogy of the question of the real in western economics and management. *Society and Business Review* 2 (2): 193–203.

———. 2009. Virtual organisation, real work. A Henryian critique of the virtual organisation of human work. *Studia Phænomenologica* IX.

———. 2014. Affects (situations stratégiques). In Franck Tannery (dir.), *Encyclopédie de la stratégie.* Paris: Vuibert,.

Fleming, Peter, and André Spicer. 2003. Working at a cynical distance: Implications for power, subjectivity and resistance. *Organization* 10 (1): 157–179.

Ford, Jackie. 2006. Discourses of Leadership: Gender, identity and contradiction in a UK public sector organization. *Leadership* 2 (1): 77–99.

Ford, Jackie, and Nancy Harding. 2011. The impossibility of the "true self" of authentic Leadership. *Leadership* 7 (4): 463–479.

Foucault, Michel. 2001. *Herméneutique du sujet. Cours au Collège de France 1981–1982.* Paris: Seuil/Gallimard.

———. 2008. *Le gouvernement de soi et des autres. Cours au Collège de France 1982–1983.* Paris: Seuil/Gallimard.

Gagnon, Suzanne. 2008. Compelling identity. Selves and insecurity in global, corporate management development. *Management Learning* 39 (4): 375–391.

Gély, Raphaël. 2007. *Rôles, action sociale et vie subjective.* Brussels: Peter Lang.

Gilardone, Muriel. 2010. Amartya Sen sans prisme. *Cahiers d'économie politique* 58 (1): 9–39.

Gilkey, Roderick, and Clint Kilts. 2007. Cognitive fitness. *Harvard Business Review* 85 (11): 53–54.

Giovanola, Benedetta. 2005. Personhood and human richness: Good and Well-being in the capability approach and beyond. *Review of Social Economy* 63 (2): 249–267.

———. 2009. Re-thinking the anthropological and ethical Foundation of Economics and Business: Human richness and capabilities enhancement. *Journal of Business Ethics* 88: 431–444.

Gorz, André. 2008. *Métamorphoses du travail.* Paris: Gallimard.

Greisch, Jean. 2006. Vers quelle reconnaissance ? *Revue de métaphysique et de morale* 50: 149–171.

86   2 Rethinking Management

Gschwandtner, Christana. 2012. What about non-human life? An "Ecological" reading of Michel Henry's critique of technology. *Journal of French and Francophone Philosophy* XX (2): 116–138.

Guéguen, Haud, and Guillaume Malochet. 2014. *Les théories de la reconnaissance*. Paris: La Découverte.

Hamraoui, Éric. 2013. Le besoin de temps. Entre travail et politique. *La Pensée* 376: 69–86.

Han, Byung-Chul. 2014. *La Société de la fatigue*. Paris: Circé.

Hancock, Philip. 2016. Recognition and the moral taint of sexuality: Threat, masculinity and Santa Claus. *Human Relations* 69 (2): 461–481.

Hancock, Philipp, and Melissa Tyler. 2001. Managing subjectivity and the dialectic of self-consciousness: Hegel and organization theory. *Organization* 8 (4): 565–585.

Hassard, John, Ruth Holliday, and Hugh Willmott. 2000. *Body and organization*. Londres: Sage.

Hatem, Nicole. 2006. Le secret partagé: Kierkegaard-Michel Henry. In *Pensée de la vie et culture contemporaine*, ed. Michel Henry. Paris: Beauchesne.

Henry, Michel. 1963. *L'Essence de la manifestation*, 4th ed. 2011. Paris: PUF. English version: Henry, Michel. 1973. *The essence of manifestation* (Trans. G. Etzkorn). The Hague: Nijhoff.

———. 1976. *Marx, I & II, Une philosophie de l'économie*. Paris: Gallimard. English version. Michel Henry, *Marx. A philosophy of human reality* (K. McLaughlin, trans.). Bloomington, IN: Indiana University Press, 1983.

———. 1985. *Généalogie de la psychanalyse*. Paris: PUF. English version. Michel Henry, *The Genealogy of Psychoanalysis* (D. Brick, Trans.). Stanford, CA: Stanford University Press, 1993.

———. 1988. Schopenhauer et l'inconscient. In *Schopenhauer et la force du pessimisme*, ed. Jean-Pierre Bertrand. Monaco: Le Rocher.

———. 1996. L'ontologie de Kierkegaard. Discussion. In *Annales de philosophie*, ed. K.E. Løgstrup, vol. 17, 1–13. Université St Joseph.

———. 2000. *Incarnation. Une philosophie de la chair*. English version. Paris: Seuil. Henry, Michel. (2015). *Incarnation. A Philosophy of Flesh* (Trans. K. Hefty). Evanston: Northwestern University Press.

———. 2003. *Phenoménologie de la vie, I. De la phénoménologie*. Paris: PUF.

———. 2004. *Phénoménologie de la vie, III, De l'art et du politique*. Paris: PUF.

———. 2005. *Entretiens*. Cabris: Éditions Sulliver.

———. 2008a. *La Barbarie*. 2nd ed. Paris: PUF. English version. Michel Henry, *Barbarism* (trans. S. Davidson). London and New York: Continuum, 2012.

———. 2008b. *Du communisme au capitalisme: Théorie d'une catastrophe*. L'âge d'homme.

———. 2011a. *L'Essence de la manifestation (1963)*. 4th ed. Paris: PUF. English version. Michel Henry (1973), *The essence of manifestation* (trans. G. Etzkorn). The Hague: Nijhoff.

———. 2011b. *Phénoménologie de la vie, II, Sur la subjectivité*. Paris: PUF.

———. 2011c. *Notes sur l'expérience d'autrui*. Revue Internationale Michel Henry. No. 2.

———. 2013. Notes préparatoires à 'L'Essence de la manifestation': la subjectivité'. *Revue internationale Michel Henry* 3.

Hibou, Béatrice. 2012. *La Bureaucratisation à l'ère néolibérale*. Paris: La Découverte.

Hilgendorf, Linden, and B.L. Irving. 1978. Decision criteria in person recognition. *Human Relations* 31: 781–789.

Holmer-Nadesan, Majia. 1996. Organizational identity and Space of Action. *Organization Studies* 17 (1). https://doi.org/10.1177/017084069601700103.

Honneth, Axel. 1995. *The struggle for recognition: The moral grammar of social conflicts*. Cambridge: Polity Press.

———. 1997. Recognition and moral obligation. *Social Research* 64 (1): 30–32.

———. 2004. La théorie de la reconnaissance: une esquisse. *Revue du Mauss* 23: 133–136.

———. 2006. *La Société du mépris*. Paris: La Découverte.

Honneth, Axel, and Stéphane Haber. 2008. Réification, connaissance, reconnaissance: quelques malentendus. *Esprit, Juillet*: 96–107.

References

Ibarra-Colado, Eduardo, Stewart Clegg, Carl Rhodes, and Martin Komberger. 2006. The ethics of managerial subjectivity. *Journal of Business Ethics* 64 (1): 45–55.

Inkson, Kerr. 2008. Are Human Resource? *Career Development International* 13 (3): 270-279.

Islam, Gazi. 2012. Recognition, reification, and practice of forgetting: Ethical implications of human resource Management. *Journal of Business Ethics* 111: 37–48.

Jackall, Robert, and Moral Mazes. 1988. *The world of corporate managers*. New York: Oxford University Press.

Jean, Grégori. 2014. *Force et vitalisme. Essais sur la phénoménologie vitaliste de Michel Henry*. Paris: Hermann.

Jones, Campbell, and André Spicer. 2005. The sublime object of entrepreneurship. *Organization* 12 (2): 223–246.

Knights, David, and Glenn Morgan. 1991. Corporate strategy, organizations and subjectivity: A critique. *Organization Studies* 12 (2): 473–489.

Lazzeri, Christian, and Alain Caillé. 2004. La reconnaissance aujourd'hui. Enjeux théoriques éthiques et politiques du concept. *Revue du Mauss* 23: 88–115.

Le Blanc, Guillaume. 2008. L'épreuve sociale de la reconnaissance. *Esprit. Juillet* 127–143.

Letiche, Hugo. 2009. Reflexivity and affectivity. *Culture and Organization* 15 (3–4): 291–306.

Mackenzie, Alec. 1972. *The time trap: Managing your way out*. New York: Amacom.

Maesschalck, Marc. 2000. La forme communautaire du jugement éthique chez M. Henry. Filiation et fraternité. In J.-M. Longneaux (dir.), *Retrouver la vie oubliée. Critiques et perspectives de la philosophie de Michel Henry*. Namur: Presses Universitaires de Namur.

Marion, Jean-Luc. 2002. *In Excess: Studies of Saturated Phenomena*. Fordham University Press.

Maris, Bernard. 2014. *Houellebecq économiste*. Paris: Flammarion.

Martin, Yann. 2011. Une ontologie de la vie intérieure. *Les Cahiers philosophiques de Strasbourg* 30 (2): 67–81.

Martinet, Alain-Charles, and Yvon Pesqueux. 2013. *Épistémologie des sciences de gestion*. Paris: Vuibert/FNEGE.

Mead, George Herbert. 1934. *Mind, myself and society*. Chicago: University of Chicago Press.

Mitchell, Ronald, Bradley Agle, and Donna Wood. 1997. Toward a theory of stakeholder identification and saliance. Defining the principle of who and what really counts. *Academy of Management Review* 22 (4).

Nelson, Bob, and Dean Spitzer. 2003. *The 1001 rewards and recognition Fieldbook*. New York: Workman Publishing.

O'Doherty, Damian, and Hugh Willmott. 2001. The question of subjectivity and the labor process. *International Studies of Management & Organization* 30 (4): 112–132.

Painter, Mollie, Mar Pérezts, and Ghislain Deslandes. 2020. Understanding the human in stakeholder Theory: A phenomenological approach to affect-based learning. *Management Learning* 52 (2): 203–223.

Painter-Morland, Mollie. 2013. The relationship between identity crises and crises of control. *Journal of Business Ethics* 114 (1): 1–14.

Parker, Follet Mary. 1919. Community is a process. *Philosophical Review* XXVIII: 576–588.

Parker, Martin. 1999. Capitalism, subjectivity and ethics: Debating labour process analysis. *Organization Studies* 20 (1): 25–45.

Pierre Guillet de Monthoux. 2000. Performing the Absolute. Marina Abramovic Organizing the Unfinished Business of Arthur Schopenhauer. *Organization Studies* 21 (1).

Pierson, Françoise. 2011. Pour un apprentissage de la lutte et de la résistance des cadres pour limiter leur souffrance au travail: les apports de la théorie de la reconnaissance d'Axel Honneth. *M@n@gement* 14 (5): 351–370.

Pless, Nicola, and Thomas Maak. 2004. Building an inclusive diversity culture: Principles, processes and practice. *Journal of Business Ethics* 54 (2): 129–147.

Puyou, François-Régis. 2013. Les individus et leurs rôles: l'apport des personnages au travail vivant. In *La Vie et les Vivants. Rereading Michel Henry*, ed. Grégori Jean, Jean Leclercq, and Nicolas Monseu. Louvain: Presses Universitaires de Louvain.

Puyou, François-Régis, and Éric Faÿ. 2013. Cogs in the wheel or spanners in the works? A phenomenological approach to the difficulty and meaning of ethical work for financial controllers. *Journal of Business Ethics* 128 (4): 863–876.

Rappin, Baptiste. 2014. *Au fondement du management. Théologie de l'organisation.* Vol. 1. Nice, Ovadia.

Reed, Michael. 1988. The problem of human Agency in Organizational Analysis. *Organization Studies* 9 (1): 33–46.

Renouard, Cécile. 2011. Corporate social responsibility, utilitarianism, and the capabilities approach. *Journal of Business Ethics* 98: 85–97.

Rhodes, Carl, and Edward Wray-Bliss. 2013. The ethical difference of organization. *Organization* 20 (1): 39–50.

Ricoeur, Paul. 1960. *Philosophie de la volonté, II, 2 t. L'homme faillible.* Paris: Aubier.

———. 2004. *Parcours de la Reconnaissance.* Paris: Stock.

Rocha, Hector, and Sumantra Ghoshal. 2006. Beyond self-interest revisited. *Journal of Management Studies* 43 (3): 585–615.

Rosa, Harmut. 2010. *Acceleration. Une critique sociale du temps.* Paris: La Découverte.

———. 2012. *Alienation and acceleration. Vers une critique de la modernité tardive.* Paris: La Découverte.

Sabelis, Ida. 2001. Time Management. Paradoxes and Patterns. *Time and Society* 10 (3).

Sandel, Michael. 2020. *The tyranny of merit: What's become of the common good?* Straus and Giroux: Farrar.

Schopenhauer, Arthur. 2000. *Le fondement de la morale.* Paris: Le livre de poche.

Schwartz, Yves. 2012. *Expériences et connaissance du travail.* 2nd ed. Paris: Éditions Sociales, 1998.

Sen, Amartya. 1987. *On ethics and economics.* Oxford: Basil Blackwell.

Sennett, Richard. 1998. *The corrosion of character. The personal consequences of Work in the new capitalism.* New York/London: W. W. Norton & Company.

Seyler, Frédéric. 2009. Michel Henry et la critique du politique. *Studia Phenomenologica* IX: 351–377.

Simone, Raffaele. 2012. Face à une droite hédoniste, la gauche n'a que l'effort à proposer. *Philosophie Magazine* 58.

Stiegler, Bernard. 2006a. *Mécréance et Discrédit, t. II, Les Sociétés incontrôlables d'individus désaffectés.* Paris: Galilée. English version. Bernard Stiegler, *Uncontrollable Societies of Disaffected Individuals: Disbelief and Discredit, 2,* Cambridge: Polity Press, 2013.

———. 2006b. De l'économie libidinale à l'écologie de l'esprit. Entretien avec Frédéric Neyrat. *Multitudes* 2006/1 (24): 85–95.

Tansley, Carole, and Simone Tietze. 2013. Rites of passage through talent Management progression stages: An identity Work perspective. *The International Journal of Human Resource Management* 24 (9): 231–250.

Taylor, Charles. 1992. *Multiculturalism and « the politics of recognition », an essay.* Princeton University Press: Princeton.

Thomas, Robert, and Warren Bennis. 2002. *Speed leading: Do you have what it takes.* Harvard *Management Update.*

Thoroughgood, Christian, Art Padilla, Samuel Hunter, and Brian Tate. 2012. The susceptible circle: A taxonomy of followers associated with destructive leadership. *The Leadership Quarterly* 23 (5): 897–917.

Townley, Barbara. 1993. Foucault, power/knowledge and its relevance for HRM. *Academy of Management Review* 18 (3): 518–545.

———. 1994. *Reframing human resource management. Power, ethics and the subject at Work.* Thousand Oaks: Sage.

Ventrice, Cindy. 2003. *Make their day! Employee recognition that works.* San Francisco: Berret-Koehler Publishers.

References

Voswinkel, Stephan, Isabelle Bernet, and Emmanuel Renault. 2007. L'admiration sans appréciation. Les paradoxes de la double reconnaissance du travail subjectivisé. *Travailler* 18: 59–87.

Wieviorka, Michel. 2013. Le travail aujourd'hui. L'hypothèse de la reconnaissance. *La nouvelle revue du travail* 2: 1–60.

Xenophon. 1933. *Economique. Notice par Pierre Chambry*. Paris: Garnier.

Chapter 3
Rebuilding Management

Abstract This last chapter aims to rebuild management by starting with a paradox and an analysis. The paradox of excellence concerns the forgetfulness of their limits by managers who are supposed to have all the qualities and talents. However, it is within the framework of a dialectic between strengths and vulnerabilities, between reign and burdens, that 'capable' management can be reconsidered. As for the emergence of joy in the context of collaborative work, which we attempt to analyse in the current pandemic context, and which only occurs in the amplification of individual power and the experience of conviviality (where individuals see their desire to live amplified). In the last sub-chapter, a definition of management is then put forward as a "vulnerable force in organizations subject to the pressure of numbers and endowed with a triple power of constraint, imitation and imagination exercized at the subjective, interpersonal, institutional and environmental levels". These different notions are finally discussed in an attempt to test a philosophical understanding of management, one that is free from the obsolescence of ancient "protomanagement" and the outdated and dubious prescriptions of "scientific management".

Keywords Business education · Containment · Free qualities · Joy at work · Managerial condition · *Negotium* · Paradox of excellence · Powerlessness · Suffering · Tyranny of numbers · Vulnerability

3.1 Leadership or the Powerlessness of the Powerful

> If power is essentially force and capacity for action and government, why should it assume the rigid, cumbersome and 'glorious' form of ceremony, cheering and protocol? What is the relationship between economy and glory?
>
> Giorgio Agamben, *Homo Sacer, II, 2: Reign and Glory. For a theoretical genealogy of economy and government.*

© The Author(s), under exclusive license to Springer Nature
Switzerland AG 2023
G. Deslandes, *Postcritical Management Studies*, Ethical Economy 65,
https://doi.org/10.1007/978-3-031-29404-4_3

3.1.1 The Paradox of Excellence

Questions of authority and the ability to command, and the relationship between managerial power and the success of organizations, have been fundamental facets of management sciences since their inception.[1] In the writings of Henri Fayol in particular, the manager is the one most clearly endowed with a certain set of qualities (moral qualities, general culture, intelligence), not least among which are bodily power, health and physical vigour.[2] The enumeration of the manager's talents, of his mastery of the tools as well as of himself, is at the heart of the many definitions of the ideal archetype which have succeeded these very first orientations. The field of *leadership* research has gradually been added to this literature, spawning a large body of texts devoted to the positive capacities and characteristics of the manager/leader. Two words that we hardly dissociate here, a point on which I will explain later, as one can be considered as a "superior variation" of the other.

It is interesting to note the multiplicity of the terms used to define this power: charismatic,[3] heroic,[4] authentic,[5] virile,[6] transformational,[7] shared,[8] distributed,[9] visionary,[10] etc. These notions are forever jostling to grasp the essence of this particular force that is *leadership*, which nevertheless seems to be slipping away, as at least two recent schools of thought argue.

The first of these axes is to be linked to *critical leadership studies*, perhaps best embodied by Simon Kelly's article which proposes to define this force on a principle of non-substantiality, not as an object of knowledge in itself, made up of personality traits, practices or *processes*, but as a signifier that would contain nothing in itself but emptiness.[11] The latter is thus a space of "absent presence" in which are expressed the plural expectations and hopes emanating from the desire for leadership that we experience, not least because of its seductive side (more than management in any case), its sacred character, and finally its infinite adaptability/plasticity.[12] A negative ontology of this kind allows us to glimpse the fundamentally renegotiable character of leadership, highlighting the fact that, within a given cultural and psychological context, it is always more or less arbitrary.

---

[1] This chapter reproduces the conference given at CRESO, Research Centre for Social Entrepreneurship, in September 2014, entitled "Vulnerability in business: the challenge of a renewal of ethical aims".

[2] H. Fayol 1916.

[3] J. M. Howell 2005.

[4] C. Manz and H. Sims 1991.

[5] W. Gardner et al. 2011.

[6] G. Powell and D. Butterfield 1979; C. Kulich et al. 2007.

[7] B. Avolio and B. Bass 1985.

[8] C. Pearce and A. Conger 2003.

[9] K. Grint 2010.

[10] H. Ibarra and O. Obadaru 2009.

[11] S. Kelly 2014.

[12] K. Grint 2010.

3.1 Leadership or the Powerlessness of the Powerful 93

The second line of research can be credited to Thomas DeLong and Sarah DeLong who note, in an article in the *Harvard Business Review*, that leadership capacities "are diminished when *high* achievers (exceptionally successful managers) are unable to recognise their weaknesses, their weak points, their "limitations."[13] Therefore, for these authors, it is by confessing one's mistakes to the people one works with, by admitting the uncertainty that most often guides decision-making, that one finally shows oneself in the best light, hence the title of the article in question: "The Paradox of Excellence." This orientation is partly reminiscent of Peter Drucker's criticism of charismatic leadership theories, published as far back as 1986.[14] Drucker argues that such ideas prove to be the downfall of leaders who believe they are invested with superior powers, which in reality makes them inflexible, because they perceive themselves as infallible and are unable to change their position when the environment changes.[15] In fact, not admitting one's vulnerability "can have disastrous consequences"[16] by preventing other managers from recognising their own difficulties; we are here opposed to attempts to define leadership on the basis of its strength alone (charismatic, heroic, visionary, etc.), and which fail to explore its negative side, that of vulnerability and powerlessness.

I hope to show that, in *leadership*, power is not separable from impotence and arbitrariness. To do so, I will begin by identifying a dialectic of strength and vulnerability, and then turn to an anthropological analysis based on the notions of capacities and incapacities, with particular reference to the work of Paul Ricœur.

3.1.2 Activity or Burden: Managerial Polarities

The emergence of the term *leader* in this field of management research – and of the more general theme of leadership – must be understood as the logical consequence of this inflation of traits that define the leader of a well-performing organization. As Jonathan Gosling and Henry Mintzberg have rightly noted, we must not be too hasty to separate management from leadership, to make one the counterpoint of the other, under the pretext that management without leadership would lack style and that leadership without management would encourage the negative power of *hubris*.[17]

If leadership very rapidly emerged as a subject of management research (for Mary Parker-Follet or Chester Barnard, for example), it is surely because it is a natural and almost immediate extension of management, embodying the power of the effective leader. It is also, as Birgit Schyns and Michelle Bligh rightly note, because attributing the success or failure of an organization to its leader is,

---

[13] T. DeLong and S. DeLong 2011:119.

[14] P. Drucker 1986.

[15] C. Manz and H. Sims 1991.

[16] T. DeLong and S. DeLong 2011:122.

[17] J. Gosling and H. Mintzberg 2003.

compared to all other potential factors, the simplest explanation.[18] This tendency to believe that organizational phenomena can be explained simply by the actions and decisions of the leader(s) finds its first scientific expression in *Great Man Theory*. It is extended, in a constructivist perspective, by the work initiated by Meindl, Ehrlich and Dukerich around the notion of the *romance of leadership*[19] (or RoL). Taken as an implicit theory of organizations, this notion allows us to better understand the mythical and symbolic character of the terms used in the field of leadership, and to explain how leaders give it its own radiance and power.

To avoid separating leadership from management too abruptly, let's return to the word *oikonomia* as Marie-José Mondain identifies its different meanings in Byzantine literature, including "different terms such as incarnation, plan, design, administration, providence, office, accommodation, lie or trickery."[20] The term is therefore polysemic to say the least. It is understandable that in administrative management – in an economic-managerial environment, at any rate – the aim is to guide each other's behaviour in order to achieve certain goals. However, if we go back to Aristotle's *Economics*,[21] a twofold direction emerges from the outset, which has already been discussed here: on the one hand, what he calls *chrematistic*, which is the method available to increase wealth, and on the other, something more qualitative, which has to do with the well-being of the city, its *administration*. This ancient definition of proto-management allows us to establish a dynamic imbalance between *managerial power* and *managerial charge*.

What elements allow us to establish this double polarity of the notion? Later, well after the Greeks, during the first centuries of our era, among the Fathers of the Church in particular, we find the term *oikonomia* employed to designate "the whole of providential nature, the incarnational plan and the strategic adaptation of the means to the ends which will be subsumed by one and the same concept."[22] "It is because God is *oikonomos*, i.e. the supreme administrator and manager, that the whole of his creation in the universe is *oikonomia*."[23] For Paul, it also refers to "God's purpose for the salvation of mankind."[24] The first polarity of management is that of sovereignty, dignity and strength. And that is not all; as Giorgio Agamben shows, *oikonomia* is "something that is entrusted: it is therefore both an activity *and a burden*,"[25] i.e. a responsibility, a weight, a liability, a charge. We have here a second polarity, the potential for fragility, less power, almost no power. In support of this idea, Giorgio Agamben explains:

> What Aristotle tries to conceive of in the *Treatise on Metaphysics* is not power as a mere logical possibility but the actual modalities of its existence. This is why, in order for power not to vanish each time immediately in the act but to have its own consistency, it must also

---

[18] B. Schyns and M. Bligh 2007.

[19] J. Meindl et al. 1985; J. Meindl and S. Ehrlich 1987; Meindl 1990.

[20] Here we rely on M.-J. Mondzain 1996: 27.

[21] With Xenophon's *Economics*.

[22] M.-J. Mondzain 1996: 34.

[23] *Ibid.*: 52.

[24] *Ibid.*: 47.

[25] G. Agamben 2008: 48.

3.1 Leadership or the Powerlessness of the Powerful

be able not to pass to the act, whether it is constitutively the *power not to* (do or be), or, as Aristotle says, whether it is also impotence (*adunamia*).[26]

Is it actually through non-action that leaders truly reveal their power, by not doing something which is within their power?

> That which has the power to exist can just as well exist or not exist. The power to be and not to be are thus one and the same [...] This deposition of powerlessness does not mean its destruction but, on the contrary, constitutes its fulfilment, the way in which power turns towards itself in order to 'give itself to itself'.[27]

Here we have a possible theoretical interpretation of the article by Thomas DeLong and Sarah DeLong: maintaining the option of renouncing its own power, true power retains the possibility of denying itself.[28] Ultimately, true power recognises its vulnerability according to the expression used by Pierre Chambre in his introductory note to Xenophon's Economics:

> Economics is a science that can be taught, but a lot of talented people, capable of putting this science into practice, are hindered by their passions, and remain *embarrassed*.[29]

This is the paradox of *oikonomia*: it will either be synonymous with strength or with embarrassment and fragility. In management, as Marie-José Mondzain shows, there is certainly an articulation of "the incessant coming and going between the visible and the hidden, between the enigma and the mystery,"[30] but also, in the very dynamic of the concept, a permanent tension between the statement of authority and the expression of doubt, of feverishness, a tension that we now need to decipher.

3.1.3 Reign and Charges

Oikonomia finally appears to be on the side of the "reign", and therefore of a desire.[31] It embodies this persevering power, it oversees it through norms, agendas, constraints, gratification. It thus implies a power-over, and may resort to certain capacities such as trickery or manipulation in order to concentrate power and deprive others of all power to act (power to confer impotence, one might say). Being above all a force, it is immediately on the side of politics because it concerns the balance of power between men and, to a certain extent, the government of consciences: to produce "zealous, conscientious and diligent workers"[32] is in the first place the means and the goal of "ménagement" (or management). The natural bent of the

---

[26] *Ibid.*: 54.

[27] *Ibid.*: 55.

[28] T. DeLong and S. DeLong 2011

[29] P. Chambry in Xenophon 1933: 327.

[30] M.-J. Mondzain 1996: 57.

[31] G. Agamben 2008.

[32] Xenophon 1933: 420.

manager, we could just as well say of the leader, is *hubris*,[33] the impression of being able to control everything, of being able to "deliver."[34]

One author who very clearly elucidates the propensity and intention (yet another translation of *oikonomia*) of the will to dominate is Blaise Pascal.[35] This temptation is also very well illustrated in an important book on management by American scholar Robert Jackall, *Moral Mazes: The World of Corporate Managers:* "Power struggles are a constant and recurring feature in business, fundamentally shaping the experience and perspectives of managers."[36] To understand the managerial arena is to venture into a realm where measurement devices and calculation tools help to orient human behaviour in a certain direction, to the benefit of the person who controls this environment. This is also why, necessarily, the position of the manager is envied. And the manager has no chance of escaping this mimetic situation.[37]

In his *Three Discourses on the Condition of the Greats*, Pascal very clearly demonstrates that behaving as a "Great" (in his mind, a person who has means that others do not have) is about being the master of men's desires and having the capacity, if need be, to satisfy them. The powerful should therefore have no illusions about the deep reasons for their authority; it consists in using the strength that their social position and the means at their disposal give them to, as Xenophon would add, "do good, by Zeus, whenever the gods grant us some abundant harvest."[38] The power of the manager consists in the devotion of those who work to increase the *oikos*, which depends on the share of prosperity that will be reserved for them in case of a good harvest: it is "the one who gains most from the conservation of the patrimony and who loses most from its decadence, [who] is most interested in watching over it,"[39] Xenophon reminds us. Pascal, faithful to his theory of orders, offers this even more radical and abrupt formulation in his Third Discourse:

> Satisfy their just desires, meet their necessities, take pleasure in being beneficent. Advance their interests as best you can and you will act as a *true king of concupiscence (ie lust)*.[40]

3.1.4 Management as a Charge

If strength is indeed the first word, is it also the last word of management? There is reason to doubt it. *Oikonomia is* translated by charge, as we have said, but also by accommodation. There is something negative in management, something that resists it.

---

[33] M. Kroll et al. 2000; R. Brown and N. Sarma 2007.

[34] R. Damien 2013.

[35] G. Deslandes 2011.

[36] R. Jackall 1988: 24.

[37] "Wealth exposes its possessor to the covetous gaze of others. It does not matter that others covet what does not deserve to be coveted, what counts is the covetous gaze itself," J.-P. Dupuy 2012: 25.

[38] Xenophon 1933: 388.

[39] *Ibid.*: 378.

[40] B. Pascal 2006: 14–15.

3.1 Leadership or the Powerlessness of the Powerful

An executive supposedly high up in the hierarchy may be *de facto* devoid of effective power (lack of legitimacy, lack of authority, short-circuiting by his or her subordinates, etc.), and conversely, an employee at the bottom of the hierarchical line may exercise power that exceeds the official prerogatives of his or her position. [...] In an organization, everyone exercises power, no matter how fragmented and minimal it may be.[41]

The manager has to face resistance, but also ambiguity, uncertainty and change. Managing is also about coping, dealing with it. It is the role of techniques, and of raising them to a theoretical, even scientific level, to serve as a support point and to help the manager in his decisions.

This negative aspect has scarcely been addressed in the management literature. An important exception is David Sims' 2003 article 'Between the millstones: a narrative account of the vulnerability of middle managers' storying.' The author draws upon numerous testimonies to illustrate the 'loneliness, precariousness and vulnerability,'[42] of the middle manager, who is placed in an impossible relational triangle: she has to show her authority vis-à-vis the teams she is in charge of, while at the same time what she says is particularly fragile in that her hierarchy can question her at any time. It is a question of communicating meaning to others, while knowing that this meaning becomes senseless when the strategy evolves, when the regime of "successive truths" is set in motion. For this is precisely what characterises *middle management* in the eyes of *top management*: its inability to influence strategic decisions, which in turn is the responsibility of another level, the political level that is supposed to define seniority in management.[43]

In short, line managers are caught between a hierarchical superiority, to which they are legally subordinate, and employees who generally wish to rise in the hierarchy. David Sims explains: "It is when managers reach the middle levels of the hierarchy that they have the least control over the plot of the stories they tell and experience on a daily basis."[44] The major problem is that middle managers, squeezed between the expectations expressed by their team and their characteristic 'political' powerlessness, end up in a moral crisis, knowing that they are unable to keep their promises if the course of events changes significantly (a new strategy, a new shareholder, a new customer, more frequently a new boss, etc.). However, as David Sims points out, perhaps paradoxically it is at the higher level that this weakness becomes even more obvious:

The survivors [among the middle-managers] of this process go on to be called senior managers; they often find that, like the mountain climb where an apparent summit turn out to have been obscuring higher peaks behind it, there were constraints on their senior managers' story telling of which they knew nothing previously. The hope that one more stop would take them out of range of the millstones may be unfounded.[45]

---

[41] M. Barabel et al. 2013: 81.

[42] D. Sims 2003: 1195.

[43] A top manager is defined by his or her ability to influence the strategic decision by participating in the committees responsible for defining it.

[44] D. Sims 2003: 1208.

[45] *Ibid.*

98   3 Rebuilding Management

Thus, the strength of the manager is relative; it would rather be an effect of strength or a sign of strength, but not real strength. This is why, to 'reign', explains Giorgio Agamben, *oikonomia* must necessarily add 'glory'.

> How can one show that one has plurality for oneself, i.e. the strength of several arms, if not by signs: hair, embroidery, ribbons, etc., as Louis Marin describes it, signs which are less those of beautiful finery and noble appearance in the eyes of the people than effects of strength. [...] The strongest "speaks" only to express his triumph. He may well say: 'Justice is unjust;' this statement is an expression of his domination.[46]

But by this very fact, the Reign shows its limits, an indication of its non-substantiality, its vicariousness.[47] If strength shows itself to be so strong as to become a doxology, a prayer of praise, particularly addressed to this kind of manager called leaders, it is because it knows itself to be vulnerable, subject to precariousness.[48] Agamben describes this glory as an "uncertain zone:"

> If power is essentially force and effective action, why does it need to receive ritual acclamations and songs of praise, to put on bulky crowns and tiaras, to submit to painful ceremony and immutable protocol – in short, why must operativity and *oikonomia* stand still in hieratic glory?[49]

Isn't this "hieratic immobilisation in glory" precisely what we see in the spectacle of the business press, for example? As they are presented in this type of media, "leaders" appear by definition flawless, over-powerful, they embody power itself, they are omniscient, efficient, dominating. However, this "sporting"[50] image of management and leadership seems to contradict the findings of countless studies which show how much less powerful managers are today than we imagine. As Jean-Philippe Bouilloud points out, the life of a senior executive is "beset by storms and the risk of destruction, and where one runs the permanent risk of definitive failure. In short, behind the amiable and virile games, there is a very clear battle for survival."[51] The executive is under permanent tension, torn between regal and vicarious postures, assigned to a constraining and supposedly free organization; hence

---

[46] L. Marin 1981: 35. Compare Pascal's evocation of frivolous finery in this passage from *Les Pensées*: "Our magistrates have known well this mystery. Their red robes, the ermine in which they wrap themselves like furry cats, the courts in which they administer justice, the fleurs-de-lis, and all such august apparel were necessary; if the physicians had not their cassocks and their mules, if the doctors had not their square caps and their robes four times too wide, they would never have duped the world, which cannot resist such an original presentation. If magistrates had true justice, and if physicians had the true art of healing, they would have no occasion for square caps; the majesty of these sciences would of itself be venerable enough. But having only imaginary knowledge, they must employ those silly tools that strike the imagination with which they have to deal; and thereby in fact they inspire respect" (Laf. 44).

[47] An organ which, through its own functioning, makes up for the functional deficiency of another organ.

[48] G. Agamben 2008: 215.

[49] *Ibid.*: 297.

[50] J.-Fr. Chanlat 1998.

[51] J.-Ph. Bouilloud 2012: 11.

3.1 Leadership or the Powerlessness of the Powerful

these phenomena of fatigue, stress, "paradoxical injunctions"[52] and suffering at work, which form a paradoxical and anxiety-provoking zone around the managerial function. It is as if these outer displays of strength conceal an underlying impotence, as if managers were "partly the bearers of the discourse and ways of thinking that they endure and deplore."[53]

Accepting fragility is anathema to the self-representation of management and leadership. Viewing management as a theatrical simulation that takes the place of reality, as a game of appearance, as a spectacle,[54] is not a new idea; Adam Smith himself considered the economy as an arena in which the members of a society tell stories to one another,[55] a tacit and unifying lie, held together by a spirit of reciprocity, so that anybody seeking to step outside this framework will inevitably cause a disturbance to public order. This deception ("Admit that I am a leader, I will pretend to believe that you are a doctor") is the ground on which "leaders" establish themselves by "grimaces," by a "body of signs."[56]

3.1.5 Between Capacities and Incapacities

Approaching this problem from another analytical angle, this time anthropological, we can interpret this twin polarity of management in terms of capacities and incapacities, with particular reference to the already mentioned philosophical work of Paul Ricœur.[57] His analysis is an anthropological one, because it contains a reflection on the condition of man in the world. In *Finitude and Guilt. Fallible Man*, which constitutes the second volume of his *Philosophy of the Will*,[58] Ricoeur draws on Pascal's *Pensées*, and in particular on the passage referring to the two infinites, entitled "Disproportion of Man". What does Pascal say?

> Returning to himself, let man consider what he is in comparison with all existence; let him regard himself as lost in this remote corner of nature; and from the little cell in which he finds himself lodged, I mean the universe, let him estimate at their true value the earth, kingdoms, cities, and himself. What is a man in the Infinite?[59]

---

[52] "This is particularly the case for Marc, responsible for evaluating client risk, but whose department reports to the business manager, who has nothing to gain from having Marc put too many obstacles in the way of his teams. Thus the paradoxical injunction mentioned above is very clearly reflected in Marc's dual dependency, in relation to his function and the activity in which he is engaged," J.-Ph. Bouilloud 2012: 105.

[53] *Ibid.*: 44.

[54] G. Debord 1992.

[55] J.-P. Dupuy 2012.

[56] L. Marin 1981: 36.

[57] P. Ricœur 1960; G. Deslandes 2012a.

[58] P. Ricœur 1960. Translated in the United States in 1986.

[59] Pascal, *Pensées*, ed. L. Brunschwig, 72.

As man is placed in this uncomfortable situation between the two infinites, the infinitely large and the infinitely small, he has nothing fixed to which to relate, so his action is never perfectly mastered, never quite certain. As Pierre Magnard puts it, nobody is quite sure whether man is at rest or in movement.[60] Ernst Wolff elaborates:

> In the heat of the moment, the exercise of a capacity leads to the manifestation of a disability – the specific relationship between capacity and disability revealing the degree of competence of the organisation in carrying out a set of actions.[61]

Elsewhere, Wolff pursues this line of reasoning as follows:

> To say that incapacity and capacity are not simply two mutually exclusive dimensions of action, but are constitutive of each other, means that incapacity, despite its 'negative' character, contributes to making the agent capable of doing things; similarly, capacity, despite its 'positive' character, contributes to making the agent incapable of doing other things or doing them in other ways.[62]

Here we are once again faced with what we must call a paradoxical definition of human capacities. Ricoeur's proposed solution to this paradox hinges on the concept of *practical wisdom*.[63] The capable man, for Ricoeur, is to be found on the side of Aristotelian *phronésis* (prudence). There is no doubt that, in Paul Ricoeur's case, this capacity inevitably passes through a stage of consultation, of debate among the members of the community, giving the lie to the pure verticality of political power. It is in fact a question of developing a legitimate capacity for judgement *in a situation*; for Ricœur, the *phronimos*, the one who expresses the prudential judgement, is sometimes unable to exercise his/her judgement alone.

In his work on medical judgement, he shows that the capacities of each individual can compensate for the shortcomings of others, with each playing a differentiated role. The man of action can be considered capable when he shows himself to be attentive to his own inadequacies, demonstrating an ability to listen to the claims of others, situating himself within the logic of the probable, the plausible.[64] According to Ricœur, this is the most important feature of the individual in action: the "capacity to choose for a reason, to prefer this to that, in short, the capacity to act *intentionally*."[65]

3.2 Working Without Joy?

> There are rare natures [...] who would rather perish than work without joy.
> Nietzsche, *The Gay Science*, §42.

---

[60] P. Magnard 1997.

[61] E. Wolff 2014.

[62] E. Wolff 2013: 54.

[63] G. Deslandes 2013.

[64] G. Deslandes 2012a.

[65] P. Ricœur 1991: 257.

3.2 Working Without Joy?

Can a book whose objective is to redefine management really afford to avoid the question of work?[66] Surprisingly enough, many authors appear to think so. However it is no easy task to discuss management in relation to work, in its original sense, which traces its roots back to the Latin *labor*, punishment, or *trepalium*, an instrument of torture. Management, on the other hand, is often presented as a performance mechanism intended to achieve satisfaction, completion, and the positive exaltation of effort.[67] Nonetheless, management professionals would do well to remember that it is precisely because of the laborious nature of work, its arduousness, that management exists. The task of management is to define work, to say what it should be, what form it should take, with the aim of reward – essentially salary – but which may take various other forms of recompense or recognition. It therefore implies a logic of finality.[68]

Moreover, if work, which most often amounts to nothing more than being paid to serve the interests of others, were only a pleasure, a joy, would we still need management to be efficient? In the end, is it work that needs management or management that needs work? Management always appears to have an ambiguous relationship with work: it regards work as indispensable, while at the same time belittling it, since the role of management is to cut down on work, to streamline it – as demonstrated, for example, by Taylor's "systematic study" of the time required to perform physical actions and tasks, as discussed by Armand Hatchuel.[69] The aim appears to be to cancel work as an experience, as a test, in order to replace it with an expert methodology devoted to rationalising production. Why is it those who do not "work" who are most interested in defending it?

This equivocal relationship will be the first topic studied in the present chapter, by means of a critical analysis of work. I will argue that the strength of a "collaboration" is defined by the extent to which it allows each "collaborator" to access the same shared life experience. I will define this experience, when it occurs, as joy. Since work itself is not necessarily joyful (which is why the title "working without joy" speaks to everyone), what might joy at work look like; what does it mean to work joyfully?

Philosophy, on the other hand, is interested in work and very little in management. The philosophy of work covers, as the philosopher François Dagognet explains,

> questions that affect the whole city – wages, prices, company relocation, automation of tasks, industrial society – questions that fall within the discipline of philosophy; and it is these questions that have laid the foundations for an initial analysis of work.[70]

---

[66] This section is based on an article published under the title "Le travail désaffecté ou la joie, enjeu managérial et social," *Le Portique*, 35/2015, document 4: http://leportique.revues.org/2818

[67] S. Fineman 2006. This text shows the agony of "*fun*" and "*feeling happy*" at work.

[68] E. Berns 2000.

[69] Ar. Hatchuel 1994: 60–61.

[70] Fr. Dagognet 2013: 24.

André Gorz and Michel Henry, who can be numbered among the contemporary thinkers most interested in this subject, agree that the very nature of work precedes not only all forms of collaborative organizations, but also the economy itself. For the latter, work is presented as the very power to create value and therefore cannot, in itself, be compared to any other value in particular. It is precisely the place where the economy can be thought of from the outside, where the "being" of action occurs. This position is at odds with the economic analysis of labour, according to which it is one value among others, but treated as a negative quantity – hence the notion of disutility, or negative utility, in economics. Labour is seen as a costly effort, through which the worker obtains a wage that allows him or her to benefit from advantages, in this case purchasing power.

For Henry, on the other hand, work is the necessary condition for all forms of economic organization, as well as of the economic sphere itself. Without work, the economic world is without reality and therefore without value.[71] This is precisely what theorists of political economy have never been able to understand, according to Henry, as they devote themselves to their favourite themes without ever questioning the nature of reality, which by definition eludes them. André Gorz concedes that wealth is created through work, only to then contrast this work with real work, work on oneself, especially the work of the author, artist or researcher, which is its own "primary goal, and not an exchange value."[72] Work as understood from the ontological angle, the being of work, constitutes a second angle from which to approach this classic philosophical question.

3.2.1 Work, Suffering and Joy

It should be pointed out that the individual at work has been the subject of number of studies by sociologists and contemporary psychiatrists, as well as philosophers, encompassing various themes such as creation[73] or suffering.[74] As Yves Schwartz notes, however, the multidisciplinary analysis of work poses "a problem of epistemological recomposition: where the sociologist will speak of 'integration into the company', the economist will see an increase in profitability through the liberation of working capacities, and the psychologist of 'joy at work'. In this concrete example, we see the disadvantage of a 'narrow positivism' which claims to 'compartmentalise' and separate into different dimensions that are totally integrated into reality."[75] For what can these notions of suffering work and creative work mean to the philosopher, where joy – whether it is missing or occurring – seems to be the tipping point?

---

[71] M. Henry 1976, 2003.

[72] A. Gorz 1988: 220.

[73] P.-M. Menger 2009.

[74] Ch. Dejours 2009.

[75] Y. Schwartz 2012: 848.

3.2 Working Without Joy?

Jacques Noiray selects this significant passage from Jean Giono's novel *Que ma joie demeure*:

> When the daffodils are in bloom, Mme Hélène, perhaps not yet convinced, will ask her question again: 'And what are you going to do with them, Jourdan?' – 'Nothing,' he'll say, 'it's just for fun. I'm tired of doing sad work.'[76]

Giono appears to draw a rather classical contrast between action for pleasure and the utilitarian character of work. This opposition between utilitarian value and expressive value is found in many authors, with variations: in Hannah Arendt (*The Human Condition*), work serves to provide the means of satisfying bodily necessities (food, shelter, etc.), while works plural (*l'œuvre*) are a matter of cultural experience. In Sigmund Freud's conception of work, there is a very clear and irreconcilable opposition between *labour* (always more or less hetero-determined and excluding joy from the field of possibilities) and *opus*, where the motivation is intrinsic,[77] coming closer here to creative work of any kind (scientific, philosophical, literary in particular) and which supposes the pursuit of objectives that do not fall into the category of necessity. From this point of view, joy at work in its primary sense seems to be clearly distinguished from joy in the managerial sense of the term: joy at work would be intrinsic to the work itself and secondarily to the production of a work of capital importance for its author (and whose evaluation, incalculable, would remain subjective). Managerial joy, meanwhile, is more narrow in its focus, not on the work itself but purely on results, calculable and defined in relation to predetermined goals.

Workers are thus held to be concerned about themselves and their work, or themselves as work, while managers use their own work and the work of others to achieve heterogeneous objectives, generally of a quantitative nature. On the one hand a higher form of possible joy, on the other hand a form of equivocal pleasure, often disqualified in the eyes of philosophers, a kind of pleasure irremediably linked to economic well-being which, as economist Tibor Scitovsky notes, even when it grows regularly does not necessarily make us happier.[78]

Lurking behind this contradiction between the concrete joy of the worker and the questionable pleasure (i.e. without real substance) of the manager, we find Karl Marx. He placed real work at the centre of his philosophical system, recognising its central role in human activity, making work the main factor in the realisation and emancipation of the human being. Dominique Méda and Patricia Vendramin quote the young Marx, who wrote the following in 1844:

> Let us suppose that we had carried out production as human beings. Each of us would have in two ways affirmed himself and the other person. In my production I would have objectified my individuality, its specific character, and therefore enjoyed not only an individual manifestation of my life during the activity, but also when looking at the object I would have the individual pleasure of knowing my personality to be objective, visible to the senses and hence a power beyond all doubt.[79]

---

[76] J. Noiray 2002: 71–72.

[77] C. Dejours 2009.

[78] T. Scitovsky 1976.

[79] D. Méda and P. Vendramin 2013: 31.

104   3 Rebuilding Management

He adds:

> I would have been for you the mediator between you and the species, and therefore would
> become recognised and felt by you yourself as a completion of your own essential nature
> and as a necessary part of yourself, and consequently would know myself to be confirmed
> both in your thought and your love. In the individual expression of my life I would have
> directly created your expression of your life, and therefore in my individual activity I would
> have directly confirmed and realised my true nature, my human nature, my communal
> nature.[80]

Thus, at work, an absolutely positive value is recognised as a revelation of the real
power of my personality and my life, since my creative abilities are manifested,
which is to say, to use a buzzword beloved of contemporary management-speak, the
specificity of my *talents*.[81] Also, adds Marx, this revelation of the self through production – production as work on oneself – finds its corollary in an increase in socia-
bility: it would be like a mirror reflecting the importance of others, of their
recognition revealed even in the works of labour. This position of course contains an
implicit criticism of forms of work that would be something other than a power of
revelation for oneself and for others. Even if Marx "believes in the civilising mission of big industry,"[82] his work always contains an insurmountable ambiguity
between this vision of work as emancipatory and vital, and the idea of work as
punishment, as the dominant classes constantly "improve" its restrictive character.

In Nietzsche, on the contrary, the social character of work is the object of strong
criticism. Shouldn't we rather avoid expecting too much of it? In *The Dawn of Day*
he writes:

> In the glorification of 'work,' in the tireless speeches on the 'blessing of work,' I see the
> same ulterior motive as in the praise of impersonal and useful acts: namely the fear of
> everything that is individual.[83]

It is not the self-reflective character of labour that is called into question here, but
rather the notion of "mirror production" for the benefit of society as a whole. For
Nietzsche, this notion only aims at "powerfully hindering the taste for reason,
desires, the taste for independence."[84] Apologies for work serve the interests of
those who do not want to hear about the singular worker, this worker-individual who
refuses "the petty goal" that is "constantly presented to him at the sight" of "easy
and regular satisfactions."[85] In The *Gay Science* he adds that "there are those of a
[...] rare nature, who prefer to perish rather than work without joy."[86]

This reflection from Nietzsche, and the double drama that inspires it – work
without joy and its disastrous consequences, appear to have a direct bearing on the

---

[80] *Ibid.*

[81] A term that hides a number of difficulties. See M. Painter-Morland et al. 2019.

[82] Y. Schwartz 2012: 755.

[83] Fr. Nietzsche Daw of the day, 1880, & 173.

[84] *Ibid.*

[85] *Ibid.*

[86] Nietzsche The Gay Science, 1989, § 42.

3.2 Working Without Joy?

subject of this book. The dual posture inherent to management, caught between dominance and vicariousness, appears to leave managers with an impossible task. The imbalance of this dual posture, as we have seen, is already present in the notion of *oikonomia* itself. Indeed as we noted at the outset, managers are the socio-professional category most affected by stress,[87] fatigue, *burn-out*, etc., but also by all kinds of health problems such as MSDs (musculoskeletal disorders, nervous depression, excessive consumption of anxiety medication, skin, heart and tension problems, etc...). Pascal Chabot has devoted a book-length study to this large-scale social phenomenon:[88]

> Today, *burn-out* is becoming a real epidemic in many countries around the world. We are not to blame, it is the world and the *nature of work* that has fundamentally changed. The world of work – be it in companies, hospitals, schools or public services – has become cold, hostile and demanding, both economically and psychologically. Individuals are emotionally, physically and spiritually exhausted. The daily demands of work, family and everything else have ended up eroding their energy and enthusiasm. The joy of success and the satisfaction of having achieved one's goals are becoming harder and harder to achieve, and professional *dedication and* commitment are disappearing.[89]

Why managers are often more affected than others by this moral and spiritual exhaustion is open to question. How can they be both tormentors and sufferers at the same time? Managers are sometimes the standard-bearers for an impoverished discourse on work, far removed from any notion of *gaudium* (Latin for joy), and of which they are the first victims. "How can one objectively complain about a situation to which one has long adhered, and from which one has hoped, and sometimes obtained, real benefits?" Jean-Philippe Bouilloud asks.[90] Real benefits which make one think of the easy and regular satisfactions evoked by Nietzsche, which abolish quality in favour of quantity, and which add to the "systemic stupidity" of the elites described by Bernard Stiegler, "deprived of knowledge about their own logic."[91] Deprived of knowledge, unconscious victims of some deceased economist, as Sumantra Ghoshal says using Keynes,[92] and who no longer even have the capacity to defend capitalism "against itself."[93]

At this point I should perhaps make it clear that I have no intention of taking the hunter-gatherer of the Palaeolithic age, or indeed the craftsman of the medieval world, as a model for the future.[94] My goal is to open up perspectives on living

---

[87] "More than one in four employees say they are regularly exposed to stress at work. Occupations are exposed to stress in different ways. [...] It is frequent in management functions (36%)," D. Méda and P. Vendramin 2013: 130.

[88] The latter itself draws upon the work of Christina Maslach, Professor of Psychology at the University of California, Berkeley, author of the *Maslach Burnout Inventory*.

[89] P. Chabot 2013: 27.

[90] J.-Ph. Bouilloud 2012: 44.

[91] B. Stiegler 2009: 68.

[92] S. Ghoshal 2005.

[93] B. Stiegler 2006: 174.

[94] P. Chabot 2013.

work, for the benefit of future collective and collaborative action.[95] Vincent de Gaulejac is right to say that "leaders are [today] unable to produce alternative models while remaining within positivist, functionalist and utilitarian paradigms. In fact, they are going around in circles."[96] Management no longer appears to be capable of transcending the management models (Toyotism, *downsizing*, etc.) set down in the last century.

3.2.2 Management and the Being of Work

Management studies may be interested in work – at least to a certain extent – but never in the *being* of work. The same is true of Smith's political liberalism, which deals with the basis of the economy but never with the nature of work itself. For the historic strain of Marxism whose doctrine was formed before the publication in 1933 of the *German Ideology*, the essence of labour is only recognised within entities such as "social classes," economic laws, the qualifiers generally reserved for skilled and unskilled labour, etc., but never for the being of labour itself.[97] In short, as a representation of concrete work, of real work in the objective/external mode constantly attacked by Michel Henry throughout the two volumes of his *Marx*:

> It is Marx's analysis which taught us that the exchange of goods was nothing original but a secondary phenomenon which refers, in its founding possibility, to this act of establishing individual labour as social labour from the outset, that is to say, to the substitution of abstract labour for real labour. In this process, which consists of substituting ideality for subjectivity, lies the constitutive alienation of the market economy [...] Quantifying labour, when subjective *praxis* is elusive, means replacing it with a system of objective and ideal equivalents, essentially quantifying the *time* spent working.[98]

Is it not rather within ourselves, at the heart of our emotional experiences, in the world of life, that the reality of work is anchored and rooted? The idea brings the work of Simone Weil to mind.[99] It is in the powers of our subjectivity and their extension into all life experiences that the actual reality of work itself must be situated and evaluated, *praxis* rather than *poiesis*, where the very movement of life itself is revealed as a need:

---

[95] "Is economy violence, as a tradition from Marx to the current critique of capitalism affirms? Is the economy the remedy against violence, as a liberal tradition from Montesquieu to Hayek thinks? Is the economy a remedy or a poison?" J.-P. Dupuy 2012: 49. Management can be remedy or poison, remedy and poison: it is neither good nor evil in itself. There is good management just as there is bad management. There is no reason to believe that the end of capitalism should entail the disappearance of management (it would perhaps be intensified).

[96] V. de Gaulejac 2012: 64.

[97] M. Henry 2008b.

[98] *Ibid.*: 89.

[99] Of which Joël Janiaud notes that "the factory diary is turned towards understanding the working world, between the omnipresence of things, which must be analysed, *and the presence of the human, which must be experienced,*" J. Janiaud 2009: 613.

3.2 Working Without Joy?

> Whether through food, sexuality, clothing, work, art, religion, etc., all these actions are only possible because of a need that drives the living self to work to fill that need. It must be stressed that these needs are needs produced by life and for life.[100]

This is as far removed as one can imagine from the Heideggerian unveiling, which considers *praxis* to be insignificant in the sense that it is a "fabrication" identical to the productions of nature. As such, it is not the machines that work, nor any tool or mechanism whatsoever. It is through reality itself that the nature of work can be grasped, and this reality is the reality of subjectivity and affectivity which alone has the power to bestow value upon objects and things.

For Henry, therefore, the economy finds its foundation in life. It is in life that use value finds its principle and its end;[101] life, where the values themselves are created, where the power to create values and to attribute them to things is found, whence the reality of action[102] also springs. Society as a whole is based on this power of life as an increase in the constant creation of new use values. All of which stands in stark contrast to the following description, proffered by Michel Henry in 2008:

> Being separated from living work, the world of tools has also lost all meaning and all conceivable finality: broken machines from which all movable parts have been stripped away, husks of engines, idle workshops, deserted hangars with broken windows, building sites closed for months, for years, barrows with outstretched arms that no human hand will grasp – these are not even simple objects, existing in the way that stones or soil exist: they are inhabited by a colossal sense of loss, eating away at their dying presence, and it is indeed death that has taken over this world, suddenly no longer wanted by life, to which it has ceased to communicate the miracle of its strength and its joy.[103]

3.2.3 The Dialectic of Suffering and Joy at Work

Let us now attempt to summarize a number of elements which shall be important going forward. First of all, Michel Henry retains from Marx the essential point that *praxis*, real action, is always subjective. Work is not the only example of a transformation and attempt to master the outside world. He also draws heavily upon Nietzsche's analysis of strength and weakness.[104] The weak and the strong do not inhabit their characters in the same way: for the weak, it is a question of maintaining an identity at all costs, whatever its discordance with their deep emotional life and its associated feeling of unease (*burn-out*). For the strong, it is a matter of resisting the temptation to conform to a civil identity that is constantly reconfigured by the gaze of others, but always to retain the strength that comes from the increase in their power to act.

---

[100] O. Ducharme 2012: 62.

[101] G. Dufour-Kowalska 1980.

[102] G. Jean 2011.

[103] M. Henry 2008a: 131.

[104] M. Henry 1985.

But how, then, are we to understand the state of suffering at work? For Michel Henry, there is no possible representation of suffering. If such a representation were possible in any form for an individual, it would mean that he or she had finished suffering.

Slipping out of oneself into the beneficial separation that would unburden it from itself, into a noematic unreality that would be nothing more than the representation or thought of suffering, is what, in its suffering reality, suffering can never do.[105]

There is no possible distance between the terms here. The one who suffers is her suffering because it is unquestionable, no one can deny in her place this suffering that she is.[106] It cannot be the subject of collective deliberation because it concerns the subject who experiences herself in all points of her being.[107]

Thus suffering is a pure feeling, a "material" reality in the sense of Michel Henry, i.e. it is neither visible nor objective. It is therefore not measurable. Its opposite is therefore not health, which is indeed measured, visible and statistically objectifiable, but joy. If suffering is the disease of life, then health is joy. Suffering and joy are here the fundamental apriorical structures of the self-involved being, without deviation or the possibility to get rid of oneself. These two ontological tones of affectivity are not separable from each other either. Michel Henry adds:

Don't all our impressions pass away, do they *not* constantly change, *not in the non-being of the past at the moment they vanish*, but in another and always "new" impression – uneasiness in well-being, desire in appeasement, hunger in satiation, anxiety in rest, suffering in joy, despair in bliss?[108]

I am therefore as heavy as my working day has been, and as light as the satisfactions it has brought me, condemned to bear its weight as well as to experience its elevation. Suffering is undoubtedly fragility, passivity, but it is also power, because it is the test of oneself, the testing of oneself as suffering, its unveiling.[109] It reveals the individual to herself, and puts her in a position to create the conditions that will allow her to "grow," to get out of her original and suffering passivity.

---

[105] M. Henry 2000: 85.

[106] "As far as those who suffer are concerned, the very project of behaving towards their suffering as if it were something we could appreciate, circumscribe, explain, relieve, *know, disregards it in* principle, neglects the decisive fact that suffering occurs entirely in a dimension of being to which there *is no other access than that suffering itself*" (1985: 325).

[107] It is as if correlated to the self. To put it in the words of Pascale Molinier: "What makes me suffer in work is *myself in the* situation, it is my own actions, what I do and what I disagree with, what I do not do and suffer from not being able to do; but also, and perhaps above all: what I do without really knowing why I do it and whether I do it *well*. [...] But this "doing better" does not respond to an external injunction to the subject, it cannot be instrumentalized; it is part of a goal of doing well – of living well – *relative to oneself*," P. Molinier 2002: 137–138.

[108] M. Henry 2000: 83 (italics in the original).

[109] F. Martins 2006.

3.2 Working Without Joy?

Deep down, failing to escape suffering is a good thing (we can detect Henry's Pascalian side here[110]), even if we constantly try to get rid of it without ever succeeding, for it is a revelation of the affective life, that is to say, of the very possibility of gaining access to enjoyment. It is by depriving ourselves of the possibility of suffering, which would in fact amount to annihilating the self-affective life itself, that we not only deprive ourselves of the possibility of enjoyment, but also potentially increase the platitude of our existence, which amounts to creating the conditions for another form of suffering, of a life questioning its own destiny and direction.

3.2.4   Joy and Cooperation

As our reflection advances in this direction, one difficulty becomes increasingly clear. Management makes cooperation an essential principle and requirement; management would not even be a valid topic of discussion if the possibility of cooperation did not exist. However, although the existing literature in the field of management has largely obscured the care-of-the-self that managers owe to themselves (as much as they should be mindful, to a certain extant, about the care that others owe to themselves),[111] the fact remains that, by definition, it focuses primarily on collective action and collaborative modes of action. As such, the question remains as to how self-growth at work benefits from the collaborative aspects of management. And how can collective action, because of its unpredictability, its natural tendency to iron out differences between individuals, its propensity also to submit one's own work to the judgement of others, be at the same time a factor in amplifying the power of individual action? By what miracle could this be possible, or even conceivable?

The classic response of management studies would surely invoke common interests, or even, to adopt an "ethical" approach: this is the role of the *credo*, for example, which companies use to assert their values loud and clear in order to define their territory, their culture, the organizational identity shared by the members. But what values are we talking about? In Michel Henry's opinion, there is only one value that allows collective action to cohabit with individual dynamics, and that single value is life.

It is precisely by experiencing solidarity, sometimes conviviality, in the ordeal of work, that individuals see their desire to live increase. Enthusiasm at the heart of cooperation, rooted in the experience of living the same life (the principle of metaphysical equality), is the best way to recognise in others the selfhood they cannot fail to have. As Éric Faÿ writes:

> When our heart is in our work (metaphor of the desire of the Other in action) and our actions admit of a desire for that which is beautiful, good and just (Aristotle), and a taste for a job well done in the interest of others, work becomes a matter of craft or even creation. [...] The

---

[110] T. Berlanda 2013.

[111] G. Deslandes 2012a.

110   3 Rebuilding Management

> desire of the Other then manifests itself as an unconscious, creative power granted to all, the
> power to create together, by speaking, listening to each other, activating and combining
> singular powers and capacities.[112]

What seems important is the original definition we have here of living together in
the experience of work. Simone Weil "writes in her *Factory Journal* that she has
gained from her experience of workers' misfortune an ability 'to intensely savour
every moment of freedom or camaraderie, as if it were to be eternal – a direct contact with life'."[113] In the very subjective and pathetic experience of life itself, to
work is to establish links with others that are capable of accentuating joy or suffering. Our affective states depend to a great extent on this relationship with the original community of the living with whom we experience work. From this point of
view, Bernard Stiegler is right to suggest that "business is always an exchange of
know-how *and savoir-vivre*. This is why the French word "commerce" can also be
used to refer to conversation, and more generally to any form of fruitful social
relationship."[114]

This shared *savoir-vivre*, made possible by work, amounts to a sharing of the
experience of life with several living people, in which we can test the hypothesis of
a dialectical transformation of suffering into joy. Provided that we perceive expressions of fraternity in the resolution of a problem, in an appropriate response to a
difficulty arising in the context of the experience of work; provided that this gesture
of fraternity allows the sometimes absurd or often contradictory rules of a working
environment to be brought into line with the concrete activity of a *praxis*, even if
this convergence does not involve the transgression of common rules, or even the
avoidance of the prescriptions of the work commissioned.[115] In such circumstances
it becomes possible to transcend the impulsive character of a life relentlessly
attached to itself, crushed beneath its own burden, constantly seeking to shift this
burden, by means of an opposing movement which allows life itself to be more joyful.

In fact, the "transgression of pre-established rules" is not unrelated to this transformation.[116] One thinks here of the Bergson of *Mind Energy* (from which Michel
Henry thought he was so far removed):

> Joy always announces that life has succeeded, gained ground, conquered. All great joy has
> a triumphant note accent. Now, if we take this indication into account and follow this new
> line of facts, we find that wherever there is joy, there is creation; the richer the creation, the
> deeper the joy. [...] The merchant developing his business, the manufacturer seeing his
> industry prosper, are joyous, – is it because money is gained and notoriety acquired? No
> doubt, riches and social position count for much, but it is pleasures rather than joy that they
> bring; true joy, here, is the feeling of having started an enterprise which goes, of having
> brought something to life. Take exceptional joys – the joy of the artist who has realized his
> thought, the joy of the thinker who has made a discovery or invention. You may hear it said

---

[112] É. Faÿ 2014: 16.

[113] J. Jannicaud 2009: 624; OC, II, 253.

[114] B. Stiegler 2009: 27.

[115] Ch. Dejours 2009; V. de Gaulejac 2012.

[116] O. Babeau and J.-Fr. Chanlat 2008.

that these men work for *glory* and get their highest joy from the *admiration* they win. Profound error! We cling to praise and honours in the exact degree in which we are not sure of having succeeded.[117]

The triumphal character is also very present in Michel Henry. Joy is a triumph over impulse, over suffering, over death. We value joy, not solely when we are not sure that we are directing our efforts in the right direction, but when life is being tested more and more, when it has gained ground over the world, beyond "glory" and "admiration".

3.3 Dialectics of Containment

The successive periods of confinement experienced over the last three years have provided ample opportunity to experience a new "condition," existing simultaneously inside and outside of organizations, notably due to the displacement of professional activities into the domestic sphere through remote working, profoundly altering what it means to be "at home" (in every sense of the term).[118]

The first period of lockdown, lest we forget, also saw the Italians solemnly singing the *Canto della Verbena* from their windows, while the French attempted to temporarily escape the loneliness of social distancing, and assuage a certain sense of guilt, by taking part in applause sessions in honour of the medical staff fighting the pandemic.[119] One could see in these exercises in spontaneous conviviality the appearance of a form of diversion, of entertainment, in the sense intended by philosopher Blaise Pascal. Also in evidence, perhaps unconsciously, was a longing to escape the structures of our *confined* condition, a sign of our flagrant inability "to remain at rest in a room",[120] but also an unexpected, undeniable and perhaps more fundamental way of recognising our belonging to the same shared life, to a collective experience, to a sort of *affectio societatis*, as suggested before. In any case, these virtual *aperitivo* moments lay bare the emptiness of our lives, suddenly partitioned and turned in on themselves, suddenly stripped of recreation, diversion, frivolity and conviviality. Never is this emptiness so apparent as when we are deprived of communication (hence Pascal's decision to abandon his explorations of mathematics and physical sciences), which is why staying in contact becomes, strange as it may seem, the absolute number one priority at times of existential and detrimental

---

[117] H. Bergson 1919 (translation by H. Wildon Carr).

[118] This section is based on an article published in French in the *Revue économique et sociale* under the title "Nouvelles expériences touchant au trop plein", n°78 (1): 15–21, 2020b.

[119] https://theconversation.com/ce-que-les-manifestations-publiques-revelent-de-notre-rapport-au-monde-en-confinement-135090. Co-authored with Mar Pérezts.

[120] Br. 139.

112   3 Rebuilding Management

crisis. All this in spite of the fact that communication, and entertainment in general, provide only temporary solutions to the emptiness of existence.[121]

But lockdown also witnessed a surge in digital activity, the sudden advent of a form of digital overload contrasting with the "emptiness" of our lives. It is as if we were forever faced with a dialectical choice: overload, or the void. Like a pendulum swinging back, the end of lockdown brought about another change in the order of things, the emptiness of our confined, insecure existences giving way to the sensory overload of our disorganized – and sometimes disoriented – lives.

Let us now try to decipher these 'new experiences' of (the return of) overload, in relation to the "void" of lockdown, while trying to draw some provisional lessons for management as a discipline, and the condition of today's managers.

3.3.1 *"Feeling the Void" in Times of Lockdowns*

Let us therefore take the void as our starting point, the void that Pascal describes in the following terms:

> Nothing is so unbearable to man as to be in full repose, without passions, without business, without entertainment, without application. He then feels his nothingness, his abandonment, his insufficiency, his dependence, his powerlessness, his emptiness.[122]

The emptiness is to be understood here as a mixture of evanescence, damage and vanity. The self empties itself of its so-called substance, which is only a kind of arrogance, a chimera: everything has been evacuated, everything has been extinguished except the sense of absence.[123] The vacancy of the self is never so evident as when business time is over. And for Pascal there is no way out of this circle of activity and rest, because when activity has ceased, when rest has been hard won, then we feel abandoned, as if isolated, and we cannot bear it. The absence of movement, the interruption of our social lives was accompanied by an overload of information, bad news and boredom, laying bare our emptiness, our most fundamental inadequacy.

This is the point of departure from which we must attempt to make sense of the many complaints, quite unrelated to the disease itself, that lockdown has generated. Rather than providing us with a period of rest in which to reflect, to read, to "recharge," to meditate, to free ourselves from our habits and determinisms, the lockdown was in fact perceived as a missed opportunity. During periods of confinement, we either poured our efforts into distraction/entertainment, or into a sense of exclusion, or both. Suddenly deprived of our social life, we found ourselves in the state in which Pascal would have expected to find us. Weary of ourselves, listless, incomplete, defeated.

---

[121] For soon enough, as Pascal also says, "diseases come" (Laf. 407).

[122] *Laf.* 622.

[123] T. Berlanda 2013.

3.3 Dialectics of Containment

This glimpse into the void offered by lockdown is nothing new. What is new, however, is the contrast with the hyperactivity, speed and intensity of our "normal" lives. However, as soon as the end of lockdown was in sight, we immediately felt a surge in the number of tasks to be done, *deadlines* to be met, obligations to be managed. The world of yesterday and the day before came back with a vengeance, plunging us once again into the frantic rhythm of the "big now," into the almost uninterrupted acceleration of our ordinary rhythms, resulting in a renewed sense of overload: always so many things to do, others to catch up on, and a diminished capacity for mobilisation after months of apathy and anguish. No one more than the managers can testify to this process of simultaneous filling in and speeding up.

There are no happy tomorrows in the evening of existential emptiness, no break between sluggishness and *burn-out*, to evoke this "disease of the good American" as Pascal Chabot (2013) calls it. This disease, which is more dangerous to health than heavy smoking, is affecting more and more people at work, sparing no hierarchical level, and is a symptom against which the battle is far from won in the contemporary world of work, still dominated by management models[124] which leave no room for subtlety.

3.3.2 Contemporaneity of 'Too Much'

One author has recently spoken indirectly about this overflow that besets everyone by referring to what he calls a 'question of size'.[125] Drawing on the work of the jurist and political theorist Leopold Kohr, Rey explains that it would seem that 'there is only one cause behind all forms of social misery: excessive size. Excessive size appears to be the one and only problem permeating all creation. Wherever something is wrong, something is too big'. Something is actually overflowing, the container can no longer be contained. According to Kohr, the problem with our lives and structures is that we no longer have a sense of proportion, as gigantism, speed, *pleonexia* and other factors have increased the number and complexity of the problems we have to solve, so that we are no longer able to cope with them.

The therapeutic approach that he deploys aims to restore what the Greeks called *metron* (measure) to our arsenal of tools. The notion features prominently in the *Philebus*, signifying that nothing, neither truth nor the arts, can be worth more than this sense of measure which is the sovereign criterion. Everything must be subject to this essential condition of just proportion, harmony, balance and concordance between the parts. The danger to be avoided at all costs is overload, uncontrolled expansion, hyper-intensity, excessive growth – or decrease. The right thing would be to strike a balance, to respect the limits that must not be exceeded, to establish a sort of harmonious relationship between too much and too little, restricting growth

---

[124] Toyotism, Taylorism, downsizing etc.

[125] Rey 2014.

to manageable proportions. This is of considerable significance for the management of organizations.

In fact, this idea is not new either. In the *Nicomachean Ethics*, Aristotle extols the wisdom of standing on a *via media*, an in-between, a ridge between excess, or overload, and lack, the void. But is this virtuous philosophy, already mentioned above, in which the individual must equip herself with *phronesis* (which can be translated as prudence or even sagacity, depending on whether we are interested in ethics or strategy), still useful today? How are we to interpret it in the age of governance by numbers, the quest for maximum intensity, and the impossibility, at whatever level, of situating one's action in the long term?

Philosopher Pascal Chabot, cited above, recently questioned the value of measuring progress exclusively in terms of quantity, arguing instead for a more 'subtle' understanding of progress, progress considered from the angle of quality.[126] In some respects this brings us back to the quandary posed by Eubulides of Miletus in the fourth century BC, concerning the impossibility of defining the word "heap" in arithmetical terms.

This reflection forms the basis for Chabot's concept of 'qualitarism', a philosophy for a future world based on overcoming – or at least contesting – the tyranny of quantity and the logic of maxima, so prevalent in contemporary social life. For Chabot, it is a question of preserving the underground world of relationships and webs from which a society is constituted, its solidarities and its deep attachments. This preservation requires the maintenance – invalidated by Descartes in the seventeenth century, according to him – of (free) qualities that cannot be controlled or calculated and that are primarily associated with our subjectivities and sensibilities. *Tact* and *delicacy, the spirit of finesse* too, are invoked as means of offering our busy lives a qualitative alternative where, out of irony or elegance, we are content to keep our distance from emptiness as well as from surplus.

Moreover, the recent health crisis, which at the time of writing is far from over, has highlighted the inability of our calculocracies to position themselves in relation to questions of life and death that transcend all possible calculation.[127] These are essential questions which cannot be satisfactorily resolved either by economic notions of quantity (purchasing power, refusal to pay taxes, etc.), or by the scorecards generally used to inform decision-making.

3.3.3 De-intensification Strategies

Another way of apprehending this painful oscillation between emptiness and overflow could be to consider it from the angle of *intensity*, the main constituent of what Tristan Garcia rightly describes as "the ethos of humanity". If we reach the sphere

---

[126] P. Chabot 2019; G. Deslandes 2020a.

[127] J-P. Bouilloud and G. Deslandes 2020; M. Henry 1963.

3.3 Dialectics of Containment

of "overflow" it is by virtue of a principle of addiction: to fight against emptiness, the banal and uninteresting life, without strong emotions, without electricity, we devote ourselves to practices that quickly become addictive and which, by the same token, end up overflowing on the rest of our activities (alcohol, gambling, etc., but more generally the mobile phone, speed, mobility).

This intensity that we impulsively seek, constantly stoked by the advertising messages we absorb either willingly or by force, is not bad in itself: for a romantic experience, or a trip, or a relationship to be intense, taking us beyond the petty calculations of bourgeois life, is only regrettable or dangerous insofar as it implies a continual raising of the thresholds. The author quotes Thomas de Quincey: "every organism [...] which has received morphine for some time feels the need to receive it in increasing doses: it is a somatic need". In other words, without a strategy of de-intensification, without a strategy of preserving our inner electricity, this irresistible amplification of doses pushes us to overload, which then appears as a logical consequence, as something inescapable. Desperate as we are to escape the emptiness of existence (zero electricity), we must never neglect the risk of overload (maximum electricity), or else run the risk of permanently damaging our nervous systems.[128]

Finally, the experience of overload is perceptible as soon as managers everywhere open their diaries. It is the sheer number of things to manage, to think about and to do that give the sense of life overflowing. Managers in particular are subject to the injunction of stopwatches, clocks, deadlines and handover dates. Business time is forever at odds with more intimate and subjective times, neglected because we have no time to think about them. However, it is in this intimate space that we as individuals can reconnect with ourselves, and it is here, on an individual but also collective scale, that our action must be constructed for the long term. The time of full agendas, of constantly-growing "to-do" lists, is essentially an infinite extension of the domain of the short term. If societies today are incapable of setting the conditions for an ecological upsurge, for example, it is precisely because they are submerged by an overload of inessential and hurried questions.

Here again, it seems that a better division between social time and subjective time, between the small necessities of daily agendas – which achieve the improbable feat of being both empty of meaning and filled to the brim – and the requirement of long time – necessary for scientific and philosophical effort – in the resolution of the great economic and political questions of our time, are among the conditions of possibility of an authentic *care for oneself* that fights against *horror vacui* and all forms of saturation. This is a way of exercising the free qualities of which they are capable, a way of constantly renegotiating the imposed temporality and the level of intensity of their own lives in the direction of a better availability to themselves and to others.

---

[128] Moreover, among the possible strategies, three seem to me to show real potential: procrastination (against restlessness and superfluity; cf. Hodgkinson 2018), disconnection (from the smartphone and social media) and slowness (cf. M. Kundera 1997).

Of course, the conditions for regaining control of their capacity for attention and their availability to themselves and the world are also political.[129] However, self-regulation has a role to play in regaining a taste for slowness, silence and calm that can help decision-makers to become truly attentive once again. So that, serenely facing the void as well as the overload, and distancing themselves from both, they can, if only this once, philosophically agree with an economist, namely John Maynard Keynes when he writes, in his *Letter to our grandchildren*:[130] "a day will come when we will know how to 'honour [...] the charming beings who know how to take pleasure in things, the lilies of the field who neither work nor spin.'"

3.4 Redefining "Management"

In the light of these various philosophical investigations, I propose to define management as "a vulnerable force, subject to the pressure of numbers, with a triple power of constraint, imitation and imagination at the subjective, interpersonal, institutional and environmental levels". Let us try to take each of these elements and examine them in turn.

3.4.1 A Strength

If management is, as Boltanski and Chiapello state, "the global mechanism capable of inspiring all the functions of the organization,"[131] then we must admit that it is first and foremost an *impetus*, a vital impulse: a force. In managerial studies, this force irremediably reminds us of the 'visible hand' of managers as formulated by Alfred Chandler in a now classic work in which he describes the rise of managerial power in American capitalism.[132] On a philosophical level, this power is to be understood in the manner defined by Blaise Pascal, that is to say, a power which first of all concerns the hierarchical relations, and therefore the *political relationship* between people.[133] For Pascal, man has a will to dominate; can we truly hope to understand management without taking this domineering aspect of strength into account? The association with ideas of strength and force implies that management must also be understood, as I have argued, as a political concept.

---

[129] M. Crawford 2015.

[130] Quoted in Hodgkinson 2018.

[131] L. Boltanski and E. Chiapello 1999.

[132] A. Chandler 1989.

[133] G. Deslandes 2011, 2013.

3.4 Redefining "Management" 117

Jackall's book *Moral Mazes* book is exemplary in this respect. The sociological analysis of bureaucratic organizations necessarily involves a study of the system of power, privilege and domination.[134] The world of organizations is driven by the quest for power and the benefit that the person who controls it for his own benefit derives from it: "the boss gets what he wants."[135] It is particularly in the hands of leaders that the power to decide is, by definition, concentrated. In order to exercise this power, one must show his strength, the number of people under his supervision, "show by his hair that he has a valet, a perfumer, etc."[136] These are images that can be seen in all representations of the business world, as if, to use Giorgio Agamben's expression,[137] dominance requires glory. In Pascal's case, this starting point concerns what he calls the quest for "big jobs," i.e. the desire to keep the person who has reached the top of the bureaucratic ladder in his job ("the weariness felt when leaving pursuits to which one has become attached"[138]). It is not so much truth that dominates the social world as power, especially that of the principal social agent in whose hands the power to decide is concentrated.[139]

As Pascal also explains, force is a condition for justice. Disarmed justice – without force (financial force, media force, power of seduction, force of norms etc.) – runs the permanent risk of being challenged by a force more powerful than itself. The force of justice, to put it more simply, is without force. For "there are always bad people",[140] he reminds us, to contradict and accuse it, to say that justice is unjust and seize it by force.

For Pascal, justice must be strong, or else it cannot be exercised in the world. It is therefore the *ethical* question of the use of force that is constantly raised. Force must be thought of in terms of its "performance," but also in terms of those on whom it is exercised.

3.4.2 A Vulnerable Force

Management, if it is a capable force in organizations, is also a vulnerable one. The manager is capable, but he is also fallible, and can experience success as well as failure. If managerial power is often presented as an omnipotent, flawless and efficient force, in the business press in particular, this image has lost credibility. Paul Ricœur

---

[134] R. Jackall 1988: 10.

[135] *Ibid.*: 36.

[136] Pascal, *ibid.*, Br. 316.

[137] G. Agamben 2008.

[138] Pascal, *ibid.*, Br. 128.

[139] "This is the reality of our society," acknowledges one of the people interviewed by Robert Jackall, "I have to acknowledge that I am part of this society and I live with it. Our society is the way it is. It is based on money and power, it's as simple as that. The truth has nothing to do with it. We just accept the world as it is and live with it," R. Jackall 1988: 186.

[140] Pascal, *ibid.*, Br. 298.

118

has clearly highlighted, especially in some of his last writings, the singular position occupied by decision-makers, halfway between almighty power to act and radical fragility.[141] The manager is capable, the manager is fallible. Managers must define themselves, their narrative identities, in relation to these two poles, between capacities and vulnerabilities. The vulnerability and fragility of the manager also condition her capacity to question, to strengthen her autonomy and judgement. In short, beneath these considerations of strength and vulnerability, the question of justice remains.

Managers are indeed subject to the dictates of the markets and shareholders, but also to the wishes of the customer and the ever-shifting feelings of the partners. Management is not immune to the growing predominance of strictly financial logic. The economic world is becoming more complex every day,[142] and we know that not even the biggest companies are immortal (AIG, Leman Brothers, Enron, MCI Worldcom etc...). Managers in particular are the first victims (although certainly not the only ones) of the tyranny of numbers:[143] for the evaluation of their performance, compared to that of their competitors, but more generally in their daily life (permanent *reporting*, line-by-line accounting results, the omnipresence of statistical tools, etc.). From this point of view, the mastery of management *techniques* and best *practices*, in a mathematical economy, is crucial for managers who want to survive and endure. However, techniques are not everything, since, as the psychologists of the Palo Alto School have shown, managers are subject to many *paradoxical injunctions*:

> The profession of management is fast becoming an 'impossible practice' due to the proliferation of paradoxical situations, between internal demands focused on maximising profit through increased monitoring of the use of resources, and development imperatives which, on the contrary, increasingly place demands upon these same resources; between the demand for collective commitment and the individualisation of assessments, which leads to a permanent tension between competition and cooperation, etc.[144]

This is why I consider that know-how and life experience are central elements in the so-called art of management. Contemporary managers could do worse than recall the words of Socrates, for whom "care" is a matter of practical wisdom,[145] *sophrosune*, a form of virtue dependent upon human skills. Between its capacities and its vulnerabilities, between its mastery of techniques and the confrontation with incessant paradoxical injunctions, by questioning and reinforcing its autonomy, management can finally increase its capacities of judgement (*phronesis*). I will also study later on how this dialectical relationship between strength and vulnerability, between the weakness of strength and the strength of weakness, as it were, suggests the conditions of possibility of a "weak management" likely to renew our most outdated conceptions of the managerial function.

---

[141] P. Ricœur 2001.

[142] "When we listen to some leaders, we have the impression that their profession is a vulcanology: they certainly have seismographs that send back information that enables them to predict what is going to happen, but they are always surprised by certain movements, by certain expressions of agitation in their institution and its environment," J.-Ph. Bouilloud 2012: 111.

[143] D. Boyle 2001.

[144] J.-Ph. Bouilloud 2012: 27.

[145] D. Moberg 2007.

3.4.3 A Triple Power of Constraint, Imitation and Imagination

The power of constraint, through norms, rules, experts and exploitation (in the sense defined by James March),[146] is the other major political aspect of organizations. Management is a "dispositif", i.e. a set of practices and knowledge that aim to orientate in some way the collective action; this notion, which has met with great success in the social sciences in recent decades, particularly under the influence of Giorgio Agamben,[147] is essential in management because it allows us to study the way in which managers build structures and develop standards to achieve their goals. It should never be forgotten that the ability to "deliver", to finish the action undertaken or to close a file, is absolutely central in management. The manager is the one who finishes the programme and completes the mission: we find here Hannah Arendt's distinction between the two Greek verbs '*archein*' (to begin, to guide, and finally to command) and '*prattein*' (to cross, to go to the end, to finish).[148] There are many examples of apparatus to be found within organizations: codes of ethics, profit-sharing schemes, cost accounting, progressive career management, supply chain management and marketing management are just a few examples. Of course, they concern the *technical* aspects of management, but also managerial *praxis*, since these techniques are intended to be used in order to influence behaviour in a way that is useful to the action being taken.

The power of imitation is also an unavoidable phenomenon. Management is certainly not immune to the sort of competitive mimesis analysed by the anthropologist René Girard,[149] where intersubjectivity is analysed from the perspective of the desire of others.[150] Indeed, the desire of others counts more than the desired object, and this impulse can lead to escalation, which may go as far as the designation of a scapegoat as a temporary remedy.[151] In organizations, this process corresponds to that of institutional isomorphism. Faced with the complexity of the economic world, organizations and managers, as Paul Di Maggio and Walter Powell[152] have shown in scientific terms, copy one another in order to reduce uncertainty, but also to increase their legitimacy on the markets.

Finally, imagination is what limits the impact of constraint and imitation. It corresponds to the exploratory phase of management highlighted by James March,[153] the one that imagines alternative systems, that creates, innovates, even transgresses.[154] Power is freer and less likely to abuse its strength when it is capable of recog-

---

[146] J. March 1991.

[147] G. Agamben, see also H. Dumez 2014.

[148] A. Hannah 1993; H. Dumez 2014.

[149] R. Girard 1978.

[150] J.-P. Dupuy 2012.

[151] See on this point R. Jackall 1988.

[152] P. Di Maggio and W. Powell 1983.

[153] J. March 1991.

[154] O. Babeau and J.-Fr. Chanlat 2008.

nizing its own system of constraints (linguistic, financial, cultural, spiritual, etc.). The notion of moral imagination consists of reformulating moral conflicts in order to imagine morally acceptable alternatives that resolve the dilemmas faced by managers.[155] Moral imagination can therefore be defined as a faculty that accompanies, during the resolution of a problem, the overcoming of perceived norms, social roles and the usual relationships maintained by the actors involved. It is an ability to discover solutions to ethical questions that are not strictly determined by circumstances, nor by the usual mental models, nor by a series of previously prescribed rules or techniques.

3.4.4 Subjective, Interpersonal, Institutional and Environmental Levels

The powers of management must be thought of in terms of the four relationships – objective, interpersonal, institutional and environmental – in which they are exercised: the micro level, i.e. personal[156] and interpersonal,[157] the meso level, i.e. institutional,[158] and the macro level, which might also be described as societal and environmental.[159] Here we have four different relationships: the relationship to oneself (the subjective part), the relationship to others (the interpersonal part), the relationship to the institution (the institutional part) and the relationship to society as a whole (the environmental part). Faced with the globalisation of the economy, it is on each of these levels that both efficiency and responsibility can be assessed.

The inclusion of the relationship to oneself may come as a surprise, making room for subjectivity in an increasingly systemic and controlled universe; however, this aspect seems to us to be an *unsurpassable* foundation. In his final lectures at the Collège de France, Michel Foucault explored, with particular reference to Socrates, this relationship of self to self and what it means politically for those who have, or will have, the responsibility for the government of others. In the words of Foucault, a political thinker par excellence, "one saves oneself inasmuch as the city-stated is saved, and inasmuch as one has enable the city to save itself by taking care of oneself."[160] To govern others well, one must first be seen to be capable of having an autonomous relationship with oneself, in relation to one's social function, in relation to one's everyday activities. Otherwise, the manager acts as a *stultus*, remaining

---

[155] P. Werhane 2002; R. Rorty 2006.

[156] M. Alvesson and Gabriel 2013.

[157] D. Bevan and H. Corvellec 2007; D. Byers and C. Rhodes 2007; J. Desmond 2007; and R. Durand and R. Calori 2006.

[158] R. Subbady et al. 2010.

[159] P. Crifo and V. Forget 2012; C. Flammer 2013.

[160] M. Foucault 2001: 169, G. Deslandes 2012b.

open to all representations, but without questioning, as Foucault recommends, what they represent.

Subjectivity is therefore directly linked to the phenomenon of management insofar as it is above all a human affair; it concerns a world of living beings and not of resources, as those who believe that life can be covered with the modest veil of objectification would have us believe. Any criticism of management must bring us back to the basis of direct experience of "living work." The living are endowed with a *pathos*, i.e. a capacity for self-affection, which allows subjects to experience themselves as such.[161] Thus management should pay more attention to the radical immanence of the subjective action of living beings, their effective capacity for initiative and growth; it is best defined by the general concern to take care of humans affected by the activity of the organization for which it is made responsible. This is its ultimate goal, as well as its point of origin.

References

Agamben, Giorgio. 2008. *Homo sacer, II. Le Règne et la Gloire.* trans. Joël Gayraud and Martin Rueff, Paris: Seuil.

Alvensson, Mats and Yiannis Gabriel. 2013. Beyond formulaic research. In praise of greater diversity in organizational research and publications. *Journal of Management Studies* 50 (1).

Avolio, B. J., and Bass, B. M. 1985. *Charisma and beyond*. Paper presented at the annual meeting of the Academy of Management, San Diego, CA.

Babeau, Olivier, and Jean-François Chanlat. 2008. La transgression, une dimension oubliée des organizations. *Revue Française de Gestion* 183 (3): 201–219.

Barabel, Michel, Olivier Meier, and Thierry Teboul. 2013. *Les Fondamentaux du management*. Paris: Dunod.

Bergson, Henri. 1919. L'énergie spirituelle: Essais et Conférence. Trans. Wildon Carr. *Hibbert Journal* 18: 184.

Berlanda, Thierry. 2013. Michel Henry. Une nostalgie pascalienne. In *La Vie et les vivants. (Re-) read Michel Henry*, ed. Grégori Jean, Jean Leclercq, and Nicolas Monseu. Louvain: Presses Universitaires de Louvain.

Berns, Egidius. 2000. Philosophie de l'économie. *Rue Descartes* 28: 9–20.

Bevan, David, and Hervé Covellec. 2007. The impossibility of corporate ethics: For a Levinassian approach to managerial ethics. *Business Ethics: A European Review* 16 (3).

Boltanski, Luc, and Ève Chiapello. 1999. *Le Nouvel Esprit du capitalisme*. Paris: Gallimard.

Bouilloud, Jean-Philippe. 2012. *Entre l'enclume et le marteau*. Paris: Seuil.

Bouilloud, Jean-Philippe, and Ghislain Deslandes. 2020. *Life is not a quantity: Philosophical fragments concerning governance by numbers*, Impact paper 2020-20-EN. ESCP Research Institute of Management.

Boyle, David. 2001. *The tyranny of numbers: Why counting cannot make us happy*. New York: Harper Collins.

Brown, Rayna, and Neal Sarma. 2007. CEO overconfidence, CEO dominance and corporate acquisitions. *Journal of Economics and Business* 59 (5): 358–379.

Byers, Damian, and Carl Rhodes. 2007. Ethics, alterity and organizational justice. *Business Ethics: A European Review* 16 (3).

---

[161] Puyou and Faÿ 2013.

Caroline, Flammer. 2013. Corporate social responsablity and shareholder reaction: The environmental awareness of investors. *Academy of Management Journal* 56 (3): 758–781.

Chabot, Pascal. 2013. *Global burn-out*. Paris: PUF.

———. 2019. *Traité des libres qualités*. Paris: PUF.

Chandler, Alfred. 1989. *The visible hand of managers*. trad. fr. Fr. Langer, Paris: Economica.

Chanlat, Jean-François. 1998. *Sciences sociales et management – Plaidoyer pour une anthropologie générale*. Canada/France: Les Presses de l'Université de Laval. Editions Eska.

Crawford, Matthew. 2015. *The world beyond your head: On becoming an individual in an age of distraction*. Farrar: Straus and Giroux.

Crifo, Patricia, and Vanina Forget. 2012. Think global, invest responsible. Why the private equity industry goes green. *Journal of Business Ethics* 116 (1): 21–48.

Dagognet, François. 2013. *Philosophie du travail*. Paris: Encre marine.

Damien, Robert. 2013. *Eloge de l'autorité. Généalogie d'une (dé)raison politique*. Paris: Armand Colin.

de Gaulejac, Vincent. 2012. *La Recherche malade du management*. Quae: Versailles.

Debord, Guy. 1992. *La Société du spectacle*. Paris: Gallimard.

Dejours, Christophe. 2009. *Live work. Travail et émancipations*. Vol. 2. Paris: Payot.

DeLong, Thomas, and Sarah DeLong. 2011. The paradox of excellence – High achievers often undermines their leadership by being afraid to show their limitations. *Harvard Business Review*, June, 119-123.

Deslandes, Ghislain. 2011. In search of individual responsibility. The dark side of organizations in the light of Jansenist ethics. *Journal of Business Ethics* 101 (1): 61–70.

———. 2012a. Power, profits, and practical wisdom: Ricœur's perspectives on the possibility of an ethics in institutions. *Business and Professional Ethics Journal* 31 (1): 1–24.

———. 2012b. The care-of-self ethic with continual reference to Socrates: Towards ethical self-Management. *Business Ethics: A European Review* 21 (4): 325–338.

———. 2013. *Essai sur les données philosophiques du management*. Paris: PUF.

———. 2023. *Erotique de l'administration*. Paris: PUF.

———. 2020a. *A propos du management et d'un problème plus général*. Paris: PUF.

———. 2020b. Nouvelles expériences touchant au trop plein. *Revue économique et sociale* 78 (1): 15–21.

Desmond, John. 2007. Levinas: Beyond egoism in marketing and Management. *Business Ethics: A European Review* 16 (3): 227–238.

DiMaggio, Paul, and Walter Powell. 1983. The iron cage revisited: Institutional isomorphism and collective rationality in organizational fields. *American Sociological Review* 48 (2): 147–160.

Drucker, Peter. 1986. *The practice of management*. Perennial Library.

Ducharme, Olivier. 2012. *Michel Henry et le problème de la communauté. Soi, communauté, habitus,* doctoral thesis in philosophy under the supervision of Sophie-Jan Arrien, Laval (Québec), Université de Laval.

Dufour-Kowalska, Gabrielle. 1980. *Michel Henry, un philosophe de la vie et de la praxis*. Paris: Vrin.

Dumez, Hervé. 2014. Qu'est-ce qui fait la spécificité des sciences de gestion? Dispositifs et performance. *Libellio d'Ægis* 10 (1): 65–68.

Dupuy, Jean-Pierre. 2012. *L'Avenir de l'économie. Sortir de l'écomystification*. Paris: Flammarion.

Faÿ, Éric. 2014. Affects (situations stratégiques). In Franck Tannery (dir.), *Encyclopédie de la stratégie*. Paris: Vuibert,.

Fayol, Henri. 1916/1999. *Administration industrielle et générale*. Paris: Dunod.

Fineman, Stephan. 2006. On being positive: Concerns and counterpoints. *Academy of Management Review* 31 (2): 270–291.

Foucault, Michel. 2001. *Herméneutique du sujet. Cours au Collège de France 1981–1982*. Paris: Seuil/Gallimard.

References

François-Régis Puyou et Éric Faÿ. 2013. Cogs in the wheel or spanners in the works? A phenomenological approach to the difficulty and meaning of ethical work for financial controllers. *Journal of Business Ethics* 128 (4): 863–876.

Gardner, William, Claudia Cogliser, Kelly Davis, and Matthew Dickens. 2011. Authentic Leadership: A review of the literature and research agenda. *Leadership Quarterly* 22 (6): 1120–1145.

Ghoshal, Sumantra. 2005. Bad Management theories are destroying good Management practices. *Academy of Management Learning and Education* 4 (1): 75–91.

Gorz, André. 1988. *Métamorphoses du travail*. Paris: Galilée.

Gosling, Jonathan, and Henri Mintzberg. 2003. The five minds of a manager. *Harvard Business Review* 81 (11): 54–63.

Grint, Keith. 2010. The sacred in leadership: Separation, sacrifice and silence. *Organization Studies* 31 (1): 89–107.

Hannah, Arendt. 1993. *Condition of the Modern Man*, tr. fr. Georges Fradier. Paris: Calmann-Lévy.

Hatchuel, Armand. 1994. Frédéric Taylor: an epistemological reading. L'expert, le théoricien, le doctrinaire. In *L'Invention de la gestion. Histoires et pratiques*, ed. Jean-Philippe Bouilloud and Bernard-Pierre Lecuyer. Paris: L'Harmattan.

Henry, Michel. 1963. *L'Essence de la manifestation*, 4th ed. 2011. Paris: PUF. English version: Henry, Michel. 1973. *The essence of manifestation* (Trans. G. Etzkorn). The Hague: Nijhoff.

———. 1976. *Marx, I & II, Une philosophie de l'économie*. Paris: Gallimard. English version. Michel Henry, *Marx. A philosophy of human reality* (K. McLaughlin, trans.). Bloomington, IN: Indiana University Press, 1983.

———. 1985. *Généalogie de la psychanalyse*. Paris: PUF. English version. Michel Henry, *The Genealogy of Psychoanalysis* (D. Brick, Trans.). Stanford, CA: Stanford University Press, 1993.

———. 2000. Speech and religion. The word of God. In Dominique Janicaud & Jean-François Courtine (dir.), *Phenomenology and The Theological Turn: The French Debate*. New York: Fordham University Press.

———. 2003. *Phénoménologie de la vie, I. De la phénoménologie*. Paris: PUF.

———. 2008a. *La Barbarie*. 2nd ed. Paris: PUF. English version. Michel Henry, *Barbarism* (trans. S. Davidson). London and New York: Continuum, 2012.

———. 2008b. *Du communisme au capitalisme. Théorie d'une catastrophe*. Paris: L'Âge d'Homme. English version. Michel Henry, *From Communism to Capitalism. Theory of a Catastrophe* (S. Davidson, Trans.), London: Bloomsbury Academic, 2014.

Hodgkinson, Tom. 2018. *L'Art d'être oisif... dans un monde de dingue*. Paris: Les liens qui Libèrent.

Howell, Jane. 2005. The role of followers in the charismatic Leadership process. Relationships and their consequences. *Academy of Management Review* 30 (1): 96–112.

Ibarra, Herminia, and Otilia Obadaru. 2009. Women and the vision thing. *Harvard Business Review*.

Jackall, Robert. 1988. *Moral mazes. The world of corporate managers*. New York: Oxford University Press.

Janiaud, Joël. 2009. Les hommes et les choses : de Simone Weil à elle-même en passant par Levinas. *Archives de philosophie* 72 (4): 607–626.

Jean, Grégori. 2011. Présentation of "l'expérience métaphysique d'autrui" to "intersubjectivité en première personne". *Revue Internationale Michel Henry* 216–70.

Kelly, Simon. 2014. Towards a negative ontology of Leadership. *Human Relations* 67 (8): 905–922.

Kroll, Mark, Leslie Toombs, and Peter Wright. 2000. Napoleon's tragic march home from Moscow: Lessons in hubris. *The Academy of Management Executive* 14 (1): 117–128.

Kulich, Clara, Michelle Ryan, and Alexander Haslam. 2007. Where is the romance for women leaders? The effects of gender on Leadership attributions and performance based pay. *Applied Psychology* 56 (4): 582–601.

Kundera, Milan. 1997. *Le lenteur*. Paris: Folio Gallimard.

March, James. 1991. Exploration and exploitation in organizational learning. *Organization Science* 2 (1): 71–87.

Magnard, Pierre. 1997. *Pascal, ou l'art de la digression*. Paris: Ellipses.

Manz, Charles, and Henry Sims. 1991. Superleadership: Beyond the myth of heroic Leadership. *Organizational Dynamics* 19 (4): 18–35.

Marin, Louis. 1981. *Le Portrait du roi*. Paris: Minuit.

Martins. Florinda. 2006. L'autre: le corps vivant. In Jean-François Lavigne (dir.), *Michel Henry. Pensée de la vie et culture contemporaine*. Paris: Beauchesne.

Méda, Dominique, and Patricia Vendramin. 2013. *Réinventer le travail*. Paris: PUF.

Meindl, James. 1990. *On leadership: An alternative to the conventional wisdom. Research in Organizational Behaviour* 12.

Meindl, James, and Sanford Ehrlich. 1987. The romance of Leadership and the evaluation of organizational performance. *Academy of Management Journal* 30 (1): 91–109.

Meindl, James, Sanford Ehrlich, and Janet Dukerich. 1985. The romance of Leadership. *Administrative Science Quarterly* 30 (1): 98–102.

Menger, Pierre-Michel. 2009. *Le Travail créateur. S'accomplir dans l'incertain*. Paris: Gallimard/Seuil.

Moberg, Dennis. 2007. Practical wisdom and business ethics. *Business Ethics Quarterly* 17 (3): 535–561.

Molinier, Pascale. 2002. Souffrance et théorie de l'action. *Travailler* 1 (7): 131–146.

Mondzain, Marie-José. 1996. *Image, Icône, Economie. Les sources byzantines de l'imaginaire contemporain*. Paris: Seuil.

Noiray, Jacques. 2002. Utopie et travail dans *Que ma joie demeure* de Jean Giono. *Travailler* 1 (7): 63–76.

Painter-Morland, Mollie, Susan Kirk, Ghislain Deslandes, and Carole Tansley. 2019. Talent management: The good, the bad, and the possible. *European Management Review* 16 (1): 135–146.

Pascal, Blaise. 2006. *Trois Discours sur la condition des Grands et six liasses extraites des Pensées*. Paris: Gallimard.

Pearce, Craig, and Jay Conger. 2003. *Shared leadership: Reframing the hows and whys of leadership*. Londres: Sage.

Powell, Gary, and Anthony Butterfield. 1979. The "good manager": Masculine or androgynous? *Academy of Management Journal* 22 (2): 395–403.

René, Girard. 1978. *Des choses cachées depuis la fondation du monde*, 1978. Paris: Grasset.

Rey, Olivier. 2014. *Une question de taille*. Paris: Stock.

Ricoeur, Paul. 1960. *Philosophie de la volonté, II, 2 t. L'homme faillible*. Paris: Aubier.

———. 1991. *Lectures 1: Autour du politique*. Paris: Seuil.

———. 2001. *Le Juste, 2 t*. Paris: Éditions Esprit.

Rodolphe, Durand, and Roland Calori. 2006. Sameness, otherness? Enriching organizational change theories with philosophical considerations on the same and the other. *Academy of Management Review* 31 (1). https://doi.org/10.5465/amr.2006.19379626.

Rorty, Richard. 2006. Is Philosophy relevant to applied ethics? *Business Ethics Quarterly* 16 (3): 369–380.

Schwartz, Yves. 2012. *Expériences et connaissance du travail*. 2nd ed. Paris: Éditions Sociales, 1998.

Schyns, Birgit, and Michelle Bligh. 2007. Introduction to the special issue on the romance of leadership. In Memory of James R. Meindl. *Applied Psychology: An International Review* 56 (4).

Scitovsky, Tibor. 1976. *The Economy without Joy*. tr. fr. Martie Fiorini and Amanda Wilson, Paris: Calmann-Lévy.

Sims, David. 2003. Between the millstones: A narrative account of the vulnerability of middle managers' storying'. *Human Relations* 56 (10): 1195–1211.

Stiegler, Bernard. 2006. *Mécréance et Discrédit, t. II, Les Sociétés incontrôlables d'individus désaffectés*. Paris: Galilée. English version. Bernard Stiegler, *Uncontrollable Societies of Disaffected Individuals: Disbelief and Discredit, 2*, Cambridge: Polity Press, 2013.

———. 2009. *Pour une nouvelle critique de l'économie politique*. Paris: Galilée. English version. Bernard Stiegler, (2010) For a New Critique of Political Economy, Cambridge: Polity Press.

References

Suddaby, Roy, Kimberly Elsbach, Royton Greenwood, John Meyer, and Tammar Zilber. 2010. Organizations and their institutional environments. Bringing meaning, values, and culture back in. *Academy of Management Journal* 53 (6): 1234-1240.

Werhane, Patricia. 2002. Moral imagination and systems thinking. *Journal of Business Ethics* 38: 33–42.

Wolff, Ernst. 2013. Compétences et moyens de l'homme capable à la lumière de l'incapacité. *Études ricœuriennes/Ricœur Studies* 4 (2): 50–63.

———. 2014. *Who gets organised? Capacities and incapacities of the organisational man. Un plan de recherches*. Ricoeur/Ehess Fund Study Day. 16 April 2014.

Xenophon. 1933. *Economique. Notice par Pierre Chambry*. Paris: Garnier.

Conclusion: Postcritical Perspectives

Even sinners do the same. If you lend when you are sure you will be repaid, what gratitude can you expect? Even sinners lend to sinners so that they can be repaid. On the contrary, love your enemies, do good and lend without expecting anything in return" (Luke 6:32–34) (...) In this last phrase, which is likely to go unnoticed, we discover an essential feature of human relationships which we have not yet reflected on and which will constitute - therein lies the paradox - the reason for their condemnation by Christ: reciprocity.
Michel Henry, *Words of Christ.*

Is the lack of influence and legitimacy of management studies within the social sciences inevitable? An analysis of the Greek origins of the concept has shown us its richness, which can be understood as a set of techniques, a science in the making, a ratified collection of professional practices, an applied ethic or a form of political reasoning. The moderns have preferred, according to their epistemological or even ideological choices, to favour this or that approach to the detriment of the other four, making managerial discourse sometimes destitute and often inaudible. The era of postcriticism, at its beginning, would like to distinguish itself from this compartmentalised approach to the problem, with a willingness to 'narrate instead of judge' and to 'accept weakness instead of pretending to be strong'[1], based on a new conception of the managerial condition likely to confront the systemic stupidity of organizations with some chances of success. An era to which this essay would like to contribute in its own way, and which constitutes nothing more than a little step in that direction, aiming in particular to open the way – in managerial thought – to other philosophical approaches stemming from the developments of phenomenology.

By favoring a more multidimensional path, and by calling upon different approaches to contemporary management research, new perspectives will open up, enabling us to reconstruct the richness of the managerial imagination as first glimpsed by Xenophon. For that reason, I have proposed a new definition of the

---

[1] De Sutter 2019: 233.

© The Author(s), under exclusive license to Springer Nature
Switzerland AG 2023
G. Deslandes, *Postcritical Management Studies*, Ethical Economy 65,
https://doi.org/10.1007/978-3-031-29404-4

128 Conclusion: Postcritical Perspectives

term, affording priority to symbolic points of reference and philosophical concepts conducive to offering such perspectives, and temporarily putting to one side the conflict of interpretation that has been raging within the discipline from its earliest days. To this end, I have insisted on three key points: the dialectic of strength and vulnerability, which constitutes the basis of managerial action; its power of constraint, imitation and imagination; the framework of action situated in a quadruple concern for oneself, for people, for institutions and for the environment.

If I have urged on highlighting the twin polarity of management, of strength with regard to vulnerability and vulnerability with regard to strength, it is because the harmonious balance between politics and ethics seems to be a fundamental point; as long as it is strong and all-powerful, and only thus, management is true to its own projected image, its own staging, its own vanity. But when the feeling of fragility, weakness, confusion is mixed in, then the secret of politics falls like a mask.[2] "The secret of the absolute monarch," explains philosopher and semiologist Louis Marin, "is that he is not; this thought is hidden, never spoken, perhaps never thought."[3] Never thought through the illusion of power. "To be a superintendent, chancellor or first president,"[4] as Pascal says (and we might add editor-in-chief, deputy general manager or chairman of the board of directors etc...), essentially amounts to being surrounded by helpful people who prevent each of these "decision-makers" from having a lucid relationship with themselves. The feeling of vulnerability must act as a counterforce, and at least as a "double thought," as Pascal understands it when he describes this King, alone on an island and experiencing being "reduced to his royal substance." This double thought, through the demystification it brings about, stripping away the theatrical fripperies of the world, provides the necessary political outlet, that is to say, from the truth of the relationship with oneself and the concern for others as people in their own right.[5]

Managers, and particularly the "leaders" among them, are rightly placed to appreciate their real situation. Hence their adoption of strategic behaviours that try to adjust evolving collaborative situations. This can lead to absurd situations such as the one Matthew Crawford describes in his *Shop Class as Soulcraft*:

> For executives, the rule is therefore to avoid making real decisions, which may end up damaging their careers, but to know how to concoct *a posteriori* stories that will enable them to interpret the slightest positive result in their favour. To this end, executives are exclusively dedicated to manipulating abstractions, leaving the operational details to their subordinates.[6]

---

[2] Deslandes 2020.

[3] Marin 1981: 289.

[4] Pascal, ed. Brunschwig, 126.

[5] "From then on, the field of politics is immanently split between its own field, which is that of the lie and the conning of the subjugated by the one who governs them, and a section of this field which, set aside and apart, constituted in secret, witnesses withdrawal of politics into ethics, itself very generally defined as a reflection of oneself on oneself, as an autoposition of the subject in the reflection. Ethics is obtained by an operation of internal exclusion - if one dares to use this expression - from politics, it is the secret of politics, or this withdrawal of the subject from politics even by reflection on oneself. Ethics is the secret of politics in the sense that it is constituted by the place where the political is absent from itself, this place which is, however, that of the subject-supporter of politics," Marin 1981: 287.

[6] Crawford 2009: 61.

Conclusion: Postcritical Perspectives

This is as far as removed as it is possible to get from the initial promises of power, revealing in their place a kind of continuous fragility and underlying insecurity that prevents the slightest action.

At the very heart of the role of manager/leader, there is therefore a dual position to be held, with the political and social aspect of the function on the one hand and, on the other, the relationship with oneself. But these two aspects appear to be tailor-made for conflict, rendering the task particularly arduous. How can we 'manage' this point of tension and find the sweet spot where uncertain arrangements (another word for *oikonomia*) and precarious reconciliations between social, economic, political and ethical demands[7] can be created and imagined?

According to Robert Jackall's description of the state of the managers he met during his research, there is nothing left to save.[8] And yet, one cannot help but feel that the actor must have something more real to fall back upon than the remnants of the character s/he plays on the stage... because if the economic sphere were merely a theatre, how could a manager (or managed employee) be profoundly affected by it, much more so in any case than a simple spectator could be by a performance seen on a stage? How can managers (or those they manage) maintain their probity, whatever roles they are asked to play over the course of their careers, other than through the "compartmentalisation" of existence?[9] Finally, let us ask ourselves the question: can the life of managers/executives be reduced to a series of actions exterior to them?

If the 'compartmentalisation' of the self is indeed possible at the level of social functions, with the constraints this implies, it can never be effective at the immanent and affective level. This is not a set of "specifications" for managers, or any other person, to put into practice; it is the seat of their "life power."[10] Managers never cease to be people, people who experience themselves, outside of any social determination, or prior to any professional experience. This emotional growth operates on the same level of self-experience as the actualisation of one's work force, which is never more vigorous than when it is shared with others.[11] This is why all communities can trace their origins to encounters situated within social frameworks, where each person necessarily plays a visible role, but on a more fundamental level these are encounters between living people, within the community of the living, a community rendered all the more powerful by the fact that it exists outside of direct worldly experience.

Burn-out is a hell of mismatched roles, it is the manager reduced to the status of camel (Nietzsche), a beast of burden, tired of being human, not expecting anything

---

[7] To quote André Gorz on this point: "Professional and private life are dominated by radically different, even contradictory, norms and values. Thus, the private virtues of the good father, good husband, appreciated by his neighbours, may go hand in hand with the professional efficiency of the civil servant passing indifferently from the service of the Republic to that of the totalitarian state and vice versa," Gorz 1988: 66–67.

[8] Jackall, 1988.

[9] McIntyre 1999; Rozuel 2011.

[10] Gély 2007: 54.

[11] Deslandes 2012b.

130 Conclusion: Postcritical Perspectives

important for herself from her professional life, except to waste her life earning a living.[12] The self must constantly submit to the desire to be affected by life in the deepest part of oneself. But life is never so closely connected to the self as when it achieves the sense of joy evoked above. Failure to reach this condition drives a wedge between life and the self. If affectivity were not itself malleable and fragile, it would not have the capacity to be constantly reborn to itself, to experience itself with greater intensity.[13]

Drawing on Michel Henry, the psychoanalyst Christophe Dejours,[14] who has produced important research on the causes of suffering in the world of work, very rightly explains that "the person who is insufficiently sensitive is inevitably a clumsy person. He breaks the machines because he does not know how to feel emotionally when they are struggling. The clumsy carer destabilises the patient because he does not affectively recognise the anguish of the other. In order to experience reality affectively and therefore to know the world, we need a body, first of all, because it is with the body that we experience affects". The intelligence of the body, especially at work, shows itself precisely when a solution is found, that is, when the world is pertinently deciphered by the body in a space that Henry calls *Corpspropriation*, "where a subjective and affective familiarity between the body and the real is revealed".[15] So that new competences, new skills, new *savoir-vivre* and know-how always come from this encounter between a subjective and bodily experience on one side, with this real that resists them in the other.

Re-examining Our Managerial Condition

Thinking about organizations from a phenomenology of life or an ontology of vital praxis therefore[16] amounts, in the end, to taking on all the representationalist and materialist presuppositions, so prevalent in managerial literature, of 'production' and social relations. It suggests a question of returning to a real, sensitive and pathetic subjectivity of individuals, to the detriment of the 'pure' objective and the

---

[12] In exposing this will to power of the lion manager (*thus spoke Zarathustra*), has one finally, as Nietzsche thinks, lost all negativity, all weakness, all vulnerability? Are we certain that we are still driven by this desire to increase the power of life, which is basically the basis of what we have called 'strength'? There is reason to doubt it. As Raphaël Gély (2007: 12) shows, we must acknowledge "the intrinsic vulnerability of this desire".

[13] But in Michel Henry's work, as Olivier Ducharme (2012), Grégori Jean (2011) and Raphaël Gély (2007) have all remarked, this emotional debate is never experienced as deeply as it is at the moment of encountering other lives, and with the principle of the same connection. It can appear as if it were "by inner resonance" that others and I discover each other, "so that what others say, what they express and what they do is spoken, said or 'repeated' to each other, co-born 'in me' in such a way that I become 'contemporary'," Jean 2011: 58.

[14] Dejours 2021: 102.

[15] *Id.*, 103.

[16] Faÿ 2007a, 2007b, 2009.

Conclusion: Postcritical Perspectives 131

traditional modes of representation, particularly visual, of contemporary organizations. For the management of "human resources" as well as for questions of leadership and power, this radical phenomenological reading of the human condition as a *relationship to oneself in life* seems to offer important "philosophical data"[17] in order to have a more precise idea of the proper responsibility of management, its "ethics", as well as its true meaning.

For in all human experience, even economic, the question of the meaning of action should always be philosophically questioned, in order to avoid submersion in what Bouveresse (2011) in his text *"Can managers have an ideal?"* calls a sea of "realities and facts" that leads to absolute disenchantment and ultimately to the delegitimisation of managerial activities. What Bouveresse wants to denounce is a separation between, on the one hand, the men/women of reality, who swim to the point of suffocation in this sea of 'realities and facts', and, on the other hand, the idealists, those 'intellectuals who specialise in this kind of presentiments and inner jeremiads'. However, he also notes optimistically that this division of labour between intellectuals, capable of ideals, and merchants, is being reduced, particularly under the influence of the growing interest in philosophy within companies, and within management research (see, for example, the publication in 2015 of a special issue of the journal *Rue Descartes* devoted to "Variations on the philosophical question of management").[18]

This point is not foreign to the Henryian approach to organization developed in these lines. In his view, we can only intuit the world through our sensitive and living subjectivity, through pathos, through individual effort, through transcendental affectivity. It is thus strongly opposed to the quantifiable and mathematizable abstractions with which, since political economy was brought into being, we have been trying to evaluate work, so that the object of this science becomes a gigantic abstraction that no longer has anything in common with individual effort (which are called 'resources'). Overall, he only renews the Kierkegaardian effort, which he himself would acknowledge, by separating as clearly as possible the objective, communitarian, generic and normative side of morality (norms, laws, tradition) and its subjective side, which is of particular interest to us here, where the *I* poses itself as a critical force of appropriation.[19] This effort thus leaves an important place to what the Danish philosopher calls the individual-singular (*den enkelte*), to the personality, to the self, in a particularly original and significant way for managerial ethics, notably in the relationship with others. Thus, the Kierkegaardian conception of subjectivity is the opposite of a dreamy, narcissistic withdrawal, but the mediation of an exit from oneself in the direction of the other, with whom *I* enter *into* essential relationships that bring *me* into concrete existence. However, as Levinas (1976) also notes, the interiority of the other remains hidden. How, then, can we resolve this paradox and lack of transparency in the relationship with others?

---

[17] Deslandes, 2013.

[18] http://www.ruedescartes.org/numero/?numero=RDES_091.

[19] Politis 2002.

132   Conclusion: Postcritical Perspectives

In these pages I have sought to highlight the necessary conditions for a management that looks beyond quantity, beyond instrumental rationality, a management centred on vital *praxis* rather than on data or information flows. A vision of management which strives, if not to escape the idea of measurement altogether (how could the world of organizations do this? Would it even be desirable?), at least to recognise its share of incommensurability and invisibility.

In fact, recent events in economic life, such as the Volkswagen case (sometimes called "dieselgate"), have highlighted the limitations of a discourse which maintains that only that which can be measured has any value. The cost of moral mistakes is incalculable in advance, which is what makes them special but also gives them their particular importance in the business world: the BP case shows that the price paid by stakeholders can only be "calculated" – if ever it is – many years after the fact.

At this juncture we might well recall the distinction formulated by Philippe Corcuff between the "logic of social justice (as a response to the capital/labour contradiction) and a logic of development of singular individualities (as a response to the capital/individuality contradiction)."[20] This book has cleaved to the latter: to a vision of management no longer centred on the exteriority of quantitative objectives, a theory only reduced to mere objects relations, but also on a culture of collaboration between living beings.

Certainly the individual, the 'man of action' in particular, is generally defined by his desire to be the strongest. Yves Clot interprets this desire very accurately:

> The logic of competition, marketing and consumption, in which this entrepreneurial activity takes place, is a logic of denial of fragility and loss, a logic of repressed fear. In the capitalist market economy, individual entrepreneurs and consumers build, buy, sell, struggle, innovate, keep busy and creative, seek success and opportunities for growth, all to delay the realisation of their ultimate metaphysical loss, i.e. their fragility and mortality.[21]

I have endeavoured to show that this desire can only be fulfilled by accepting one's share of fragility, negativity and vulnerability. It is when the leader removes her mask of glory that she becomes fallible, but also capable.[22]

The managerial "I can" – its power – is inseparable from the "self-testing" that constitutes it,[23] and allows it to recognise itself as capable and responsible. Thus management appears as it was at the moment of its birth, at once a power and a burden. The philosopher Yves Michaud notes that the main lesson to be drawn from this duality is the "return to a human conception of control: neither complete (the fantasy of control), nor impossible (abandonment), but relative and measured."[24] Qualities that can hardly be considered exceptional, but which are representative of "a real being, present to things and to others as well as to itself."[25] It is imperative to

---

[20] Corcuff 2010: 250.

[21] Clot 2008: 217.

[22] Boubeker 2011; Ricœur 2001.

[23] Henry 1963.

[24] Michaud 2013: 229. See also Deslandes 2020.

[25] *Ibid.*, 209.

Conclusion: Postcritical Perspectives

get away from the heroic postures which, if we are to believe François Jullien,[26] characterize the western strategist more than any other. Rather than seeking to conform to the fictional archetype of the manager who is so sure of her methods and achievements, the usual heroic figure of the business press, managers would do better to show more concern for themselves and for others, having the strength to recognise the limits of their knowledge in the face of the intrinsic uncertainty, shifting contours and constant ambiguity of management situations.

So what remains of the managers and the managed? The living. Living people, not resources, defined by their *pathos*, that capacity for self-affection which ultimately underpins all reality. Living beings situated within the worldly configuration that falls to them, and whose joy comes from the ability to "allow" the growth of oneself and others. Management is thus essentially a matter of taking care of those living beings affected by an organization's activity. This encompasses concerns such as suffering at work and health in the workplace, major issues for contemporary organizations.[27] It is also worth noting that this concern for health at work predates Taylorism.[28] In this respect, management is definitively moving away from its Taylorian definition, which tended to disregard individuality and focus only on the activity itself. Management is therefore indeed a *pharmakon,* in the sense that Bernard Stiegler insightfully employed that term, i.e. a remedy, a medication, that can always become a poison (side effects being always possible).[29]

The solution proposed by Pascal Chabot is essentially a matter of defending and promoting what he calls, as opposed to useful progress, "subtle progress."[30] The word "subtle," used in much the same way that Blaise Pascal employs the term "finesse," seems judicious insofar as it denotes both ingenuity and perspicacity. It means astute, as well as complicated, piercing, cunning or flexible, words which are themselves linked to the etymological and historical meaning of the word management.[31,32]

---

[26] In his *Conference on Effectiveness*, he maintains that this conception belongs to the modern West alone: "Strategy is the opposite of heroism, as the Greeks already knew. So there is no glory in good management. I have known many entrepreneurs who have told me, after listening to me: indeed, I managed my company by exploiting all its assets, by unfolding all its possibilities. Nothing sensational, nevertheless its capital has never stopped growing, its sectors have diversified, its establishments have multiplied: it has never stopped strengthening and imposing itself. But when I left, no one thought of praising me." Fr. Jullien 2005: 42.

[27] Dejours 2009.

[28] As T. Le Texier explains: "We will first consider the primary meaning of the term 'management', which predominated in the XVIIth and XIXth centuries, and according to which (it) is an art of care": T. Le Texier 2011, p. 13. And further on: "This principle of care covers the prevention of moral and physical degradation and, if necessary, the application of medical treatment," *Ibid.* p. 18.

[29] Stiegler, 2008.

[30] Chabot 2013: 75.

[31] Agamben 2008; Mondzain 1996.

[32] The points discussed here are taken from the article "Le travail désaffecté ou la joie, enjeu managérial et social," *Le Portique* 35, document 4, URL: http://leportique.revues.org/2818.

134 Conclusion: Postcritical Perspectives

In fact, the figure of the manager often appears to be constantly caught between "the famous and sinister figure of the foreman[33] "and the "extraordinary, superior, learned leaders" who know how to inspire "pride in individual and collective discipline and joy at work, when it is necessary to work."[34] How can we escape the twin caricatures of the little boss and the great man, our stereotypes of those in power?

There is something negative in management, an elusive component, which obliges us to recognise its intrinsically fallible side. Accepting this fragility may damage the manager's aura of "glory,"[35] but it may also provide the courage required to shed that camouflage. Recognising one's own fragility, one's own fallibility,[36] and that of others – shared fragility, therefore – is to recognise the importance of autonomy. This is the price to pay for managerial authority: power (of technique, science, practice) is inseparable from *pathos,* from the "self-testing" that constitutes me as a human being,[37] and that allows me to recognise in myself a capable nature. Activity, vulnerability and responsibility are therefore reciprocal.

A better understanding of this difference between useful and subtle progress can only be achieved by highlighting, when this happens, the tyranny of measuring instruments. As the economist Tibor Scitovsky explains:

> Modern economists are not concerned with whether work is pleasant or not. They believe that its ungratefulness increases (or that its pleasantness decreases) with time and the amount of work done. Marginal work (i.e. the last extra work done) is, in their view, unpleasant and is done only for the income it brings.[38]

I have been quite critical of this definition of marginal work, insomuch as what we do for ourselves or for others in the context of work is ultimately denied and considered to be outside the economy (despite the existence of unpaid voluntary work, for example). In an essay entitled *The Tyranny of Numbers. Why Counting Cannot Make Us Happy,* Boyle convincingly demonstrates that flows of statistics, tons of figures and ratios actually merely simplify the problems, without resolving the big questions.[39] No one has ever met *"Mr. or Mrs. Average,"* the average person who serves as the point of reference for all forms of statistics. There are invisible dimensions to all organizations, they are underpinned by various strains of formal and informal logic, each with its own dose of the irreducible and the immeasurable,[40] remaining stubbornly out of reach of the prevalent calculocracy.

---

[33] Foucault 2001: 516.

[34] Xenophon 1933: 419.

[35] Agamben 2008.

[36] Ricœur 2001; Deslandes 2012b.

[37] Henry 1963.

[38] Scitovsky 1976: 98.

[39] Boyle 2001.

[40] As Tibor Scitovsky further states, "it is impossible to make even an approximate calculation to determine the value of the following four categories [...]: personal and self-acquired satisfaction, reciprocal stimulation, externalities, job satisfaction," Scitovsky 1976: 109.

Conclusion: Postcritical Perspectives

The question that then arises is how to "account for" the fact that managerial activity cannot be reduced to a simple series of calculations. One way would be to leave more room for the appreciation of beauty in management.[41] Another possible way would be to cultivate the sense of play or ironic distance.[42] We could add humour and wit, as envisaged by the philosopher and historian of philosophy Denis Kambouchner[43] in relation to education. It would then be a matter of promoting, according to the expression used by the author, an atmosphere of "enjoyment" within organizations.

This last point requires further reflection on subjectivity at work. Who are the individuals at work? Social roles? Agents in the system? Images? Resources? Talents? For my part, I have defined the individual at work as one with pathetic and emotional potential. However, nothing seems more harmful than to deprive an individual of the affective power with which she feels she is endowed. Michel Henry describes the consequences with searing accuracy:

> The whole immense process of resentment and bad faith that traverses the human world and gives it its dreadful aspect rests on an unshakeable foundation, on the ground formed by the suffering of the one who can no longer bear herself.[44]

For instance, one could note that contemporary French cinema has clearly seen this urgency. Aurélie Jeantet and Emmanuelle Savignac explain that it is "most often the subjective relationship to work that is the most fully-realised aspect of films, through the interiority of a central character."[45] *Whatever* (Extension du domaine de la lutte), *Work hard play hard* (Violence des échanges en milieu tempéré), *Louise Michel*, *Mammuth*, etc.[46] all movies that show the world of work as a struggle waged by individuals who can no longer stand themselves.

Tackling Systemic Stupidity

Let us attempt to consider how the pharmacological approach to technology within organizations, as evoked in Chapter 1, might help us to arrive at a new understanding of ethical reflexivity within organizations.

---

[41] Dejours 2009, Bouilloud and Deslandes 2012.

[42] Fleming and Spicer 2003.

[43] Kambouchner 2013.

[44] Henry 1985: 297.

[45] Jeantet and Savignac 2012: 44.

[46] The authors note that the Dardenne brothers' films "have gone from documentary to fiction, notably to adapt their cinema to this change, work being less and less the stake of collective struggles to become more and more an individual and subjective issue. (...) Fiction would then be better able to capture, through the staging of singular destinies, the responses given to the precariousness of work and employment," *ibid.*, 44.

The importance of "ethical reflexivity"[47] and "team reflexivity"[48] is among some of the most frequently encountered topics in contemporary business ethics literature. Schneider (2015, p. 525) asserts that this reflexive capacity, be it "self-reflexivity or critical reflexivity" (Fatien Dichon and Nizet, 2019), and whether it operates on a profound interior level or is manifested in changes to organizational structures and practices, has "the potential to initiate processes of collective learning and could eventually bring about the realization of business models that integrate economic, ecological, and social considerations." But it is precisely this reflective mode of ethics which appears to be the first casualty of automation and systemic stupidity, as outlined above. If we do not always have the option of asking managers for an explanation, if we do not even have the power to override decisions taken on our behalf by advanced information systems, it seems evident that our reflexive capacities will be reduced, or even dismissed from the field of decision-making altogether.

At this juncture it seems appropriate to look more closely at the ethical programme proposed by Stiegler (2008), whose work in these issues seems unavoidable, founded in part on the notion of *aidos*. This key concept in Greek philosophy is broadly equivalent to the feeling of dignity, so that to behave ethically is first and foremost a matter of nurturing a sense of dignity within oneself and towards others. In Stiegler's view this involves a desire to rise above our base impulses, to transcend them in a certain manner, a desire which sets us apart from other species.

But it is important to note that the concept of *aidos* has already been invoked by researchers in business ethics as a term which "symbolizes honor, humility, and restrained pride".[49] Ultimately *aidos* is a virtue,[50] embodying the importance of retaining one's dignity as far as possible. For Petit and Bollaert, for example, it is one of the virtues – along with justice (*dike*) – which enable managers to avoid the pitfalls of immoderation ("hubristic CEO"[51]). In a more general sense, the existing literature in the field of business ethics attaches great importance to the notion of dignity, a concept memorably deployed by Kant to highlight those things in life which are truly priceless,[52] and which might also be considered as "unspoken but accepted conventions of mutual respect in everyday life".[53] Ultimately this is a manner of asserting the centrality of people as the true beneficiaries of all economic activities, whatever form they may take,[54] a cause served in organizations by the use of reason[55] as well as the presence of the arts.[56]

---

[47] Kandathil and Joseph 2019.

[48] Lyubovnikova et al. 2017.

[49] Petit and Bollaert 2012: 276.

[50] Sison 2015.

[51] Petit and Bollaert 2012: 278.

[52] Pirson et al. 2016.

[53] Noronha 2020: 554.

[54] Mea and Sims 2019.

[55] Sison et al. 2016.

[56] De Colle et al. 2017.

Conclusion: Postcritical Perspectives

But are we even capable of retaining our dignity in the age of automated decision-making and organizational stupidity? In fact, faced with the rise of digital technical objects, we need to engage in a process of *mnemotechnic therapy*, ensuring that the externalisation of knowledge to machines "makes possible the reinternalization of new knowledge enabling us to think for ourselves".[57] The loss of knowledge as a result of automation (trading software, GPS, decision-making tools etc.) means that people no longer have any individual identity at work. They are "dissociated from their milieu"[58] and from themselves. From this point of view, intelligence cannot be gauged solely on the basis of personal intellectual capacities[59] or the quality of a specific technical environment. Whenever we use our faculties of learning and critical thinking, Stiegler contends that there is always a certain degree of *unlearning* involved, a reframing of what we know or think we know. We remain capable of making this constant effort to unlearn as long as our capacity for attention is preserved, but our attention spans are slipping away as the opportunities to allow our behaviour to be digitally guided continue to proliferate. Unlearning assumes special significance when it comes to fighting back against the defining force reshaping our contemporary economy: the rise of what Stiegler calls the *proletarianisation* (or cretinisation) of elites. In this respect unlearning becomes a synonym for another key term in the philosopher's lexicon: deproletarianisation.[60]

It is worth looking more closely at what Stiegler means by this unusual term, particularly when applied to business leaders. He insists that proletarianisation should be understood in a cultural, and not strictly economic, sense. Because what is at stake here is a loss of skills and knowledge, a growing inability to appropriate our own knowledge, to remain attentive (Crawford 2015). A person is proletarianised when she is deprived of her capacity for ethical deliberation, lacking the knowledge and the ability to reassess and change this state of affairs. In Stiegler's view, attention is a prerequisite for reflection and deliberation, and not a reflex, but rather a central pillar which stands between what he calls retention (what we retain of the past) and protention, i.e. our projections for the future. Without these central pillars, which make it possible for us to accumulate knowledge of the past and project our thoughts into the future – perhaps to defend certain principles, or adopt a certain style – values such as integrity, authenticity or honesty become hollow concepts.

But what can we do to escape the "systemic stupidity" in which we are currently mired, starting with a more effective balance between living organisms, social organisms and technical objects. To begin with we must focus on the necessary conditions for this transformation: a new vision of work as contribution (*contributive income*) and a new understanding of work as care (*rethinking theotium/negotiumdichotomy*). Finally, it seems important to highlight the need for

---

[57] Stiegler et al. 2014: 67.

[58] Petit 2013; Simondon 2012.

[59] As measured by IQ, for example; see Alexandre 2017.

[60] Deslandes and Paltrinieri 2017.

138   Conclusion: Postcritical Perspectives

a renewal of culture and education, a prospect made possible by the digital humanities.

As we have seen Stiegler, who offers in such matters an important additional contribution to that proposed in the henryian corpus, believes that the task of renewing political economy requires us to reconnect with desire.[61] This can be achieved by nurturing the emergence of a form of industrial economy where the contributions of all stakeholders exist within a psycho-socio-technical network in which investment (in the long term) can once again be envisaged. This requires a thorough re-examination of the "cogito-economic subject"[62] and a reconnection with the notion of the common good,[63] along with deliberative practices within companies.[64]

For this to happen we not only need to rebuild our knowledge, but also to rediscover the "flavour" which makes learning appealing (even if that means starting by unlearning), as well as ways of living together which, unlike technology and particularly digital technologies, are not driven by the sole objective of increasing value for shareholders. We must instead use such technologies to form collaborative, contributive networks which are capable of changing our relationship with work. Perhaps what is needed here is in fact a deconstruction of the notions of employment and work.[65] Employment is to be understood as the general framework within which a hierarchical relationship exists between employers and employees. Work, on the other hand, corresponds to all occupations, all manual or intellectual activity, which is not dependent upon such a contractual framework.

On this specific point, Stiegler has called attention to the examples of community-developed open software, and the special status of *intermittents du spectacle* in France. This special employment status allows people working without fixed contracts in the entertainment industry, including artists (actors, writers etc.) and technicians (cameramen/women, floor managers, operators, post-production teams etc.), to access their full social rights, including unemployment pay, as long as they meet the minimum working hours requirement set by the government. The idea behind this system is to take into account the fact that not only is much of this kind of work seasonal (at a time when many jobs in many other sectors are going the same way), but also that these workers require a certain amount of time to research, reflect and perfect their skills.

He insists upon this point to demonstrate the urgent need to offer the population as a whole the possibility of changing professions, in the face of growing technological disruption and the risk that more than half of all jobs will have disappeared by 2040.[66] He also suggests alternating between periods of activity and periods in which we focus on updating our skills, made possible by a new legal framework.

---

[61] Smith et al. 2016; Deslandes and Paltrinieri 2017; Deslandes 2023.

[62] Rhodes and Garrick 2002.

[63] Argandona 2018.

[64] Sillince 1999.

[65] Lips-Wiersma et al. 2020.

[66] Collins et al. 2016.

Conclusion: Postcritical Perspectives 139

This is the thinking behind his concept of the *contributive income*, which would form the basis of the *contributive economy*, providing a "conditional income, which can only be renewed, to borrow the term used by *intermittents*, once one has 'recharged' one's entitlement by acquiring and/or sharing knowledge, know-how and life skills".[67]

As a matter of fact, the ethics of care is largely defined by the idea that our understanding of what constitutes the autonomy of human beings, particularly in material and affective terms, is founded on false premises.[68] In truth, a truly human existence is only made possible by the support and solicitude of fellow humans who are just as vulnerable as we are, which inevitably has consequences for the way we understand collaboration in all of its many forms.[69] But Stiegler's point is that, in a technological environment where stupidity has become systemic, our vulnerability is primarily noetic and cognitive. Hence the need to rethink our understanding of work as a contributive phenomenon to retain our capacity for ethical reflexivity and thus, by extension, our dignity (as encapsulated in the concept of *aidos*).

In order to conceptualise this new relationship to work, Stiegler suggests to make a distinction between *otium*[70] and *negotium*,[71] a dichotomy to which he frequently returns. He uses these terms to refer to the classic distinction (Roman, as it happens) between humanist culture and leisure (*otium*) and the production and sale of goods (*negotium*). On one side sits necessity, utility, need; on the other lies creativity, dawdling, the time in which we truly exist.

Closely related to the Greek term *Skholé* (which gives us school, scholarship, etc.), *otium* is the time in which our ideas and theories take form, the "noetic" moment of elevation evoked earlier on in this essay, nurtured by drama, the arts, reading etc. This is also the meaning generally attributed to the term liberal arts: arts that are not subservient, not bound by any obligation of utility. As such, time devoted to these pursuits is a symbol of our sovereignty[72] which sets us apart from everyday activities, which in turn reflect our subservience to our basic needs.

Otium is by definition an object of "employment" (the status of employee), crucible of the rediscovery of work, in the sense of "the cultivation of knowledge, in any form, through the performance of an action which is part of our own singularity and that of our environment, which opens up a new world in the way that a 'work' can".[73] Without *otium*, without a noetic, humanist dimension to work[74] workers are liable to fall into a state of profound symbolic misery, which may well correspond to the phenomena of burn-out and brown-out frequently encountered in contemporary

---

[67] Stiegler and Kyrou 2016: 54.

[68] Gilligan 1982; Tronto 1993.

[69] Solomon 1998; Nicholson and Kurucz 2019.

[70] Gotsis and Kortezi 2008.

[71] Small 2013.

[72] Painter-Morland et al. 2017.

[73] Stiegler and Kyrou 2016: 52.

[74] Pirson and Lawrence 2010.

140   Conclusion: Postcritical Perspectives

organizations (Chabot, 2013). Herein lies the advantage of the system available to artists and technicians working in France's cultural sector, the opportunity to profit from their noetic know-how and skills (*negotium*), and in return to secure the time they need to constantly refresh these resources and come up with new, original ideas (*otium*).

By insisting that digital technologies, the platform economy and even certain academic institutions should be governed purely in the interests of *negotium*, we are missing an opportunity to appreciate the true value of that which cannot be calculated: the "flavour," the organizational life skills, and more generally the infractuosities, nuances and singularities of our professional paths. This perhaps explains why Stiegler makes a point of insisting that the distinction between *otium* and *negotium* needs to be transgressed. The aim here is not to add a fresh layer of paint to the Romans' insurmountable barrier between aristocratic *otium* and servile *negotium*, but rather to demonstrate that *negotium* is and always should be a component of *otium* (contradicting the technics of "governance by numbers"[75] which holds the contrary assumption that *otium* is diluted in *negotium*).

It is on these terms that Weber (1905/2002) bases his definition of capitalism, as a form of *negotium* placed under the authority and influence of ethics (Protestant, in this case). In Stiegler's view, the primacy of *otium* offers the best chance of saving capitalism itself, by setting it on a different path from that which it has followed in recent decades, successfully pivoting into the Anthropocene era and saving whatever is left to save.

But how can we reverse the proletarianisation of managers and employees? How can we help them to rediscover their own desires? How can we inure ourselves to the poisonous *pharmaka* which constantly drip-feed us with what we might call the *otium of the people*? What therapeutic solution can organizations adopt in order to escape from this systemic stupidity and enrich management research with a new degree of conceptuality?[76] What can be done to further the cause of "harming stupidity," to borrow Nietzsche's famous explanation of the role of philosophy (*The Gay Science*, §328)?

It is first at the cultural level that we must comprehend the importance of our shared *savoir-vivre*, made possible by productive activity. Work experience is a "cultural" experience in the broadest sense. As such it always requires a certain distance from production, from the work itself. The corrosion of life in work can be halted by means of a "resumption" of work outside of production itself.[77] From this point of view, the *digital humanities* and the "liberal arts" have a fundamental role to play in expanding the confines of management education beyond the paradigms

---

[75] Supiot 2017.

[76] Painter et al. 2020.

[77] "At present, these two spheres are integrated and constitute a global control where existence is totally subject to consumption patterns, which are themselves totally conformed to the necessities of production, i.e. of subsistence, of *negotium*. Now, such submission is structurally antagonistic to any *otium*, to any cultural *practice, to* which the hegemony of *negotium* substitutes 'uses', which themselves define consumption models," Stiegler 2004: 166.

Conclusion: Postcritical Perspectives

of operativity and effectiveness, calculated with the help of dashboards which tell us nothing about real work.[78] As Peter Case puts it:

> The increased sensitivity achieved by exposure to literary culture could help managers navigate more skilfully through the shifting and immeasurable currents of job motivation. [...] The pursuit of virtuous and ethical conduct in the context of the manager's daily micro-stories offers concrete hope to decision-makers who aspire to wiser leadership and a more fulfilled life.[79]

The strategy proposed by Stiegler is indeed focused on the field of digital humanities, defined as "corresponding in some respects to what would previously have been known, in the field of literature and philology, as the auxiliary sciences (epigraphy, archival work, library science, documentation etc.), repurposed for the era of digital technologies".[80] Digital humanities are thus presented as a "'transdiscipline', embodying all the methods, systems and heuristic perspectives linked to the digital within the fields of humanities[81] and the social sciences.[82]" This is why the concept of a "trading zone" evoked by Svenson[83] seems judicious, since the term "digital humanities" embraces a broad range of very different skills which have traditionally been considered separate and unrelated (the distinction between researchers and engineers, for example), spanning disciplines which are often defined in opposition to one another (e.g.: the social sciences *versus* philosophy).

It is also a matter, to use another Stieglerian term, of using the digital humanities to contribute not only to the *economy of subsistence,* but also to the *economy of existence,* and to do so by means of an exosomatic approach to the humanities, that is, by exploring all of the relationships which exist between social bodies and practices and their external tools. In this context the role of the educator is essentially to subvert[84] the use of new technologies in order to get at their underlying meaning and cultural and existential implications, amplifying the critical and creative role of the traditional humanities.

In some respects, the emergence of digital humanities represents an attempt to humanise the digital world, an attempt which would of course require our management training institutions to thoroughly overhaul their programmes to accommodate

---

[78] For John Hendry, the study of history has important assets for management education: "By moving people away from the immediate confusion of the present, history can bring a new distance and clarity to the nature of the role of managers and help them distinguish it from roles that are not theirs. The most important challenge for management educators is precisely to conceive of the discipline beyond its purely technical aspect and thus to move beyond a conception of organizations centred solely on the 'business' model," J. Hendry 2006: 279.

[79] Case 2006: 287.

[80] Stiegler 2012: 331.

[81] Michaelson 2017; Quintili et al. 2016.

[82] Transdisciplinary domains such as cultural analytics, digital curation, humanities gaming, platform studies and humanities computing offer new opportunities for uniting culture, society and technologies.

[83] See Mounier 2015: 99.

[84] Bureau and Fendt 2012.

142   Conclusion: Postcritical Perspectives

this new arrangement. But they would also need to amend their structures in order
to facilitate more horizontality, stronger connections between disciplines, more
rapid decision-making. All with a view to liberating our future "elites" from the
state of proletarianisation in which they would otherwise find themselves. This
effort would also have consequences for public education policy, and the realloca-
tion of funding to "contributive investments",[85] i.e., investments with a clear emphasis on the social economy and solidarity[86] as well as the development of "contributive"
territories, prioritising those thus far left behind by globalisation.

For a "Weak Management"

The etymological and conceptual study of *oikonomia* (household management) has
led us to the idea of weakness. Here, I would like to start from this idea as envisaged
in contemporary philosophy, particularly in postmodern theology,[87] in order to
define the contours of what would be a 'weak' management, sensitive to 'weak'
signals and capable of recognising its fallibility (and not only to display "force" as
such). This is in contrast to a 'strong' management, confident and insensitive to
uncertainty (which the current pandemic period invites us to reconsider),[88] to which
we have been accustomed in managerial studies since Fayol, in the sense that the
manager would be the one who concentrate positive qualities such as physical
health, strategic intelligence[89] and an almost innate sense of morality.

The notion of "weakness"is central to the philosophical work of Gianni Vattimo.
For this former Professor of Hermeneutics at the University of Turin, "weak"
thought must be understood as a counterpoint to metaphysical discourse, and to its
own violence.[90] Vattimo conceives of postmodernity as a critique of the idea of
foundations, as well as the modern of truth as a faithful reflection of reality. Weak
thought is distinguished by its capacity to contrast ultimate and indisputable truths,
with the aim of deconstructing firm and definitive proclamations that admit no dis-
sension or doubt. Vattimo's 'strong' thinking is always characterised by an instinc-
tive desire for power and the domination of one system of thought over another,
insensitive to difference and nuance. There is nothing derogatory in the term "weakness;" on the contrary it is this weakening, this loss of the sense of Being, as this
student of Heidegger puts it, that opens up the possibility of another ontology, an

---

[85] Stiegler 2013: 230–31.

[86] Espagne 2002; Sison et al. 2016.

[87] Caputo 2015; Vattimo 1996.

[88] This sub-chapter builds on the ideas developed in my essay published under the following reference Ghislain Deslandes, Weak Theology and Organization Studies, *Organization Studies*, 41(1):
127–139, 2020.

[89] Painter-Morland et al., 2014.

[90] Staquet 1996.

Conclusion: Postcritical Perspectives 143

ontology of incarnation.[91] Opposed as they are in many other respects,[92] on the theological level the philosophical projects of Vattimo and Caputo – an American philosopher and theologian associated with postmodernist Christianity – converge, united in their opposition to "strong theology."[93]

For Caputo, in fact, the Christian God, who "becomes incarnate" in the person of Christ, is defined more by his weakness, by the weakness of his call to us, rather than by the use of any force. In other words, God himself is not the supreme force, nor does he define himself as such.[94] In this sense, attentive to nuances and ambiguities, weak theology, this hermeneutic of 'events',[95] seems to be of primary use in studying management thought, capable of discerning the conditions of the present and doubting its certainties, and renewed, therefore, from this philosophical and theological heritage.

First of all, a management marked by the seal of "weakness" would consist in exercising a potentiality which may *or may not* be realised. True power is precisely the ability to resist one's own power, to reveal a part of non-power that constitutes a judicious exercise of this power.[96] I agree with the idea that it is when the decision-maker experiences her limits that she can have a fair representation of her capacity to act, that she can exercise her decision-making power wisely. For it is first and foremost a legitimate capacity for situational judgement, on a case-by-case basis one might say, that the *phronimos* must develop in order to express a prudential judgement (prudence, which we must remember is one of the meanings of the term *oikonomia*).

In an economic world that is increasingly difficult to predict, and in the face of the weakening of 'positive truths' in management,[97] 'weak' thinking, a philosophy of hospitality and difference, brings us back first and foremost to savoir-vivre. For Vattimo, 'weak' thinking places the figure of the Other and her vulnerability at the heart of management,[98] and therefore presupposes a renewed concern for this figure, an attitude we might define as empathy, or hospitality without calculation and the expectation reciprocity. It also implies a sense of openness, receptivity and constant vigilance.

More broadly speaking, a 'weak' manager stands in opposition to familiar managerial discourses, particularly 'masculine' tropes such as the "little chief,"[99] and of course to all abusive forms of authoritarian managerialism. This model is as much

---

[91] Zimmermann, 2009.

[92] Deslandes 2021b.

[93] Caputo and Vattimo 2007.

[94] Caputo 2006.

[95] Caputo: 323; Marion 2015.

[96] DeLong and DeLong 2005.

[97] Clegg 1989.

[98] D. Knights and O'Leary 2006; R. Greenleaf 1970; M. Painter-Morland 2006; D. Van Dierendonck 2011.

[99] Fotaki 2013; Painter-Morland and Deslandes 2014; Pullen and Rhodes 2015.

opposed to the 'Master of the Universe' managers described by Knights and McCabe as it is to the 'grandiose' discourses[100] of traditional managerial terminology ('mission', 'vision', 'strategy' etc.). In short, the manager is no longer the omniscient, omnipotent professional who can methodically solve all the organization's problems, but a vulnerable being, sensitive to the fragility of her environment, who knows that failure is always possible (and perhaps even desirable if we look at the chequered career paths of some of the most emblematic entrepreneurs of the twentieth century, beginning with Steve Jobs). As Bouilloud points out, the life of chief executives is also a place 'where one finds cases of turbulence or breakdowns, and where they constantly run the risk of a decisive failure. In short, beneath the surface of amiability and virility, we quickly see that it is a matter of survival'.[101] The exercise of managerial power is always paradoxical, like an *impossible performance* that is always called into question by the events that occur in the organization.

In this respect, the notion of 'negative capabilities' as developed by French[102] and Simpson et al.[103] from the initial intuitions of poet John Keats, and understood as a capacity to be "*capable of being in uncertainties*," seems to me particularly relevant to this impulse, specific to "weak" management, to move away from an essentially cognitive qualification of managers' actions. The leader's "negative capabilities"are concerned with openness to the world and to others without *preconceptions*, but also with an intimate resistance to the fact that we cannot know everything. They imply, in the words of Simpson et al., a form of "reflexive inaction," insofar as listening and observation are essential to the conduct of collective action, and are often neglected. In essence, negative capabilities are there to confront us with our difficulties, our limits, and sometimes our worries, so that we can better overcome them when the opportunity arises.

The second key element of "weak" management, which peels back the "mask of glory" mentioned above,[104] is linked to the notion of the "good enough manager" (GEM) as proposed by Michaud[105] and Nurick.[106] This proposal is of course based on psychoanalyst Donald Winicott's work on the ideal role of the mother, supposedly situated between the "too good" mother, who by striving to do (too) well does not give her offspring enough opportunity to develop on their own, and the "bad" mother, who can be assumed to be an anti-model. The idea is to return to a more measured understanding of control (neither too much nor too little), a vision which does not assume managers to be omniscient and omnipresent, which, as Michaud reminds us, they are not now and never have been. On the contrary, Michaud's

---

[100] Knights and McCabe 2015; Alvesson and Gabriel 2016.

[101] Bouilloud 2012: 11.

[102] French, 2001.

[103] Simpson et al. 2002.

[104] Agamben 2008; Marin 1981; Pascal 2006.

[105] Michaud 2013.

[106] Nurick 2012.

Conclusion: Postcritical Perspectives 145

model manager is an individual who listens to others and is not "all talk."[107] This is very close to Caputo's insistence upon the importance of being sensitive to nuances, to the evanescent, to a sense of ambiguity. The manager's job is first and foremost to exercise prudential judgement, which does not necessarily fit within the confines of the hypothetical-deductive approach to business administration. This tension was not lost upon the Greek philosophers who reflected seriously upon management, as showed in the first chapter of this book.

*

Faced with dualist, rational and essentialist self-definitions on the one hand, and postmodernist, fragmented and anti-essentialist self-definitions on the other, these brief philosophical investigations of managerial phenomenology has endeavoured to demonstrate how the henryian philosophical project offers a possible alternative to the many managerial studies concerned with the ontological aspect of subjectivity. Henry's perspective makes the question of the self its primary concern, upstream of the questions of identity so frequently discussed in management studies. Indeed, these questions situate questions of self in the order of representation, something I have sought to avoid for both ontological and ethical reasons.

To this end I have, of course, drawn on some of the major works devoted to this subject,[108] but it was also my hope to draw attention to a territory situated upstream of identity and reflexivity.[109] I wanted, in Henry's words, "to wrest this life from the fantasies and myths of a hinterland[110]" by putting it back where it is and whence it came, which is to say within ourselves, and to propose a conception of *subjective bodies* that is not dependent upon representation alone.

As a matter of fact, it seems to me that this is tantamount to looking at the 'invisible' side of organizations, which maybe at the core of what goes on in them. As Marie-José Mondzain noted in her aforementioned inquiry, management used to be the expression of an 'incessant back and forth between the visible and the hidden', of a constant opposition between what shows itself and what refrains from exposing itself, the realm of which is constantly expanding today (all-out digitalization, the increasingly intangible nature of assets, informal hierarchies, 'invisible' essential workers, the 'absent presence' of leadership, etc.). And what these postcritical investigations basically bring to the forefront is this ring of invisibility that surrounds organizational activities, and which stands in the way of the mere relationships between objects that most management books are content to deal with. The subjective body, as Michel Henry presents it to us, is of course the very principle of this invisibility from which everything in organizations (especially the 'human' itself) stems: anxiety about the future, (de)motivation at work, entertainment and the quest for happiness, for power, in short, for feeling alive. It is as if the subjective side of managerial rationality is appearing as the crisis of current managerial

---

[107] Michaud 2013: 209.

[108] Alvesson 2010.

[109] Rhodes 2009.

[110] Henry 1985: 9.

146 Conclusion: Postcritical Perspectives

rationality becomes apparent. Hence the urgency, perhaps, to reconsider management, or postmanagement, not only as the only place of expression for figures, discourses, technologies and representations of all kinds (logos, charts, brands, etc.), which we study within the framework of an 'organology' from which we believe we can steer the material world from the 'monotonous and stereotyped background of utilitarian objects' (according to the expression Henry uses in his book on Kandinsky). But also as the site that would require the elaboration of a proper "organosophy" instead, where the non-immediately measurable proves to be at least as indispensable to the achievement of our ends and purposes. Such a co-existence of two distinct and mixed sites implies that managers must develop objective skills, but without detracting from their faculties of discernment, sensitivity to ambiguities and 'deciphering' of management situations, which are at least as important (if not more). It is in this gap that the future of the discipline is played out, even if, as François Jullien points out in his Conference on Efficiency, in management as in all areas, "real victories are difficult to see".

This phenomenology of life also hints at new perspectives for dialogue with the philosophies of representation and the object, with both the poststructuralist current – to which we can partly associate the work of Bernard Stiegler for instance – and Freudian psychoanalysis. The Kierkegaardian term *contemporaneity* can help us to define the terms of this relationship, offering an opportunity to think together about the self and its representation, never in an impersonal way, but never from a "timeless nowhere[111] "either. Indeed, it is quite possible that the study of managers will not be able to do without the "explanation with the self[112]" of which Paul Audi speaks. The gap between the exercise of power and the realization of power is a broad one, and if managers and leaders wear the finery of this force, it is most often to mask a real deficiency. However, "character" is only incumbent on those who are able and willing to recognise what they can do and what they want. "A man *with character, a* man who has character, *is* therefore a man who does not seek to show off forces he does not possess; who does not play with counterfeit money."[113] This point of view seems to me to be quite far removed from the current epistemological climate, even in *critical management studies,* which tends to favour only structural-relationist readings. Of course, I do not deny the importance of exo-relationships in collaborative life and management, as the study of the Stieglerian hypothesis has shown, but I also believe it is necessary not to limit the importance of either endo-relationships – those that managers and the managed have with themselves – or of the individual entity as such, in our understanding of organizational phenomena. In short, a postcritical approach simply rejects the idea of "processes without subjects" – an expression which, as Jean-Pierre Dupuy[114] usefully points out, applies to

---

[111] Stokes 2008.

[112] Audi 2007: 120.

[113] *Ibid.* p. 139: "But, conversely, anyone who despairs of himself, anyone who does not support himself, anyone who hates this pure inner trial of being himself, which is called life, cannot be just - neither towards himself nor towards others," *ibid.,*: 295.

[114] Dupuy 2012: 267.

Conclusion: Postcritical Perspectives

Friedrich Hayek as much as it does to Louis Althusser – too often invoked to explain managerial facts by the prevailing relationist trend in social sciences.[115]

This contribution to a phenomenology of life in managerial studies offers a counterpoint to terms such as 'negotiate', 'cut', 'restrict', etc., classic examples of management speak which do nothing to foster an affective and human approach to the situations experienced in workplaces. For such terms, marching under the banner of science and technicality, serve only to deceive us about ourselves and our own *desires*. In fact this is what surveys on the subject keep claiming, with only a small minority of employees worldwide declaring themselves to be engaged in their work.[116] And it should thus come as no surprise that, in the professional sphere, the informal aspect of human relations, what we could call conviviality[117] or informal benevolence,[118] is at least as important as the formal, strictly political aspect. In the world of organizations, and the arena they provide for subjectivities to exchange and interact, life asserts its primacy even in our obsession with measurement, which it would be unwise to restrict only to our capacities for calculation.

References

Agamben, Giorgio. 2008. *Homo sacer, II. Le règne et la gloire*. trans. Joël Gayraud and Martin Rueff, Paris: Seuil.
Alexandre, Laurent. 2017. *La guerre des intelligences*. Paris: JC. Latès.
Alvesson, Mats. 2010. Self-doubters, strugglers, storytellers, surfers and others: Images of self-identities in organization studies. *Human Relations* 63 (2): 193–217.
Alvesson, Mats, and Yiannis Gabriel. 2016. Grandiosity in contemporary management and education. *Management Learning* 47 (4): 464–473.
Argandona, Antonio. 2018. Economics for the common good. *Business Ethics Quarterly* 28 (4): 493–496.
Audi, Paul. 2007. *Supériorité de l'éthique*. Paris: Flammarion.
Boubeker, Ahmed. 2011. L'homme capable à l'épreuve de l'invisibilité sociale. *Le Portique* (26) document 5, online available: https://journals.openedition.org/leportique/2511.
Bouilloud, Jean-Philippe. 2012. *Entre l'enclume et le marteau*. Paris: Seuil.
Boyle, David. 2001. *The tyranny of numbers. Why counting cannot make us happy*. New York: Harper Collins.
Bureau, Sylvain, and Jacqueline Fendt. 2012. La dérive « situationniste ». *Revue Française de Gestion* 38 (223): 181–200.
Caputo, John. 2006. *The weakness of God – A theology of the event*. Indianapolis: Indiana University Press.

---

[115] Piette 2014.

[116] The percentage is 20% worldwide. This is in contrast to the two-thirds who say they are disengaged, according to the Gallup study (State of the Global Workplace, Gallup Press, New York, 2021).

[117] Deslandes 2012a.

[118] Mercier and Deslandes 2020.

148 Conclusion: Postcritical Perspectives

———. 2015. L'audace de Dieu: Prolégomènes à une théologie faible. *Etudes théologiques et religieuses.* 90 (3): 317–338.

Caputo, John, and Gianni Vattimo. 2007. *After the death of God.* Columbia University Press.

Case, Peter. 2006. Management education and the philosophical life: A response to John Hendry. *Management Learning 37* (3): 283–289.

Chabot, Pascal. 2013. *Global burn-out.* Paris: PUF.

Clegg, Stewart. 1989. *Frameworks of power.* Londres: Sage.

Clot, Yves. 2008. *Work without man? Pour une psychologie des milieux de travail et de vie.* Paris: La Découverte.

Collins, Randall, Georgi Derluguian Michael Mann, Graig Calhoun, and Immanuel Wallerstein. 2016. *Le capitalisme a-t-il un avenir ?* Paris: La Découverte.

Corcuff, Philippe. 2010. Néocapitalismes et imaginaires. In *Affectivité, imaginaire, création sociale,* ed. Raphaël Gély and Laurent Van Eynde. Brussels: Publications des Facultés universitaires Saint-Louis.

Crawford, Matthew. 2009. *Éloge du carburateur: essai sur le sens et la valeur du travail.* Paris: La Découverte.

———. 2015. *The world beyond your head: On becoming an individual in an age of distraction.* Farrar: Straus and Giroux.

De Colle, Simone, Edward Freeman, Bidhan Parmar, and Leonardo De Colle. 2017. Practicing human dignity: Ethical lessons from commedia dell'Arte and Theater. *Journal Business Ethics* 144: 251–262.

De Sutter, Laurent (dir). 2019. *Postcritique.* Paris: PUF.

Dejours, Christophe. 2009. *Live work. Travail et émancipations.* Vol. 2. Paris: Payot.

———. 2021. *Ce qu'il y a de meilleur en nous travailler et honorer la vie.* Paris: Payot.

Deslandes, Ghislain. 2012a. *Le Management éthique.* Paris: Dunod.

———. 2012b. Power, profits, and practical wisdom: Ricœur's perspectives on the possibility of an ethics in institutions. *Business and Professional Ethics Journal* 31 (1): 1–24.

———. 2013. *Essai sur les données philosophiques du management.* Paris: PUF.

———. 2020. Weak theology and organization studies. *Organization Studies* 41 (1): 127–139.

———. 2021a. Branching off in the Anthropocene era. *Organization Studies* 43 (3): 468–471.

———. 2021b. *Antiphilosophy of Christianity.* Springer.

———. 2023. *Érotique de l'administration.* Paris: PUF.

Deslandes, Ghislain, and Luca Paltrinieri. 2017. Entretien avec Bernard Stiegler. *Rue Descartes* 91: 119–140. https://doi.org/10.3917/rdes.091.0119.

Ducharme, Olivier. 2012. *Michel Henry et le problème de la communauté. Soi, communauté, habitus,* doctoral thesis in philosophy under the supervision of Sophie-Jan Arrien, Laval (Québec), Université de Laval.

Dupuy, Jean-Pierre. 2012. *L'Avenir de l'économie. Sortir de l'écomystification.* Paris: Flammarion.

Espagne, François. 2002. Sur l'économie sociale et solidaire. *RECMA* 4 (286): 13–22. https://doi.org/10.7202/1022236ar.

Faÿ, Éric. 2007a. A critical and phenomenological genealogy of the question of the real in western economics and management. *Society and Business Review* 2 (2): 193–203.

———. 2007b. Phenomenological approaches to Work, life and responsibility. *Society and Business Review* 2 (2): 145–152.

———. 2009. Virtual organisation, real work. A Henryian critique of the virtual organisation of human work. *Studia Phænomenologica* IX.

Fleming, Peter, and André Spicer. 2003. Working at a cynical distance: Implications for power, subjectivity and resistance. *Organization* 10 (1): 157–179.

French, Robert. 2001. "Negative capability": Managing the confusing uncertainties of change. *Journal of Organizational Change Management* 14 (5): 480–492.

Fotaki, Marianna. 2013. No woman is like a man (in academia): The masculine symbolic order and the unwanted female body. *Organization Studies* 34 (9): 1251–1275.

Conclusion: Postcritical Perspectives 149

Foucault, Michel. 2001. *Herméneutique du sujet. Cours au Collège de France 1981–1982*. Paris: Seuil/Gallimard.

Gély, Raphaël. 2007. *Rôles, action sociale et vie subjective*. Brussels: Peter Lang.

Gilligan, Carol. 1982. *In a different voice: Psychological theory and women's development*. Cambridge, MA: Harvard University Press.

Gotsis, George, and Zoi Kortezi. 2008. Philosophical foundations of workplace spirituality: A critical approach. *Journal of Business Ethics* 78 (4): 575–600.

Gorz, André. 1988. *Métamorphoses du travail*. Paris: Galilée.

Greenleaf, Robert. 1970. *The servant as leader*. Newton Centre.

Hendry, John. 2006. Educating managers for post-bureaucracy: The role of the humanities. *Management Learning* 37 (3): 267–281.

Henry, Michel. 1963. *L'Essence de la manifestation*, 4th ed. 2011. Paris: PUF. English version: Henry, Michel. 1973. *The essence of manifestation* (Trans. G. Etzkorn). The Hague: Nijhoff.

———. 1985. *Généalogie de la psychanalyse*. Paris: PUF. English version. Michel Henry, *The Genealogy of Psychoanalysis* (D. Brick, Trans.). Stanford, CA: Stanford University Press, 1993.

Jackall, Robert. 1988. *Moral mazes. The world of corporate managers*. New York: Oxford University Press.

Jean, Grégori. 2011. Présentation of "l'expérience métaphysique d'autrui" to "intersubjectivité en première personne". *Revue Internationale Michel Henry* 216–70.

Jeantet, Aurélie, and Emmanuelle Savignac. 2012. Représentations du monde professionnel et du rapport subjectif au travail dans les films de fiction français contemporains. *Travailler* 27 (1): 37–63.

Jullien, François. 2005. *Conférence sur l'efficience*. Paris: PUF.

Kambouchner, Denis. 2013. À propos de l'École. *Cahiers philosophiques* 134: 114–126.

Kandathil, George, and Jerome Joseph. 2019. Ethical reflexivity: Normative underpinnings of direct employee participation studies and implications for developing ethical reflexivity: A multidisciplinary review. *Journal of Business Ethics* 157: 685–697.

Knights, David, and Darren McCabe. 2015. 'Masters of the Universe': Demystifying leadership in the context of the 2008 global financial crisis. *British Journal of Management* 26: 197–210.

Knights, David, and Majella O'Leary. 2006. Leadership, ethics and responsability of the other. *Journal of Business Ethics* 67: 125–137.

Le Texier, Thibault. 2011. *La Rationalité managériale. De l'administration domestique à la gouvernance*. PhD thesis in economics, under the supervision of Joël-Thomas Ravix, Nice, Sophia-Antipolis University.

Lips-Wiersma, Marjolein, Jarrod Haar, and Sarah Wright. 2020. The effect of fairness, responsible leadership and worthy work on multiple dimensions of meaninful work. *Journal of Business Ethics* 161 (1): 35–52.

Lyubovnikova, Johanne, Alsion Legood, Nicola Turner, and Argyro Mamakouka. 2017. How authentic leadership influences team performance: The mediating role of team reflexivity. *Journal of Business Ethics* 141: 9–70.

Marin, Louis. 1981. *Le Portrait du roi*. Paris: Minuit.

Marion, Jean-Luc. 2015. *Negative certainties*. University of Chicago Press.

McIntyre, Alasdair. 1999. Social structures and their threats to moral agency. *Philosophy* 74 (289): 311–329.

Mea, William, and Ronald Sims. 2019. Human dignity-centered business ethics: A conceptual framework for business leaders. *Journal of Business Ethics* 160: 53–69.

Mercier, Guillaume, and Ghislain Deslandes. 2020. Formal and informal benevolence in a profit-oriented context. *Journal of Business Ethics* 165: 125–143.

Michaelson, Christopher. 2017. Virtual special issue on humanities and business ethics. *Journal of Business Ethics* 142 (3): 409–412.

Michaud, Yves. 2013. *Qu'est-ce que le management responsable ? Confiance, décision, réflexivité*. Paris: Eyrolles.

Mondzain, Marie-José. 1996. *Image, Icône, Economie. Les sources byzantines de l'imaginaire contemporain*. Paris: Seuil.

Mounier, Pierre. 2015a. Une " utopie politique " pour les humanités numériques ? *Socio – La nouvelle revue des sciences sociales, Éditions de la Maison des sciences de l'homme, 2015, Le tournant numérique.. et après ?* 97–112.

Nicholson, Jessica, and Elizabeth Kurucz. 2019. Relational leadership for sustainability: Building an ethical framework from the moral Theory of 'ethics of care'. *Journal of Business Ethics* 156: 25–43.

Noronha, Ernesto. 2020. Saikat Chakraborty & Premilla D'Cruz, "'doing dignity Work': Indian security guards' Interface with precariousness". *Journal of Business Ethics* 162: 553–575.

Nurick, Aaron. 2012. *The good enough manager – The making of a GEM*. New-York: Routledge.

Painter, Mollie, Mar Pérezts, and Ghislain Deslandes. 2020. Understanding the human in stakeholder Theory: A phenomenological approach to affect-based learning. *Management Learning* 52 (2): 203–223.

Painter-Morland, Mollie. 2006. Redefining accountability as relational responsiveness. *Journal of Business Ethics* 66: 89–98.

Painter-Morland, Mollie, and Ghislain Deslandes. 2014. Gender and visionary leading: Rethinking "vision" with Bergson, Deleuze and Guattari. *Organization* 21 (6): 844–866.

Painter-Morland, Mollie, Geert Demuijnck, and Sara Ornati. 2017. Sustainable development and well-being: a philosophical challenge. *Journal of Business Ethics* 146: 295–311.

Pascal, Blaise. 2006. *Trois Discours sur la condition des Grands et six liasses extraites des Pensées*. Paris: Gallimard.

Pauline, Fatien Diochon, and Nizet Jean. 2019. Ethics as a fabric: An emotional reflexive sense-making process. *Business Ethics Quarterly* 29 (4): 461–489.

Petit, Victor. 2013. Vocabulaire ars industrialis. In *Pharmacologie du front national*. Paris: Flammarion (see also www.arsindustrialis.org).

Petit, Valérie, and Helen Bollaert. 2012. Flying too close to the sun? Hubris among CEOs and how to prevent it. *Journal of Business Ethics* 108: 265–283.

Piette, Albert. 2014. *Contre le relationnisme. Lettre aux antropologues*. Lormont: Le Bord de l'Eau.

Pirson, Michael, and Paul Lawrence. 2010. Humanism in business – Towards a paradigm shift ? *Journal of Business Ethics* 93 (4): 553–565.

Pirson, Michael, Claus Dierksmeier, and Kenneth Goodpaster. 2016. Human dignitiy and Business. *Business Ethics Quarterly* 26 (4): 465–478.

Politis, Hélène. 2002. *Kierkegaard*. Paris: Ellipses.

Pullen, Alison, and Carl Rhodes. 2015. Writing, the feminine and organization. *Gender, Work and Organisation* 22 (2): 87–93.

Quintili, Paolo, Carlo Cappa, and Donatella Palomba. 2016. *Université et anti-Université – les humanités dans l'idée de formation supérieure*. Paris: L'Harmattan.

Rhodes, Carl. 2009. After reflexivity: Ethics, freedom, the writing of organization studies. *Organization Studies* 30 (6): 653–672.

Rhodes, Carl, and John Garrick. 2002. Economic metaphors and working knowledge: Enter the 'cogito-economic' subject. *Human Resource Development International* 5 (1): 87–97.

Ricœur, Paul. 2001. *Le Juste, 2 t*. Paris: Éditions Esprit.

Rozuel, Cecile. 2011. The moral threat of compartmentalization: Self, roles and Responsability. *Journal of Business Ethics* 102 (4): 685–697.

Schneider, Anselm. 2015. Reflexivity in sustainability accounting and management: Transcending the economic focus of corporate sustainability. *Journal of Business Ethics* 127: 525–536.

Scitovsky, Tibor. 1976. *The Economy without Joy*. tr. fr. Martie Fiorini and Amanda Wilson, Paris: Calmann-Lévy.

Sillince, John. 1999. The Organizational setting, use and institutionalization of argumentation repertories. *Journal of Management Studies* 36 (6): 795–830.

Simondon, Gilbert. 2012. *Du mode d'existence des objets techniques*. Paris: Aubier.

Simpson, Peter, Robert French, and Charles Harvey. 2002. Leadership and negative capability. *Human Relations* 55 (10): 1209–1226.

Sison, Alejo. 2015. *Happiness and virtue ethics in business: The ultimate value proposition.* Cambridge: Cambridge University Press.

Sison, Alejo, Ignacio Ferrero, and Gregorio Guitián. 2016. Human dignity and the dignity of work: Insights from Catholic social teaching. *Business Ethics Quarterly* 26 (4): 503–528.

Small, William. 2013. Business practice, ethics and the philosophy of morals in the rome of Marcus Tullius cicero. *Journal of Business Ethics* 115 (2): 341–350.

Smith, Brett, Geoffrey Kistruck, and Benedetto Cannatelli. 2016. The impact of moral intensity and desire for control on scaling decisions in social entrepreneurship. *Journal of Business Ethics* 133 (4): 677–689.

Solomon, Robert. 1998. The moral psychology of business: Care and compassion in the corporation. *Business Ethics Quarterly* 8 (3): 515–553.

Staquet, Anne. 1996. *La pensée faible de Vattimo et Rovatti: Une pensée–fable*. Paris: L'Harmattan.

Stiegler, Bernard. 2004. *Mécréance et Discrédit, t. I, La Décadence des démocraties industrielles*. Paris: Galilée. English version. Bernard Stiegler, (2011) *The Decadence of Industrial Democracies: Disbelief and Discredit*, 1, Cambridge: Polity Press.

———. 2012. *Etats de choc – Bêtise et savoir au XXIème siècle*. Paris: Mille et une nuits. English version. Bernard, Stiegler, *States of Shock: Stupidity and Knowledge in the 21st Century*, Cambridge: Polity Press, 2015.

———. 2013. *Pharmacologie du Front National*. Paris.

Stiegler, Bernard, and Ariel Kyrou. 2016. Le revenu contributif et le revenu universel. *Association Multitudes. Multitudes* 2 (63): 51–58.

Stokes, Patrick. 2008. Locke, Kierkegaard and the phenomenology of personal identity. *International Journal of Philosophy* 16 (5).

Supiot, Alain. 2017. *The governance by numbers. The making of a legal model of allegiance.* Bloomsbury.

Svensson, Patrick. 2016. *Big digital humanities – Imagining a meeting place for the humanities and the digital*. University of Michigan Press.

Tronto, Joan. 1993. *Moral boundaries: A political argument for an ethic of care*. New York: Routledge.

Van Dierendonck, Dirk. 2011. Servant leadership: A review and synthesis. *Journal of Management* 37: 1228–1261.

Vattimo, Gianni. 1996. *Credere di credere*. Milan: Garzanti.

Xenophon. 1933. *Economique. Notice par Pierre Chambry*. Paris: Garnier.

Zimmermann, Jens. 2009. Weak thought or weak theology? A theological critique of Vattimo's Incarnational Ontology. *Journal of British Society for Phenomenology* 40 (3): 312–329.

Bibliography

Abel, Olivier. 2006. Une poétique de l'action. In *L'homme capable: autour de Paul Ricoeur*, ed. O. Abel and B. Clément, 13–26. Paris: Rue Descartes.

Agamben, Giorgio. 1997. *Homo sacer, I. Le pouvoir souverain et la vie nue*. trans. fr. Marilène Raiola,. Paris: Seuil.

Agamben, Giogio. 2007. *What is a device?* tr. fr. Martin Rueff, Paris: Payot & Rivages.

Agamben, Giorgio. 2011. *The kingdom and the glory: For a theological genealogy of economy and government*. Stanford: Stanford University Press.

Anquetil, Alain. 2011. *Textes clés de l'éthique des affaires*. Paris: Vrin.

Arendt, Hannah. 1993. *Condition of the modern man*. In *tr. fr. Georges Fradier*. Paris: Calmann-Lévy.

Arnaud, Gilles, and Stijn Vanheule. 2007. The division of the subject and the organization. A Lacanian approach to subjectivity at Work. *Journal of Organization Change Management* 20 (3): 359–369.

Avolio, Bruce, and Bernard Bass. *Transformational leadership, charisma and beyond*. Working paper, State University of New-York. *Binghamton*.

Badiou, Alain. 2007. *De quoi Sarkozy est-il le nom ? Circonstance 4*. Paris: Edition Lignes.

Blake, Allan, Cassondra Batz-Barbarich, Haley Sterling, and Louis Tay. 2019. Outcomes of meaningful work: A meta-analysis. *Journal of Management Studies* 56 (3): 500–528.

Bouilloud, Jean-Philippe, Ghislain Deslandes, and Guillaume Mercier. 2017. The leader as chief truth officer: The ethical responsibility of "managing the truth" in Organizations. *Journal of Buisness Ethics* 157 (1): 1–13.

Brocklehurst, Michael, Christopher Grey, and Andrew Sturdy. 2010. Management: The work that dares not speak its name. *Management Learning* 41.

Burell, Gibson. 1988. Modernism, postmodernism and organizational analysis 2. The contribution of Michel Foucault. *Organization Studies* 9 (2): 221–235.

Canguilhem, Georges. What is a philosopher in France today? Speech delivered on 10 March 1990 at the École normale supérieure, at the request of the Société des amis de Jean Cavaillès, online: http://www.paris8philo.com/article-4085356.html

Cardon, Dominique. 2015. *À quoi rêvent les algorithmes ?* Paris: Le Seuil.

Case, Peter. Management education and the philosophical life. A response to John Hendry. *Management Learning* 37 (3): 283–289.

Cassin, Barbara. 2004. *Vocabulaire européen des philosophies – Dictionnaire des intraduisibles*. Paris: Seuil/Le Robert.

© The Author(s), under exclusive license to Springer Nature Switzerland AG 2023

G. Deslandes, *Postcritical Management Studies*, Ethical Economy 65, https://doi.org/10.1007/978-3-031-29404-4

154 Bibliography

Chanlat, Jean-François. 1998. *Sciences sociales et management – Plaidoyer pour une anthropologie générale*. Canada/France: Les Presses de l'Université de Laval. Editions Eska.

Chia, Robert, and Robin Holt. 2009. *Strategy without Design: The Silent Efficacy of Indirect Action*. Cambridge: Cambridge University Press.

Crockett, Clayton. Technology and the Time-Image: Deleuze and Postmodern Subjectivity. *South-African Journal of Philosophy* 24 (3).

Dauzat, Pierre-Emmanuel. Introduction. In *Économique*, ed. *Aristote. tr. fr. Bernard Abraham van*.

Derrida, Jacques, Jean-Pierre Faye, Dominique Lecourt, and François Châtelet. 1998. *Le rapport bleu. Les sources historiques et théoriques du Collège international de philosophie*. Paris: PUF.

Deslandes, Ghislain. 2016. *Critique de la condition managériale*. Paris: PUF.

———. 2018. Le travail désaffecté ou la joie, enjeu managérial et social. *Le Portique* (35) document 4, online available.

Deslandes, Ghislain, and Jean-Philipe Bouilloud. 2019. Pour une éthique d'après la reconnaissance. *RIMHE* 34 (1): 88–102.

Dumouchel, Paul, and Dupuy Jean-Pierre. 1979. *L'enfer des choses. René et la logique de l'économie*. Paris: Seuil.

Durand, Rodolphe, and Roland Calori. Sameness, otherness? Enriching organizational change theories with philosophical considerations on the same and the other. *Academy of Management Review* 31 (1). https://doi.org/10.5465/amr.2006.19379626.

Dyck, Bruno, and Rob Kleysen. Aristotle's Virtues and Management Thought: an Empirical Exploraiton of an Integrative Pedagogy. *Business Ethics Quarterly* 11 (4): 561–574.

Edward, Freeman. 1984. *Strategic management: A stakeholder approach*. Cambridge: Cambridge University Press.

Enderlé, Georges. 1996. Towards business ethics as an academic discipline. *Business Ethics Quarterly* 6 (1): 43–65.

Faÿ, Éric. 2008. *Derision and management organization*. 15 (6): 831–850.

Fineman, Stephan. On being positive: Concerns and counterpoints. *Academy of Management Review* 31 (2).

Flammer, Caroline. Corporate social responsablity and shareholder reaction: The environmental awareness of investors. *Academy of Management Journal* 56 (3): 758–781.

Fotaki, Marianna, Susan Long, and Howard Schwartz. 2012. What can psychoanalysis offer organization studies today? Taking stock of current developments and thinking about future directions. *Organization Studies* 33 (9): 1105–1120.

Furetière, Antoine. Œconomie. In *Dictionnaire universel contenant généralement tous les mots françois, tant vieux que modernes, et les termes de toutes les sciences et des arts* (1690), available on Gallica http://gallica.bnf.fr/ark:/12148/bpt6k50614b.r=.langFR.

Garcia, Tristan. 2016. *La vie intense*. Paris: Editions Autrement.

Gilkey, Roderick, and Clint Kilts. Cognitive fitness. *Harvard Business Review* 85 (11).

Girard, René. 1978. *Des choses cachées depuis la fondation du monde*. Paris: Grasset.

Gosling, Jonathan, and Henri Mintzberg. The five minds of a manager. *Harvard Business Review* 81 (11): 54–63.

Hamraoui, Éric. Le besoin de temps. Entre travail et politique. *La Pensée* 376: 69–86.

Harari, Yuval Noah. 2017. *Homo Deus*. Harper: *A brief history of tomorrow*.

Henry, M. 2008d. *Le socialisme selon Marx*. Editions Sulliver.

———. 2008e. *La barbarie*. 2nd ed. Paris: PUF.

Henry, Michel. 2011d. *Philosophie et phénoménologie du corps. Essai Sur l'ontologie biranienne*. 6th ed. Paris: PUF, 1965. English version. Michel Henry, *Philosophy and Phenomenology of the Body* (trans. G. Etzkorn). The Hague: Nijhoff, 1975.

———. 2011e. La communication des consciences et les relations avec autrui – Cours d'Aix-en-Provence (1953–1954). *Revue Internationale Michel Henry* 2: 71–138.

Hibou, Béatrice. 2012. *La Bureaucratisation à l'ère néolibérale*. Paris: La Découverte.

Honneth, Axel. 2008. *La philosophie de la reconnaissance: une critique sociale*, 88–95. *Juillet: Esprit*.

Bibliography

Janiaud, Joël. Les hommes et les choses: de Simone Weil à elle-même en passant par Levinas. *Archives de philosophie* 72 (4).

Jean-Luc, Marion. 2006. *2003. Le Phénomène érotique*: The Chicago University Press.

Jones, Campbell, and André Spicer. The sublime object of entrepreneurship. *Organization* 12 (2): 223–246.

Karavanta, Mina, Nina Morgan, Edward Said, and Jacques Derrida. 2008. *Reconstellating humanism and the global hybrid*. Newcastle: Cambridge Scholars Publishing.

Khosrokhavar, Farhad. 2002. La scansion de l'intersubjectivité: Michel Henry et la problématique d'autrui. *Rue Descartes* 35 (1): 63–75.

Khurana, Rakesh. 2007. *From higher aims to hired hands. The Social transformation of American Business Schools and the unfulfilled promise of management as a profession*. Princeton: Princeton University Press.

Komporozos-Athanasiou, Aris, and Marianna Fotaki. 2015. A theory of imagination for organization studies using the work of Cornelius Castoriadis. *Organization Studies* 36 (3): 321–342.

La Boétie, Etienne. 1571. *La Mesnagerie*. Paris: F. Morel.

Latour, Bruno. 2004. Why has critique run out of steam? From matters of fact to matters of concern. *Critical Inquiry*: 225–248.

Leshem, Dotan. 2016. What Did the Ancient Greeks Mean by *Oikonomia*? *Journal of Economic Perspectives* 30 (1): 225–231.

Lévinas, Emmanuel. 1976. *Noms propres*. Paris: Fata Margana.

March, James. Exploration and exploitation in organizational learning. *Organization Science* 2 (1): 71–87.

Marion, Jean-Luc, and In Excess. 2002. *Studies of saturated phenomena*. Fordham University Press.

Martin, Kirsten, Katie Shilton, and Jeffrey Smith. 2019. Business and the ethical implications of technology: Introduction to the symposium. *Journal of Business Ethics* 160: 307–317.

Mondzain, Marie-José. 2005. *Image, icon, economy: The byzantine origins of the contemporary imaginary*. CA: Stanford University Press.

Mounier, Pierre. 2015b. Une " utopie politique " pour les humanités numériques ? *Socio - La nouvelle revue des sciences sociales, Éditions de la Maison des sciences de l'homme, 2015, Le tournant numérique.. et après ?* 97–112.

Nietzsche, Friedrich. 1870/1975. *Sur l'avenir des nos établissements d'enseignement In Ecrits Posthumes*. Paris: Gallimard.

———. 1985. *Le Gai Savoir (1882), trans.* Alexandre Vialatte. Paris: Gallimard.

Nietzsche, Friedrich. *Aurora (1880)*. Vol. 1980. tr. fr. Julien Hervier, Paris: Seuil.

Painter-Morland, Mollie. 2008a. Systemic leadership and the emergence of ethical responsiveness. *Journal of Business Ethics* 82: 509–524.

———. 2008b. *Business ethics as practice*. Cambridge: Cambridge University Press.

Painter-Morland, Mollie, and Ghislain Deslandes. 2017. Reconceptualizing CSR in the media industry as relational accountability. *Journal of Business Ethics* 143 (4): 665–679.

Parker Follet, Mary. 1919. *Community is a Process. Philosophical Review* XXVIII.

Pascal, Blaise. 1934. *Pensées (1669), Léon Brunschvicg edition*. Paris: Éditions de Cluny.

Pauline Fatien Diochon & Jean Nizet. 2019. Ethics as a Fabric: An Emotional Reflexive Sensemaking Process. *Business Ethics Quarterly* 29 (4): 461–489.

Perezts, Mar, Éric Faÿ, and Sébastien Picard. 2015. Ethics, embodied life and 'Esprit de corps': An ethnographic study with anti-money laundering analysts. *Organization* 22 (2): 217–234.

Pollard, Harold. 1974. *Developments in management thoughts*. London: Heinemann.

Reinmoeller, Patrick, and Shaz Ansari. 2016. The persistence of a stigmatized practive: A study of competitive intelligence. *British Journal of Management* 27 (1): 116–142.

Rendtorff, Jacob, ed. 2017. *Perspectives on philosophy of management and business ethics: Including a special section on business and human rights*. Vol. 51. Ethical Economy: Springer.

Ricœur, Paul. 1969. *Le conflits des interprétations – essais d'herméneutique*. Paris: Editions du Seuil.

Rifkin, Jeremy. 1997. *La Fin du travail*. Paris: La Découverte.

Sansonetti, Giulianno. 2006. Le Moi dans une phénoménologie radicale. In *Pensée de la vie et culture contemporaine*, ed. Michel Henry. Paris: Beauchesne.

Staquet, Anne. 1996. *La pensée faible de Vattimo et Rovatti: Une pensée–fable*. Paris: L'Harmattan.

Stieger, Bernard. 2008. *Prendre soin. 1. De la jeunesse et des générations*. Paris: Flammarion. English version. Bernard Stiegler, *Taking Care of Youth and the Generations*, Stanford: Stanford University Press, 2010.

Stiegler, Bernard. 2007. Questions de pharmacologie supérieure. Il n'y a pas de simple Pharmakon. *Psychotropes* 2007/3 (13): 27–54.

Stiegler, Bernard, Alice Béja, and Marc-Olivier Padis. 2014. Le numérique empêche-t-il de penser? *Esprit* 2014 (1): 66–78.

Stiegler, Bernard. 2017. Critique de la raison impure. *Entretien avec Camille Riquier. Esprit* 2017 (3): 118–129.

Tsoukas, Haridimos, and Stephen Cummings. 1997. Marginalization and recovery: The emergence of Aristotelian themes in organization studies. *Organization Studies* 18 (4): 655–683.

Weber, Max. 1905/2002. *The protestant ethic and the spirit of capitalism: And other writings*. Trans. Peter Baehr and Gordon Well: Penguin.

———. 1971. *Economics and society (1921)*. trans. fr. Paris: Plon.

Winnicott, Donald. 2008. *La mère suffisamment bonne*. Paris: Payot.

Wozniak, Anna. 2011. The missing subject found in the subject who does the thinking: Kierkegaard, the ethical and the subjectivity of the critical theorists. *Business Ethics: A European Review* 20 (3): 304–315.

Xenophon. 1885. *The first ten chapters of Xenophon's Oeconomicus or treatise on household management*. London: Simpkin, Marshall & Co.

Index

A

Affectio societatis, xxi, 52–54, 57, 60, 61, 111
Affectivity, xiv, 44–46, 54–56, 58, 59, 61, 107, 108, 130, 131
Agamben, G., ix, 94, 95, 98, 117, 119, 133, 134, 144
Alvesson, M., xiii, xiv, xx, 6–9, 16, 21, 24–27, 31, 41, 42, 120, 144, 145
Aristotle, x, xx, 13, 23, 32, 75, 94, 95, 109, 114

B

Badiou, A., 29, 30
Banality of evil, 31–33
Beyond recognition, 72–84
Body, xvi, xviii, xix, xxi, 4, 17, 30, 31, 41, 42, 45–47, 50–52, 56, 72, 81, 83, 92, 130, 141
Bouilloud, J.-P., xii, 17, 22, 54, 57, 63, 71, 72, 83, 98, 99, 105, 114, 118, 135, 144
Business education, 32, 140–142
Business ethics, xiii, xxi, 5, 6, 10, 12, 19–21, 23, 25, 26, 29, 40, 49, 51, 72, 136

C

Capabilities, 12, 50, 51, 72, 73, 75, 80, 82–84, 144
Capacities, ix, xii, xiv, 15, 18, 27–33, 44, 45, 50, 56–58, 71, 91–93, 95, 96, 99–100, 102, 105, 110, 113, 116, 118, 121, 130, 133, 136, 137, 139, 142–144, 147
Care, xiii, 3, 16–18, 28, 32, 33, 47, 52, 115, 118, 120, 121, 133, 137, 139

Chabot, P., xvii, 8, 14, 105, 113, 114, 133, 140
Chanlat, J.-F., xiv, xvi, 10, 20, 98, 110, 119
Constraint, xxi, 13, 54, 62, 64, 95, 97, 116, 119–120, 128, 129
Containment, 111–116
Continental philosophy, 6–9, 42, 44
Critical management studies, xx, 41, 42, 47, 146

D

Denoetisation, 30, 32, 33
Desaffectio societatis, 15, 52–61, 68
Digital humanities, 138, 140, 141

E

Environment, xv, 16, 18, 27, 28, 74, 76, 93, 94, 96, 110, 118, 128, 137, 139, 144
Eros, xv
Erotic turn, 32

F

Faÿ, E., xvi, xviii, 14, 39, 40, 49, 60, 61, 109, 110, 121, 130
Fayol, H., x, xx, 6, 92, 142
Foucault, M., 41, 47, 50, 80, 120, 121, 134
Free qualities, 114, 115
Functional stupidity, xx, 1–33

G

Governance by numbers, 114, 140

© The Editor(s) (if applicable) and The Author(s), under exclusive license to
Springer Nature Switzerland AG 2023
G. Deslandes, *Postcritical Management Studies*, Ethical Economy 65,
https://doi.org/10.1007/978-3-031-29404-4

H

Hubris, x, xx, 93, 96
Henry, M., xv–xxi, 40, 41, 44–51, 54–60, 67–70, 80, 81, 83, 93, 102, 106–111, 114, 127, 130, 132, 134, 135, 145, 146

I

Imagination, 7, 20, 98, 116, 119–120, 127, 128
Imitation, xxi, 24, 116, 119–120, 128
Intelligence, xi, 11, 14, 23–32, 60, 92, 130, 137, 142

J

Joy at work, 14, 53, 101–103, 107–109, 134

K

Keynes, J.-M., 17, 105, 116
Kierkegaard, S., 48, 56

L

Labour, xi, xx, 15, 42, 53, 59, 68, 102–104, 106, 131, 132
Latour, B., xiv
Leadership, xiii, 3, 25, 42, 50, 92–94, 98, 131, 141
Love, xv, 4, 62, 75, 104, 127

M

Managerial condition, 23, 127, 130–135
Managerial ethics, xx, 10–14, 72, 131
Marion, J.-L., xv, 32, 80, 83, 143
Material phenomenology, xviii, 41, 45, 54, 60

N

Negotium, 53, 137, 139, 140
Nietzsche, F., 46, 51, 63, 104, 105, 107, 129, 130, 140
Noetic, 32, 139, 140

O

Oikonomia, x, 23, 94–96, 98, 105, 129, 142, 143
Organizational stupidity, 23–33, 137
Organization studies, 41, 142
Otium, 53, 137, 139, 140

P

Paradox of excellence, 92–93
Pascal, B., 96, 111, 133, 144
Pharmakon, xxii, 30, 133
Phenomenology, xvii, xviii, 48, 49, 55, 67, 69, 80, 127, 145
Phenomenology of life, xvii, xxi, 39, 44–45, 49, 69–71, 130, 146, 147
Political science, 15, 21, 22
Postcritical perspectives, 127–147
Post-Taylorian management, ix, xii, xiv
Powerlessness, xix, xxi, 92–100, 112
Praxis, xxi, 39, 48, 50, 59, 69, 106, 107, 110, 119, 130, 132
Profit, 3, 4, 12, 118, 140
Proletarianisation, 26, 137, 140, 142
Proto-management, ix, 1–33, 94

R

Recognition, xv, xxi, 5, 49, 53, 58, 59, 72–84, 101, 104
Ricoeur, P., 10, 20, 40, 49, 81, 99, 100

S

Self, 3, 41, 99, 129
Sen, A., 12, 19, 50, 51, 82
Social acceleration, xxi, 62–71
Social roles, xxi, 48, 56–60, 120, 135
Social sciences, xviii, 5–7, 10, 25, 68, 71, 75, 119, 127, 141, 147
Socrates, 2–4, 15, 52, 118, 120
Solidarity, 14, 33, 59, 75, 79, 109, 114, 142
Stakeholder, 5, 12, 41, 51, 54, 55, 76, 78, 132, 138
Stiegler, B., xvii, xx, 25, 27–33, 57, 105, 110, 133, 136–142
Subjective bodies, xvi, xviii, 40, 41, 46, 48, 61, 145
Suffering, xvii, xxi, 10, 24, 46, 48, 54, 58, 61, 69, 77, 99, 102–111, 130, 133, 135
Sustainable, 13
Symbolic poverty, 31
Systemic stupidity, 8, 27, 31, 32, 127, 136, 137, 140

T

Taylor, F.W., x, xi, xiv, xix–xxii, 6, 14, 15, 18, 101
Taylorism, xiv, xvi, xxi, 14, 133
Tyranny of numbers, xxii, 118, 134–135

Index

V
Vulnerability, xxi, 63, 71, 93, 95, 97, 118, 128, 130, 132, 134, 139, 143

W
Weak management, xxii, 142–147

Weaknesses, x, 93, 97, 107, 127, 128, 142, 143
Weber, M., 3, 16, 30, 140
World-as-organization, 66

X
Xenophon, xx, 2, 4, 18, 52, 95, 96, 127, 134